Louie Wylie. Ballygarvey.

THE TRAGEDIE OF MACBETH.

Actus Primus. Scœna Prima.

Thunder and Lightning. Enter three Witches.

1. When shall we three meet againe?
In Thunder, Lightning, or in Raine?
2. When the Hurley-burley's done,
When the Battaile's lost, and wonne.
3. That will be ere the set of Sunne.
1. Where the place?
2. Vpon the Heath.
3. There to meet with *Macbeth*.
1 I come, *Gray-Malkin*.
All. Padock calls anon: faire is foule, and foule is faire,
Houer through the fogge and filthie ayre. *Exeunt.*

Scena Secunda.

Alarum within. Enter King Malcome, Donalbaine, Lenox, with attendants, meeting a bleeding Captaine.

King. What bloody man is that? he can report,
As seemeth by his plight, of the Reuolt
The newest state.
Mal. This is the Serieant,
Who like a good and hardie Souldier fought
'Gainst my Captiuitie: Haile braue friend;
Say to the King, the knowledge of the Broyle,
As thou didst leaue it.
Cap. Doubtfull it stood,
As two spent Swimmers, that doe cling together,
And choake their Art: The mercilesse *Macdonwald*
(Worthie to be a Rebell, for to that.
The multiplying Villanies of Nature
Doe swarme vpon him) from the Westerne Isles
Of Kernes and Gallowgrosses is supply'd,
And Fortune on his damned Quarry smiling,
Shew'd like a Rebells Whore: but all's too weake:
For braue *Macbeth* (well hee deserues that Name)
Disdayning Fortune, with his brandisht Steele,
Which smoak'd with bloody execution
(Like Valours Minion) caru'd out his passage,
Till hee fac'd the Slaue:
Which neu'r shooke hands, nor bad farwell to him,
Till he vnseam'd him from the Naue toth' Chops,
And fix'd his Head vpon our Battlements.
King. O valiant Cousin, worthy Gentleman.
Cap. As whence the Sunne 'gins his reflection,
Shipwracking Stormes, and direfull Thunders:
So from that Spring, whence comfort seem'd to come,
Discomfort swells: Marke King of Scotland, marke,
No sooner Iustice had, with Valour arm'd,
Compell'd these skipping Kernes to trust their heeles,
But the Norweyan Lord, surueying vantage,
With furbusht Armes, and new supplyes of men,
Began a fresh assault.
King. Dismay'd not this our Captaines, *Macbeth* and *Banquoh*?
Cap. Yes, as Sparrowes, Eagles;
Or the Hare, the Lyon:
If I say sooth, I must report they were
As Cannons ouer-charg'd with double Cracks,
So they doubly redoubled stroakes vpon the Foe:
Except they meant to bathe in reeking Wounds,
Or memorize another *Golgotha*,
I cannot tell: but I am faint,
My Gashes cry for helpe.
King. So well thy words become thee, as thy wounds,
They smack of Honor both: Goe get him Surgeons.

Enter Rosse and Angus.

Who comes here?
Mal. The worthy *Thane* of Rosse.
Lenox. What a haste lookes through his eyes?
So should he looke, that seemes to speake things strange.
Rosse. God saue the King.
King. Whence cam'st thou, worthy *Thane*?
Rosse. From Fiffe, great King,
Where the Norweyan Banners flowt the Skie,
And fanne our people cold.
Norway himselfe, with terrible numbers,
Assisted by that most disloyall Traytor,
The *Thane* of Cawdor, began a dismall Conflict,
Till that *Bellona's* Bridegroome, lapt in proofe,
Confronted him with selfe-comparisons,
Point against Point, rebellious Arme 'gainst Arme,
Curbing his lauish spirit: and to conclude,
The Victorie fell on vs.
King. Great happinesse.
Rosse. That now, *Sweno*, the Norwayes King,
Craues composition:
Nor would we deigne him buriall of his men,
Till he disbursed, at Saint *Colmes* ynch,
Ten thousand Dollars, to our generall vse.

King No

Facsimile (reduced) of the First Page of Macbeth, First Folio.

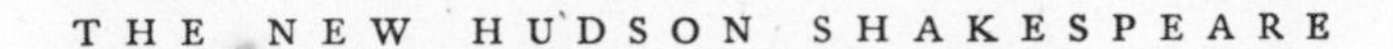

THE NEW HUDSON SHAKESPEARE

THE TRAGEDY *of* MACBETH

Introduction & Notes by
HENRY NORMAN HUDSON, LL.D.

Edited & Revised by
EBENEZER CHARLTON BLACK, LL.D.

With the collaboration of
ANDREW JACKSON GEORGE, LITT.D.

GINN AND COMPANY LTD
QUEEN SQUARE LONDON W.C. 1

THE NEW HUDSON SHAKESPEARE

GINN AND COMPANY LTD.

054211

PRINTED IN GREAT BRITAIN BY ROBERT MACLEHOSE AND CO LTD.
THE UNIVERSITY PRESS, GLASGOW

PREFACE

The text of this edition of *Macbeth* is based upon a collation of the seventeenth century Folios, the Globe edition, and that of Delius. As compared with the text of the earlier editions of the Hudson Shakespeare, it is conservative. Exclusive of changes in spelling, punctuation, and stage directions, very few emendations by eighteenth century and nineteenth century editors have been adopted ; and these, with every variation from the First Folio, are indicated in the textual notes. These notes are printed immediately below the text so that a reader or student may see at a glance the evidence in the case of a disputed reading and have some definite understanding of the reasons for those differences in the text of Shakespeare which frequently surprise and very often annoy. A consideration of the more poetical, or the more dramatically effective, of two variant readings will often lead to rich results in awakening a spirit of discriminating interpretation and in developing true creative criticism. In no sense is this a textual variorum edition. The variants given are only those of importance and high authority.

The spelling and the punctuation of the text are modern, except in the case of verb terminations in *-ed*, which, when the *e* is silent, are printed with the apostrophe in its place. This is the general usage in the First Folio. Modern spelling has to a certain extent been followed in the text variants; but the original spelling has been retained wherever its peculiarities have been the basis for important textual criticism and emendation.

With the exception of the position of the textual variants, the plan of this edition is similar to that of the earlier editions of the Hudson Shakespeare. It is impossible to specify the various instances of revision and rearrangement in the matter of the Introduction and the interpretative notes, but the endeavour has been to retain all that gave the Hudson Shakespeare its unique place and to add the results of what seems vital and permanent in later inquiry and research.

While it is important that the principle of *suum cuique* be attended to so far as is possible in matters of research and scholarship, it is becoming more and more difficult to give every man his own in Shakespearian annotation. The amount of material accumulated is so great that the identity-origin of much important comment and suggestion is either wholly lost or so crushed out of shape as to be beyond recognition. Instructive significance perhaps attaches to this in editing the works of one who quietly made so much of materials gathered by others. But the list of authorities given on page lxxi will indicate the chief source of much that has gone to enrich the value of this edition. Especial acknowledgment is here made of the obligations to Dr. William Aldis Wright and Dr. Horace Howard Furness, whose work in Shakespearian criticism, research, and collating, has made all subsequent editors and investigators their eternal bondmen.

With regard to the general plan of this edition, Professor W. P. Trent, of Columbia University, has offered valuable suggestions and given important advice; and to Mr. M. Grant Daniell's patience, accuracy, and judgment this volume owes both its freedom from many a blunder and its possession of a carefully arranged index.

CONTENTS

INTRODUCTION

THE TEXT

INDEX

ILLUSTRATIONS

INTRODUCTION

NOTE. In citations from Shakespeare's plays and nondramatic poems the numbering has reference to the Globe edition, except in the case of this play, where the reference is to this edition.

I. SOURCES

The fatal consequence of the intervention of malignant supernatural powers in human affairs has fascinated the deepest minds in all ages and in all lands. It is the theme of Greek tragedy ; it is the germ idea of the Faust legend ; it is the essential element in *Paradise Lost*. The story of Macbeth, as we have it in Shakespeare, belongs to that great cycle of temptation themes which, developing naturally from the story of the fall in the *Genesis* narrative, became in the Middle Ages the legend of the man who sells his soul to the devil in exchange for fortune, power, or universal knowledge.

THE MAIN STORY

THE MACBETH OF HISTORY

Modern research [1] has established that the Macbeth of history was, for his time, a worthy and beneficent monarch, thoroughly deserving the title of " the liberal king " given to

[1] Cf. Freeman's *The History of the Norman Conquest*, 1867–1879 ; Skene's *Celtic Scotland*, 1876–1880 ; Professor Hume Brown's *The History of Scotland* (Cambridge Historical Series) ; Robertson's *Scotland under her Early Kings*.

him by St. Berchan. He appears first in trustworthy annals[1] as the hereditary 'mormaor,' or high steward, of Moray, accompanying his grandfather, Malcolm II, on a mission of homage to Cnut, king of England, in 1031. His seventeen years' reign (1040–1057) was marked by unprecedented order and prosperity ; and, as Buchanan states in his *Rerum Scoticarum Historia*, first printed in 1582, he applied his mind to make good and useful laws, a thing almost wholly neglected by former kings. From this eleventh century king of Scotland the influence of mediæval story-telling and the wilful falsification of historical material for political purposes have created the Macbeth of myth and legend. "With the Scottish historians who followed the War of Independence it was a prime concern to produce an unbroken line of Scottish kings stretching to the fathers of the human race. As an interloper in this series Macbeth was a monster whose origin and whose actions must alike have been contrary to nature." — Hume Brown.

THE MACBETH OF LEGEND

1. *John of Fordun's Chronica.* The earliest extant version of the Macbeth legend is in the *Chronica Gentis Scotorum* (sometimes called the *Scotichronicon*,[2] of which it forms the first part), written in Latin by John of Fordun (often called John Fordun), a secular priest and canon of the cathedral church of Aberdeen, who died about the year 1385. This

[1] In the earliest records the name is spelled 'Mealbeaðe,' 'Macbeoðe,' 'Machetad,' 'Machbet.' In Dalrymple's version, "in Scottish," of Leslie's *Historie of Scotland*, printed in 1578, the name is given as 'Machabie.' In Boece the Latin form of the name is 'Maccabæus.'

[2] Edited (with a translation) by Skene, Edinburgh, 1871-1872.

chantry priest did for Scottish history and story what Geoffrey of Monmouth more than two hundred years earlier had done for the mythical history of Britain and the Arthurian story in his *Historia Regum Britanniæ.* Both gathered the floating legends and stories, facts and fables, and compacted them into " something like a chronological system," thus starting them on their literary career.

2. *Andrew of Wyntoun's Orygynale Cronykil.* About the year 1424 Andrew (Androwe, Andro) of Wyntoun (often called Andrew Wyntoun), a canon of St. Andrews who became prior of St. Serf's Inch in Lochleven, resolved to draw up a *Cronykil* out " off Latine in tyll Ynglys sawe," [1] as he puts it. He prefixed the adjective ' Orygynale ' because the *Cronykil* went back to the beginnings of men and angels. In the octosyllabic couplets of the *Orygynale Cronykil* is the earliest form of the prophecy of the Weird Sisters. This is the famous passage :

> A nycht he thowcht in hys dremying,
> That syttand he wes besyd the kyng
> At a sete in hwntyng, swa
> In till a leysh had grewhundys twa :
> He thowcht quhile he wes swa syttand
> He sawe thre wemen by gangand ;
> And thai wemen than thowcht he
> Thre werd Systrys mast lyk to be.
> The fyrst he hard say gangand by,
> ' Lo, yhondyr the Thayne off Crumbawchty ! '
> The tothir woman sayd agane,
> ' Of Morave yhondre I se the Thayne ! '
> The thryd than sayd, ' I se the Kyng ! '

[1] into English speech. Until well into the sixteenth century the Lowland Scots, though they called themselves ' Scottis ' and their country ' Scotland,' called their language ' Ynglys,' ' Inglisch,' or ' Inglis.'

Here, it is to be noted, the temptation of Macbeth by the Weird Sisters takes place in a dream. This version of the story is followed by the skeptical and rationalistic Buchanan.

3. *Boece's Historiæ.* In 1526–1527 was printed the *Scotorum Historiæ* of Hector Boece (Boetius, Boyis, Boyce), the first principal of King's College, Aberdeen. This Latin redaction added new epic and dramatic elements to the Macbeth legend. The meeting of Macbeth and three women supposed to be the Weird Sisters is now described as an actual occurrence on the road to Forres, and the story begins to take the definite shape familiar to readers of Holinshed and Shakespeare.

4. *Bellenden's Croniklis.* Under the title *Croniklis of Scotland* a very free translation of Boece's work into vigorous Scottish prose was made about the year 1533 by John Bellenden (Ballantyne), archdeacon of Moray and canon of Ross. In Bellenden's version in the vernacular, first printed in 1536,[1] the description of the temptation scene is pithy and dramatic :

> Nocht lang eftir, hapnit ane uncouth and wounderfull thing, be quhilk followit sone ane gret alteration in the realme. Be aventure, Makbeth and Banquho wer passing to Fores, quhair King Duncane hapnit to be for the time, and met be the gait thre wemen, clothit in elrage and uncouth weid. They were jugit be the pepill to be weird sisteris. The first of thaim said to Makbeth : 'Hale, Thane of Glammis !' The secound said : 'Hale, Thane of Cawder !' and the thrid said : 'Hale, King of Scotland !'

Bellenden rehearses Lady Macbeth's complicity in the plot to murder Duncan with much greater detail than is found in either earlier or later versions of the legend.

[1] Edited by Maitland, Edinburgh, 1821. Reprinted in Collier's *Shakespeare's Library*.

5. *Stewart's Cronikle.* In 1535 appeared a Scottish metrical version of Bellenden's *Croniklis*, purporting to be by William Stewart [1] and made at the command of Margaret Tudor, Queen of Scotland, for her son James V. Though this *Cronikle* was not printed till after Shakespeare's day, it is perfectly possible that he may have had access to it through the friendly relations between James VI and the "King's Company" of players, to which Shakespeare belonged. Significant verbal resemblances make this not only possible but not at all improbable.

6. *Holinshed's Chronicles.* As the numerous extracts in the notes to the text in this edition of *Macbeth* will show, Shakespeare derived the great body of his story material from the *Chronicles of England, Scotland, and Ireland*, of Raphael Holinshed (Holynshed, Hollingshead, Hollinshead), first published in two folio volumes in 1577, and again in 1586–1587, "newlie augmented and continued." [2] In this second edition are many significant changes in the text, and it is interesting to note that on the title-page *The description and historie of Ireland* precedes *The description and historie of Scotland*. The first edition has a great many quaint woodcuts inserted in the text,[3] and two of these are here reproduced in facsimile, with some lines of the text. Figure 1 represents the meeting of Macbeth and the ".iij women in straunge & ferly apparell, resembling creatures of an elder

[1] Edited by Turnbull (Rolls Series), 3 vols., 1858.

[2] In W. G. Boswell-Stone's *Shakspere's Holinshed* are given all the portions of the *Chronicles* which are of special interest to the Shakespeare student.

[3] These woodcuts were omitted in the second edition, and many passages of the original text were cancelled by order of the Privy Council "as disagreeable to Queen Elizabeth."

pictures are yet in the sayde Inche, there to be
seene grauen with the armes of the Danes, as 30

third sayde: All hayle Makbeth that hereafter
shall be king of Scotland.

Then Banquho, what maner of women 50
(saith he) are you, that seeme so litle fauourable

in his place, where contrarily thou in deede shalt
not reygne at all, but of thee those shall be borne

FIG. 1.

Malcolme prince of Cumberlande, as it were
thereby to appoint him his successor in the king-

sent, he receyued the inuestiture of the kingdome
according to the accustomed maner.

The bodie of Duncane was firste conueyed
vnto Elgyne, and there buried in kingly wise,

the sonnes of king Duncane, for feare of their
liues (whiche they might well know ẏ Makbeth

FIG. 2.

worlde"; Figure 2 represents Macbeth receiving the "inuesture of the kingdome according to the accustomed maner."

In the special title prefixed to *The Description of Scotland* in the edition of 1586–1587, given in facsimile on the following page (Figure 3), Holinshed's indebtedness to Boece and to Bellenden is clearly set forth. This is the edition undoubtedly used by Shakespeare,[1] and it is not improbable that the mention of these authorities would stimulate him to read them at first hand.

While the dramatist follows closely Holinshed's account of the reigns of Duncan and Macbeth, he transfers to the murder of Duncan such details as the drugging of the grooms, the portents, the tempest, etc., from the narrative of the murder of Duffe, Lady Macbeth's great-grandfather. Additional details taken from other parts of the *Chronicles* and woven into the plot of the play are the story of young Siward's death and the description of the English king's touching to cure 'the evil.' Furness, too, has pointed out that the hint for the 'voice' which cried "Sleep no more!" (II, ii, 35) probably came from the voice that Kenneth, who had poisoned his nephew Malcolm, heard:

> And (as the fame goeth) it chanced that a voice was heard as he was in bed in the night time to take his rest, vttering vnto him these or the like woords in effect: "Thinke not Kenneth that the wicked slaughter of Malcolme Duffe by thee contriued, is kept secret from the knowledge of the eternall God." . . . The king with this voice being stricken into great dread and terror, passed that night without anie sleepe comming in his eies.

[1] For example, 'ferly,' in the description of the dress of the Weird Sisters in the first edition, is changed to 'wild' in the second, as in *Macbeth* I, iii, 40. Boswell-Stone gives other proofs of this kind.

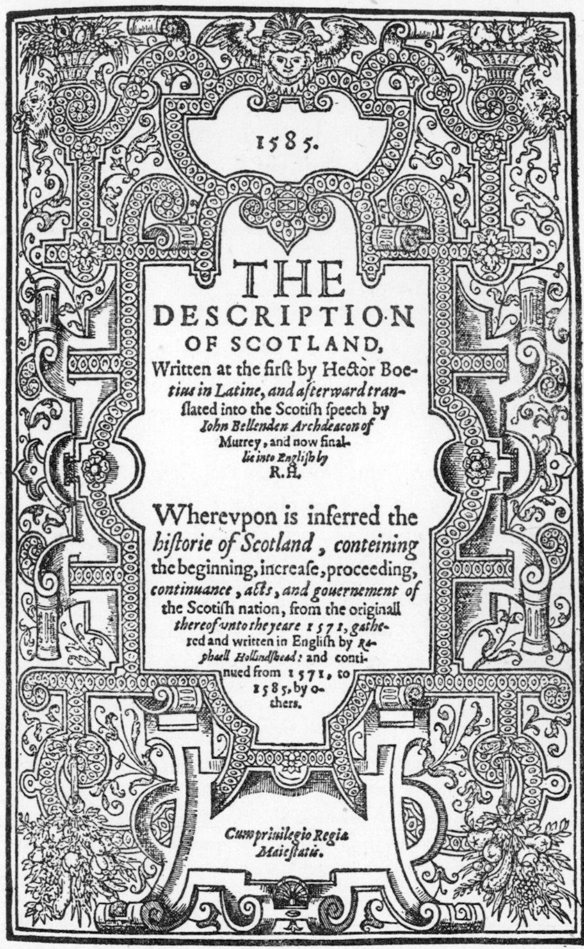

1585.

THE
DESCRIPTION
OF SCOTLAND,
Written at the first by Hector Boe-
tius in Latine, and afterward tran-
slated into the Scotish speech by
Iohn Bellenden Archdeacon of
Murrey, and now final-
lie into English by
R.H.

Wherevpon is inserted the
historie of Scotland, *conteining*
the beginning, increase, proceeding,
continuance, *acts*, *and gouernement* of
the Scotish nation, from the originall
thereof vnto the yeare 1571, *gathe-*
red and written in English by *Ra-*
phaell Hollinshead: and continued from 1571, to
1585, by o-
thers.

Cum priuilegio Regiæ
Maiestatis.

FIG. 3.

(In this connection see Buchanan's account of the conscience-stricken king quoted below.)

Notable changes in Shakespeare's use of the material furnished by Holinshed are the idealization of the character of Banquo and the simplification and compression of the action in the interests of dramatic economy. Above all, and most significant of all, the drama throbs with a passion and a moral energy of which Holinshed's *Chronicles*, with all their infusion of enchantment and the supernatural, have not the slightest trace.

7. *Buchanan's Historia.* In 1582 was printed in Edinburgh the *Rerum Scoticarum Historia* of George Buchanan, the famous tutor of James I and one of Scotland's most illustrious scholars. Of this work there was no version in English until after Shakespeare's death, but there was naturally much discussion of it in London after James ascended the English throne, and Shakespeare must have been acquainted with the book to a greater or less extent. At the close of the Macbeth narrative, Buchanan, whose attitude towards the supernatural is, as already indicated, uncompromisingly rationalistic, has this very significant sentence : " Certain of our writers here relate many things which I omit, as they seem fitter for stage representations or Milesian stories than for sober history (*theatris aut Milesiis fabulis sunt aptiora quam historiae*)." M. H. Liddell points out that the description of Kenneth's awakened conscience in Buchanan's *Historia* gives us " the picture of Macbeth's torture almost exactly as Shakespeare conceived it " :

His Mind being disquieted with the Guilt of his Offence, suffered him to enjoy no sincere or solid Mirth ; but in the Day he was vexed with the corroding Thoughts of that foul Wickedness, which would always force themselves into his Mind, and in the Night terrible Apparitions disturbed his Rest. At last, a Voice was heard from Heaven, either a true one, as some think ; or else, such an one, as his disquieted Mind suggested (as it commonly happens to guilty Consciences), speaking to him in his Bed.[1]

8. *Earlier Plays.* There is clear evidence that within a few years of the production of *Gorboduc*, the first English tragedy, Scottish legendary history was attracting the attention of dramatists as a quarry from which to take effective material. Under the influence of the passion for chronicle histories, and plays founded on romantic legend, a *Tragedie of the King of Scottes* came into existence as early as 1568 ; about 1590 Robert Greene produced *The Scottish Historie of James IV, slaine at Flodden, intermixed with a pleasant Comedie, presented by Oboram King of Fayeries* [2] ; and Henslowe in his *Diary*, under April 27, 1602, refers to a play called *Malcolme, King of Scottes.* But dealing with the Macbeth legend are two works of special interest in this connection : (1) *Macdobeth*, probably dramatic and certainly anterior to Shakespeare's play, and (2) a Latin Dramatic Dialogue given before King James at Oxford, probably anterior.

(1) *Macdobeth.* In *The Stationers' Registers* under the date August 27, 1596, is a reference to a " Ballad of

[1] This translation is from the English version of Buchanan's *History of Scotland*, published in Edinburgh, 1751. In *The Anatomy of Melancholy*, Burton quotes this passage from Buchanan.

[2] The fact that this play (in the writing of which, according to Fleay, Lodge collaborated with Greene) seems really founded on the Italian romance of Astatio and Arrenopia in Giraldi Cinthio's *Gli Hecatommithi*, 1565, does not affect the argument regarding the growing popularity of Scottish themes for dramatic treatment.

Macdobeth," and the same entry refers to " the ballad entituled The taming of a shrew." Collier held that if *The Taming of the Shrew*, which is known to be a play, was recorded as a ballad, *Macdobeth* was probably of the same character, and he sought to identify it with the " miserable stolne story " referred to by Will Kemp, a famous actor of clowns' parts, in his *Kempes nine daies wonder*, printed in 1600. In searching for a ballad-maker who had written an unauthorized account of some of his morrice-dancing adventures, Kemp says :

> I met a proper vpright youth, onely for a little stooping in the shoulders : all hart to the heele, a penny Poet whose first making was the miserable stolne story of Macdoel, or Macdobeth, or Macsomewhat : for I am sure a Mac it was, though I never had the maw to see it.

" Here the words ' to see it ' seem to show that the piece had been publicly represented, and that it was not merely a printed ' ballad.' Kemp, as a highly popular actor, would most naturally refer to dramatic performances." — Collier.

(2) *A Latin Dramatic Dialogue*. In his *Essay on the Learning of Shakespeare* (London, 1767) Farmer held that *Macbeth* was possibly suggested by " a little performance on the same subject at Oxford, before King James." This ' performance ' was a dialogue in Latin, dealing with the prediction of the " prophetic sisters " (*fatidicas sorores*) as to Banquo and Macbeth, arranged by the students of St. John's College, Oxford, on the occasion of the royal visit to the university in August, 1605. This dialogue,[1]

[1] The Latin text is given in the Appendix to Furness's *A New Variorum. Macbeth.*

written by Dr Mathew Gwynne, was found by Malone bound up with Gwynne's Latin play *Vertumnus*, and the opening lines, spoken by three students dressed to represent Sibyls, " the conceipt whereof the King did very much applaude,"[1] have certainly an interesting resemblance to the Witches' prophecy in Shakespeare's play.

Witch Lore

In sorting the materials out of which the Weird Sisters weave their incantations, and in gathering the ingredients which they compound into their hell-broth so as to " make the gruel thick and slab," Shakespeare drew upon the popular belief of his time. Into the coarse and realistic mixture he infused magic elements of that mystic symbolism which is the spirit of the Fates of the classical mythology and of the Norns of the Scandinavian — that mystic symbolism which already had so strangely idealized certain developments of witch lore in the old Hebrew story (*I Samuel*, xxviii) of Saul's visit to the witch of Endor and the reading of the future through a rising from the dead in a midnight cave.

1. *Scot's Discoverie of Witchcraft*. As the quotations in the notes to the text of the play indicate, many minor details of the witch business in *Macbeth* seem to have been derived from *The Discoverie of Witchcraft*,[2] 1584, an extraordinary impeachment of the witchcraft superstition by Reginald Scot, a Kentish man who, after years of study at Oxford, returned to his native county and gave himself to gardening

[1] A. Nixon's *The Oxford Triumph*, 1605.
[2] Edited by B. Nicholson, London, 1886.

and hop-growing.[1] *The Discoverie of Witchcraft* is a frank and able exposure of the absurdities of the popular belief, but the value of his book to-day is in the detailed account of the processes of sorcery and the minutiæ of witch lore. The scope of the work is indicated in the original title:

The discoverie of witchcraft wherein the lewde dealing of witches and witchmongers is notablie detected, the knaverie of conjurors, the impietie of inchantors, the follie of soothsayers, the impudent falsehood of cousenors,[2] the infidelitie of atheists, the pestilent practices of Pythonists, the curiositie of figure-casters, the vanitie of dreamers, the beggarlie art of Alcumystrie, the abhomination of idolatrie, the horrible art of poisoning, the vertue and power of naturall magike, and all the conveiances of Legierdemaine and juggling are deciphered, and many other things opened which have long lien hidden, howbeit verie necessarie to be knowne.

2. *King James's Dæmonologie.* In 1597 King James, a born arguer and reveler in 'counterblasts,' issued his *Dæmonologie, in Forme of a Dialogue* as a reply to Scot and other skeptics. Here, too, are interesting details of the ways and methods of witches, as this extract from the preface indicates:

The fearefull abounding at this time in this Countrey of these detestable slaues of the Diuel, the Witches or enchaunters, hath mooued me . . . to resolue the doubting hearts of many; both that such assaults of Satan are most certainely practised, and that the instruments thereof merits most seuerely to be punished: against the damnable opinions of two principally in our aage, whereof the one called *Scot*, an Englishman, is not ashamed in publike Print to deny that there can be such a thing as Witch-craft. . . . And for to

[1] He is said to have introduced hop-growing into England. His treatise on the subject, *The Hoppe-Garden*, first published in 1574, was thrice reprinted before 1580.

[2] cozeners, impostors. Cf. *The Winter's Tale*, IV, iv, 256; *King Lear*, IV, vi, 167.

make this Treatise the more pleasant and facill, I haue put it in form of a Dialogue, which I have diuided into three Bookes : The first speaking of Magie in generall, and Necromancie in speciall : The second, of Sorcerie and Witch-craft ; and the third containes a discourse of all these kinds of spirits and Spectres that appeares and troubles persons.

3. *Newes from Scotland.* In 1591 there appeared in Scotland a book called *Newes from Scotland*, in which are graphically told the doings of certain Scottish witches and "supposts of Sathan" who met "on the see . . . in riddles or seives . . . to sink the schip . . . att the Kingis returning fra Denmark." That was in 1589, when James was bringing home his Danish bride. This little book was republished in London in 1604, when the king's statute to suppress witchcraft was enacted. Steevens [1] connects the Scottish witch lore in this book with such passages in *Macbeth* as I, iii, 10–11, 25–29, but in Scot's *Discoverie* and James's *Dæmonologie* the power of witches to raise storms by sea and land is fully recognized.

4. *Golding's Ovid.* Arthur Golding's translation of Ovid's *Metamorphoses*, begun in 1565 and completed in 1575, is the probable source of much of Shakespeare's knowledge of classical mythology. "Golding's rendering of Ovid had been one of Shakespeare's best-loved books in youth." — Sidney Lee. In it we have Hecate recognized as the goddess of witches :

She went me to an Altar that was dedicate of olde
To Persys daughter Hecate (of whom the Witches holde
As of their Goddesse) standing in a thicke and secrete wood . . .
And thou, three-headed Hecate, who knowest best the way
To compasse this our great attempt, and art our chiefest stay.

[1] Cf. T. A. Spalding's *Elizabethan Demonology*, London, 1880.

The Moving Wood

The incident of the moving wood belongs to the folk-lore of both Semitic and Indo-European peoples.[1] In Wyntoun's *Cronykil* the ' flyttand Wod ' is expressly referred to as traditional. It is adumbrated in the Hebrew story of David's conquest of the Philistines following the sound and appearance as of armies moving along the tops of the mulberry trees in the valley of Rephaim. In *Poet-Lore*, May, 1890, Dr. Morris Jastrow, Jr., gives an Arabic version of the story ; and Halliwell-Phillipps transcribes a variant in an old romance life of Alexander the Great. A vigorous form of the story is in a broadside ballad purporting to be by Thomas Deloney who died about 1600. It tells of the way in which " the valiant courage and policie of the Kentish-men " enabled them to use the device of the moving wood to force William the Conqueror to recognize their rights :

> For when they spied his approch
> In place where they did stand,
> Then march'd forth they to hem him in,
> Each man with bough in hand.
>
> So that unto the Conqueror's sight,
> Amazed as he stood,
> They seem'd to be a walking grove,
> Or els a moouing wood.
>
> The shape of men he could not see,
> The boughs did hide them so,
> And how his heart did quake for fear
> To see a forest go.

[1] Some of the variants are given in Porter and Clarke's *Shakespeare Studies : Macbeth.*

Simrock[1] has shown how closely several of the *Macbeth* incidents, including this of the moving wood, correspond to the traditionary story of King Grünewald :

> A King had an only daughter, who possessed wondrous gifts. Now, once upon a time there came his enemy, a King named Grünewald, and besieged him in his castle, and, as the siege lasted long, the daughter kept continually encouraging her father in the castle. This lasted till May-day. Then all of a sudden the daughter saw the hostile army approach with green boughs : then fear and anguish fell on her, for she knew that all was lost, and said to her father, " Father, you must yield, or die ; I see the green-wood drawing nigh." [2]

Simrock claims that the legend of the moving forest originated in the German religious custom of May festivals and summer welcomings.

MACDUFF'S BIRTH

Simrock has also pointed out that the connection between an untimely birth and heroic strength and prowess as shown in the Witch's prophecy that " none of woman born Shall harm Macbeth " (IV, i, 80–81), and that Macduff satisfied this grim condition (V, viii, 15–16), is also a bit of Teutonic folk-lore, Sigurd's ancestor, Wolsung, having been a child of sorrow of this kind. Such a belief is latent in all the Aryan mythologies and is common to-day among the peasantry of many European countries. Macbeth's death at the hand of a foe not born of woman is alluded to in Wyntoun's *Cronykil*, but Shakespeare undoubtedly took his version from Holinshed's *Chronicles*, where we read : " But Makduffe . . . answered (with his naked swoord in his hand) saieng : It is

[1] K. Simrock's *Die Quellen des Shakespeare*, Hildburghausen, 1870.
[2] This is the translation given in Furness.

true Makbeth . . . I am even he that thy wizzards have told thee of, who was never born of my mother, but ripped out of her wombe."

Was Shakespeare ever in Scotland?

Whether Shakespeare visited Scotland has been the subject of much discussion. Knight, Fleay, and other scholars maintain that he did, and that *Macbeth* derives much of its 'local colour' and peculiar power from the fact that the dramatist was describing what he had seen with his own eyes. Thus, and thus alone, it has been claimed, could he have caught so marvellously both the letter and the spirit of old Highland romance. The internal evidence based on such accuracy of local description and allusion as is found in I, vi, 1–6, is strengthened by such strong external evidence as the visits of English actors to Scotland during the time of Shakespeare's connection with the stage. On October 22, 1601, the freedom of the city of Aberdeen was conferred on Lawrence Fletcher, "Comedian to His Majestie," and under a Privy Seal dated May 17, 1603, license [1] was granted to this Lawrence Fletcher, William Shakespeare, Richard Burbage, and other members of the old Lord Chamberlain's company as "the King's Men," to perform stage plays "within their now usual house called the Globe," and elsewhere in the kingdom.

Fleay [2] held that Shakespeare was in the company that went to Scotland in 1601, and that when the company was at Aberdeen he wrote a version of *Macbeth* for performance before the king there, in the winter following the Gowry

[1] The license is given in full in Collier's *Annals of the Stage.*
[2] *The Life and Work of Shakespeare*, London, 1886.

conspiracy. This he revised and enlarged after his interest had been awakened in the subject again by the dramatic dialogue given by the Oxford students in 1605. Fleay's theory is interesting and suggestive, but of course inconclusive.

II. DATE OF COMPOSITION

The date of composition of *Macbeth* falls within April 20, 1610, the later time limit (*terminus ante quem*), and 1603, the earlier time limit (*terminus post quem*). The weight of evidence favours 1605–1606.

External Evidence

1. *Forman's Diary*. In determining the date of composition, the most famous bit of external evidence gives a definite *terminus ante quem*. This is Dr. Simon Forman's account of a performance of *Macbeth* attended by him at the Globe theatre on April 20, 1610. Forman was an Elizabethan physician, astrologer, and dabbler in the black art, and in *The Booke of Plaies and Notes therof per Formans for Common Pollicie*,[1] a little manuscript volume discovered in the Ashmolean Museum in 1836, he gives a minute and particular account of the plot and leading incidents of the drama. Forman's description begins as follows:

> In Mackbeth at the glob, 16jo, the 20 of Aprill, ther was to be obserued, firste, howe Mackbeth and Bancko, 2 noble men of Scotland, Ridinge thorowe a wod, the[r] stode before them 3 women feiries or Nimphes, And saluted Mackbeth, sayinge, 3 tyms vnto him, haille mackbeth, king of Codon; for thou shalt be a kinge, but shalt

[1] for guidance in the ordinary affairs of life. Furnivall's reprint of *The Booke of Plaies* is given in the Appendix to *Transactions of the New Shakspere Society*, 1875-1876.

beget No kinge, &c. then said Bancko, what all to mackbeth And nothing to me. Yes, said the nimphes, haille to thee Banko, thou shalt beget kinges, yet be no kinge. And so they departed & cam to the courte of Scotland to Dunkin king of Scotes, and yt was in the dais of Edward the Confessor.

2. *The Puritan.* Forman's lengthy and detailed notice of *Macbeth* has been regarded as evidence that the tragedy was then fresh from Shakespeare's hand, and was in its first course of performance. But this is to mistake Forman's purpose in making his *Notes.* Besides, there are unmistakable allusions to *Macbeth* earlier than 1610. In *The Puritan, or The Widow of Watling Street*, printed in 1607, there is a very pointed reference to Banquo's Ghost: "Instead of a jester we 'll ha' the ghost i' th' white sheet sit at upper end o' th' table." [1]

3. *Marston's Sophonisba.* Professor Bradley, in his *Shakespearean Tragedy*, points out a number of parallels between *Macbeth* and Marston's *Sophonisba* (*The Wonder of Women, or The Trajedie of Sophonisba*), printed in 1606 — parallels so marked as to be conclusive that Marston was familiar with Shakespeare's play. In Marston's other plays are obvious reminiscences of Shakespeare.

4. *Warner's Albion's England.* In the 1606 edition of Warner's *Albion's England* (the first edition appeared in 1586), a *Historie of Macbeth* is added, probably in consequence of the popularity of Shakespeare's play.

5. *Latin Dramatic Dialogue.* In summing up external evidence for the date of *Macbeth* some weight is due to the Latin dramatic dialogue given before the king at Oxford in 1605, as described above.

[1] The often-quoted similar passage in *The Knight of the Burning Pestle* 1611, has no direct bearing upon the date of *Macbeth.*

Internal Evidence

The *terminus post quem* is generally agreed upon by internal evidence as 1603, the date of the accession of James I.

1. *Allusions within the Play*. (1) The specific reference to the union of the two crowns, IV, i, 120–121. (2) The description of touching for 'the evil,' IV, iii, 141–159. (3) The dramatic use of witchcraft, a subject of intense interest to the king. (4) Allusions in the Porter's speech. The references to "the equivocator," II, iii, 8–11, and "the farmer that hang'd himself on the expectation of plenty," II, iii, 4–5, are usually quoted as pointing to 1606 as the date of composition. The "equivocator" passage, especially when taken in connection with IV, ii, 45–50, and V, v, 43, is regarded by some as a reference to the trial of Henry Garnet (note, page 54, line 8). Too much has been made of the "farmer" allusion, even though special research has shown that there was an unusually abundant harvest in 1606. As a matter of fact, the jest seems to have been common in Elizabethan London and is found in Ben Jonson's *Every Man Out of His Humour*, published in 1599 (see note, page 53, lines 4–5). Another common Elizabethan jest that has been dragged into the date of composition discussion is that of the "tailor . . . stealing out of a French hose." In this connection it is well to remember that the Porter's speech is regarded by many editors as a later interpolation (see below, Shakespeare and Middleton). (5) "The fatal bellman." In a letter published in *The Athenæum*, September 13, 1902, Professor Hales points out that the surmise of the editors of the Clarendon Press Shakespeare that the full significance of the expression "the fatal bellman, Which

gives the stern'st good-night," II, ii, 3–4, lay in its "allusion to a certain Newgate custom" of Shakespeare's day, is probably correct. In 1605 Robert Dow, a merchant tailor of London, gave a sum of money to provide for, or fee, a bellman who should deliver at the prison of Newgate "a most pious and aweful admonition" to condemned criminals the night before they suffered.

2. *Style and Diction.* While certain passages in *Macbeth* are in Shakespeare's greatest, richest, and most idiomatic style, and taken by themselves might justify placing the composition of the play as near as possible to the *terminus ante quem*, the strict application of the various verse and diction tests [1] (see Versification and Diction) would make the date of composition as early as the main body of the external evidence and that drawn from the allusions within the play allow.

III. EARLY EDITIONS

Folios

On November 8, 1623, Edward Blount and Isaac Jaggard obtained formal license to print "Mr. William Shakespeere's Comedyes, Histories, and Tragedyes, soe many of the said copies as are not formerly entered to other men." This is the description-entry in *The Stationers' Registers* of what is now known as the First Folio (1623), designated in the textual notes of this edition F_1. *Macbeth* is one of the sixteen plays "not formerly entered," and it was first printed,

[1] There is an excellent summary of these tests in Dowden's *Shakspere Primer.* See also Ward's *History of English Dramatic Literature*, Vol. II, pages 47-51.

so far as is known, in this famous volume. While, as to language, it is not one of the worst printed of the plays, the peculiar nature of the errors and corruptions has given rise to an unusual amount of textual criticism and led to those interesting theories of the original version of the play which are discussed elsewhere in this Introduction and in the notes attached to the text. "Probably it was printed from a transcript of the author's MS., which was in great part not copied from the original but written to dictation. This is confirmed by the fact that several of the most palpable blunders are blunders of the ear and not of the eye." — Clar. *Macbeth* occupies pages 131 to 151 in the division of the Folio devoted to *Tragedies*, and it stands there between *Julius Cæsar* and *Hamlet*. The running title is *The Tragedie of Macbeth*. It is one of the seventeen plays in the First Folio in which is indicated the division into acts and scenes.

The Second Folio, F_2 (1632), offers an unusual number of changes in the text of *Macbeth* as compared with that of other plays. The more important of these are given in the textual notes of this edition. This Second Folio text is repeated with few changes, except in the way of slightly modernized spelling, in the Third Folio, F_3 (1663, 1664), and in the Fourth Folio, F_4 (1685).

Quartos of 1673 and 1674

In 1673 appeared a Quarto edition of *Macbeth* purporting to be as "acted at the Dukes Theatre." With the exception of songs added and changes in the witch scenes, this Quarto is a reprint from the First Folio. Furness has suggested calling it 'Betterton's Version,' after Thomas Betterton, whom Pepys regarded as the best actor in the world. In the following year appeared a Quarto with this title-page: 'MACBETH, | A | TRAGÆDY. | With all the | ALTERATIONS, | AMENDMENTS, | ADDITIONS, | AND | NEW SONGS. | *As it's now Acted at the* Dukes Theatre. | *LONDON*, | Printed for *P. Chetwin*, and are to be Sold | by most Booksellers, 1674.' This is now known as the 'D'Avenant Quarto.' It gives Sir William D'Avenant's post-Restoration revision of the play, and in it are printed now in full both Thomas Middleton's famous witch songs, "Come away, come away," and "Black spirits and white." Under the title 'The Persons Names' it contained the first list of dramatis personæ.

ROWE'S EDITIONS

The first critical editor of Shakespeare's plays was Nicholas Rowe, poet laureate to George I. His first edition was issued in 1709 in six octavo volumes. In this edition Rowe, an experienced playwright, marked the entrances and exits of the characters and introduced many stage directions. A second edition in eight volumes was published in 1714. Rowe followed very closely the text of the Fourth Folio, but modernized spelling, punctuation, and occasionally grammar.

IV. SHAKESPEARE AND MIDDLETON

In the First Folio, *Macbeth*, III, v, after line 33, is the stage direction, *Musicke, and a Song*, and after line 35 another stage direction, *Sing within. Come away, come away, &c.* Again, in IV, i, after line 43, is the stage direction, *Musicke and a Song. Blacke Spirits, &c.* In the D'Avenant Quarto, where, as mentioned above, both songs are given in full,[1] there is no sign as to the source of them, and for long they were supposed to be D'Avenant's own composition. About the year 1778 (Malone gives the date as 1779) Steevens is said to have found in "the collection of the late Thomas Pearson, esq." a manuscript play called *The Witch*, written by Thomas Middleton, one of Shakespeare's younger contemporaries and a well-known dramatist of the early seventeenth century. In *The Witch* are both songs in almost the same form as D'Avenant had given them, and it may be easily surmised why the songs were not printed in full in the First Folio. *Macbeth* was of course there printed from a playhouse manuscript; and these songs, which had formed a popular and catching part of Middleton's otherwise unsuccessful play, were introduced by the actors into *Macbeth*, and were presumed to be so well known to the actors of the play in the form it then had that a bare indication of them was enough.[2]

The date of Middleton's play has not been ascertained.[3] Various resemblances both of thought and language in the two plays — resemblances much too close and literal to be merely accidental — show that one of the authors must have borrowed from the other. Several of these resemblances

[1] See also notes, (1) page 92, lines 33, 35; (2) page 99, line 43.

[2] A. H. Bullen, in his Introduction to Middleton's *Works*, defends the Shakespearian authorship of the songs, but thinks they were probably added to and expanded by Middleton.

[3] Fleay conjectures that *The Witch* was composed in 1622, after Middleton began to write for the King's Men (Shakespeare's old company, see page xxv) at the Blackfriars theatre, by whom, according to the title-page of the manuscript, the play was first produced. The King's Men went to the Blackfriars in 1613, and Middleton wrote for the company from 1615 to 1624.

occur in those parts of *Macbeth* which are unquestionably Shakespeare's and bear the clearest tokens of his mintage Steevens, in the enthusiasm over Middleton which followed his find, held that Shakespeare borrowed from *The Witch*, but it is now clear that, whatever may be the exact date, Middleton wrote his play after the appearance of *Macbeth* ; besides, in other plays he unmistakably imitates Shakespeare. The theory of collaboration is untenable. The views of those who hold the 'interpolation' theory may be summarized thus : Middleton's own play being unsuccessful, as he admits, except probably in the lyrical passages, he was employed by the Blackfriars management to add to Shakespeare's successful play and develop the musical and spectacular features to suit the growing popular demand for this sort of thing. Of these 'interpolated' passages, the most important are : I, ii ; iii, 1–37 ; II, iii (Porter's part) ; III, v ; IV, i, 39–47, 125–132 ; iii, 140–159 ; V, ii ; v, 47–50 ; viii, 32–33, 35–75. "This theory of interpolation must be considered as in a high degree doubtful." — Dowden.

V. VERSIFICATION AND DICTION

Blank Verse

The greater part of *Macbeth* is in blank verse — the unrhymed, iambic five-stress (decasyllabic) verse, or iambic pentameter, introduced into England from Italy by Henry Howard, Earl of Surrey, about 1540, and used by him in a translation of the second and fourth books of Vergil's *Æneid*. Nicholas Grimald (*Tottel's Miscellany*, 1557) employed the measure for the first time in English original poetry, and its roots began to strike deep into British soil and absorb substance. It is peculiarly significant that Sackville and Norton should have used it as the measure of *Gorboduc*, the first English tragedy (performed by " the Gentlemen of the Inner Temple " on January 18, 1561, and first printed in 1565). About the time when Shakespeare arrived in London the infinite possibilities of blank verse as a vehicle for dramatic poetry and passion were being shown by Kyd and above all by Marlowe. Blank verse as used by Shakespeare is really an epitome of the development of the measure in connection with the English drama. In his earlier plays the blank verse is often similar to that of *Gorboduc*. The tendency is to adhere to the syllable-counting principle, to make the line the unit, the sentence and phrase coinciding with the line (end-stopped verse), and to use five perfect iambic feet to the line. In plays of the middle period, such as *The Merchant of Venice* and *As You Like It*, written between 1596 and 1600, the blank verse is more like that of Kyd and Marlowe, with less monotonous regularity in the structure and an increasing tendency to carry on the sense from one line to another without a syntactical or rhetorical pause at the end of the line (run-on verse, *enjambement*). Redundant syllables now abound and the melody is richer and fuller. In Shakespeare's later plays the blank verse breaks away from bondage to formal line limits, and sweeps all along with it in freedom, power, and organic unity.

Macbeth has a greater number of regular five-stress (pentameter) unrhymed lines [1] than is usual in a later play ; but

[1] For perfect examples of such normal lines see I, ii, 1 ; iii, 38 ; II, i, 35. The play contains 28 Alexandrines, 21 light endings, 78 feminine mid-line syllables, and 97 short lines. There are only 2 weak endings.

stress modifications of all kinds, Alexandrines, light endings, feminine mid-line syllables, and other variations and deviations from the norm give to the verse, with all its singular compactness of idiomatic expression, a rich music and a superb movement, epical as well as dramatic.[1]

Rhyme

1. *Couplets*. *Macbeth* has 108 lines of rhymed pentameter verse (rhymed couplets), an unusually large number for a later play and one that contains only 2108 lines.[2] Rhyme-tags, or couplets at the end of scenes and acts (see Abbott, § 515), are especially numerous. "In this play more scenes end with tags than in any other play in Shakespeare; the number of tag-rhymes is also greater than in any other play, including his very earliest." — Fleay. Those who believe in the Middleton influence read Middleton's heavy hand in this extraordinary prevalence of rhymed couplets.

2. *Witch Scenes*. The dominant measure in the speeches of the Weird Sisters is four-stress (tetrameter) trochaic verse catalectic — a rhythm often adopted by Shakespeare. Cf. Orlando's verses in praise of Rosalind, and Touchstone's 'false gallop' in *As You Like It*; Autolycus's song in *The Winter's Tale*, IV, iv, 220, etc. But in *Macbeth* the trochaic movement in the tetrameter is freer than in any other Shakespeare play, being varied by the introduction of three-stress lines, of iambic five-stresses, and very frequently of inversions of stress. The speeches of Hecate and the

[1] Cf. J. A. Symonds's *Blank Verse*, page 58.

[2] *Macbeth* is the shortest of Shakespeare's plays, with the exception of *The Comedy of Errors* (1778 lines) and *The Tempest* (2065 lines).

First Witch in III, v, and in IV, i, 39–43, 125–132, are in iambic verse, and this fact has been used to strengthen the arguments against the Shakespearian authorship of these passages.

Prose

In the development of the English drama the use of prose as a vehicle of expression entitled to equal rights with verse was due to Lyly. He was the first to use prose with power and distinction in original plays, and did memorable service in preparing the way for Shakespeare's achievement. Interesting attempts have been made to explain Shakespeare's distinctive use of verse and prose ; and of recent years there has been much discussion of the question "whether we are justified in supposing that Shakespeare was guided by any fixed principle in his employment of verse and prose, or whether he merely employed them, as fancy suggested, for the sake of variety and relief." [1] It is a significant fact that in many of his earlier plays there is little or no prose, and that the proportion of prose to blank verse increases with the decrease of rhyme. In *Macbeth* four kinds of prose may be distinguished : (1) The prose of formal documents, as in Macbeth's letter to Lady Macbeth (I, v). In Shakespeare prose is the usual medium for letters, proclamations, and other formal documents. (2) The prose of 'low life' and the speech of comic characters, as in the Porter scene (II, iii).

[1] Professor J. Churton Collins's *Shakespeare as a Prose Writer*. See Delius's *Die Prosa in Shakespeares Dramen* (*Shakespeare Jahrbuch*, V, 227-273) ; Janssen's *Die Prosa in Shakespeares Dramen* ; Professor Hiram Corson's *An Introduction to the Study of Shakespeare*, pp. 83–98.

This is a development of the humorous prose found, for example, in Greene's comedies that deal with country life. (3) The colloquial prose of simple dialogue, as in the talk between Lady Macduff and her little boy (IV, ii), and in the conversation of the Doctor and the Gentlewoman (V, i). In both these passages, as in the Porter scene, the prose diction gives temporary emotional relief and prepares for the heightening of the dramatic pitch in the scenes which immediately follow. (4) The prose of abnormal mentality, as in the sleep-walking scene (V, i). It is an interesting fact that Shakespeare should so often make persons whose state of mind is abnormal, or seemingly so, speak in prose.[1] "The idea underlying this custom of Shakespeare's evidently is that the regular rhythm of verse would be inappropriate where the mind is supposed to have lost its balance and to be at the mercy of chance impressions coming from without (as sometimes with Lear) or of ideas emerging from its unconscious depths and pursuing one another across its passive surface. The somnambulism of Lady Macbeth is such a condition. . . . This language (i.e. Lady Macbeth's in prose) stands in strong contrast with that of Macbeth in the surrounding scenes, full of a feverish and almost furious excitement, and seems to express a far more desolating misery." — A. C. Bradley. In previous editions of Hudson's Shakespeare the suggestion was made that the matter in the sleep-walking scene is too sublime, too austerely grand, to admit of anything so artificial as the measured language of verse, even though the verse were Shakespeare's ; and that the poet, as from an instinct of genius, saw or felt that any attempt

[1] Cf. *Hamlet*, II, ii, 171–221 ; IV, v, 172–186 ; *Lear*, III, iv, 51–64, etc.

to heighten the effect by any such arts or charms of delivery would unbrace and impair it. Is prose then, after all, a higher form of speech than verse ?

VI. DRAMATIC STRUCTURE

In regularity of construction and in symmetrical development of plot, *Macbeth* and *Julius Cæsar* are unsurpassed among Shakespeare's plays. The individual act-structure in both plays is as compact and effective as the structure of the drama as a whole.[1] Neither play has a complicating underplot ; every incident and every speech is inextricably bound up with the central personality. In both plays the setting of scenery and the accessories of supernatural phenomena harmonize subtly with incident and characterization.

Macbeth is a romantic tragedy in which is represented a conflict between an individual, or, as in this play, two persons acting together as one protagonist, and certain forces which environ, antagonize, and overwhelm. In such a drama are five essential elements : (1) the exposition or introduction ; (2) the complication or rising action ; (3) the climax or turning point ; (4) the resolution or falling action ; and (5) the catastrophe or conclusion.[2] In *Macbeth*, as in Shakespeare's other plays, the organic elements in the action do not correspond exactly to the mechanical division into acts. The exposition is contained in the first two scenes ;

[1] *Macbeth*, IV, iii, and *Julius Caesar*, IV, iii, have been censured for being too episodical, but the 'suspensive plot' theory is surely sufficient justification.

[2] Cf. Freytag's *Technik des Dramas*, Leipzig. A useful little book on the subject is Elisabeth Woodbridge's *The Drama ; its Law and its Technique*.

the complication begins with the meeting of Macbeth and the Weird Sisters and continues until the climax is reached in the murder of Banquo in the third scene of the third act. The beginning of the resolution is usually in the closest union with the climax, and the announcement by the Third Murderer that Fleance has escaped is incorporated with the Banquo murder scene. From the escape of Fleance, on through the banquet scene, the arousing of Macduff, and the retreat to Dunsinane, the fortunes of Macbeth and Lady Macbeth fall to the catastrophe.

Analysis by Act and Scene[1]

I. The Exposition, or Introduction (Tying of the Knot)

Act I, Scene i. The Witches are introduced in a desert place to the accompaniment of a storm in the physical world. The key-note of high tragic drama is struck at once. Like a prologue this brief scene foreshadows the moral and cosmic significance of an impending struggle in which Macbeth is involved (line 7).

Act I, Scene ii. Interest in Macbeth before he appears is deepened by narratives of his personal courage and military prowess. His success in battle with rebellion and invasion wins the favour of the king, who bestows on him in absence the title forfeited by the treacherous thane of Cawdor. This gift becomes an impulse towards Macbeth's own criminal 'enterprise' (cf. I, vii, 48) and carries with it a foreboding of his own treason (cf. I, iii, 116–117).

Act I, Scene iii, 1–47. With the introduction of Macbeth the dramatic exposition is complete. For the significance of Macbeth's first words, see note, line 38.

[1] "It must be understood that a play can be analyzed into very different schemes of plot. It must not be thought that one of these schemes is right and the rest wrong; but the schemes will be better or worse in proportion as — while of course representing correctly the facts of the play — they bring out more or less of what ministers to our sense of design." — Moulton.

II. The Complication, Rising Action, or Growth (Tying of the Knot)

Act I, Scene iii, 47–156. The greetings of the Witches furnish the exciting force of the drama, and the complication, or rising action, begins. The 'supernatural soliciting' (line 130) stimulates the guilty brooding of Macbeth ; he mutters to himself of 'horrible imaginings' (line 138) and murder ; and this, the temptation scene, closes with his determination to seek the king.

Act I, Scene iv. The king's announcement that Malcolm will be his successor determines in a general way Macbeth's 'black and deep desires' (line 51). The king resolves to honour Macbeth by a visit to his castle. The way is prepared for a line of action by Macbeth and for the introduction of Lady Macbeth. The king's graciousness and trust are in ironical contrast to Macbeth's dark hopes and sinister designs (cf. note, lines 13–14).

Act I, Scene v. In her quivering ambition for her husband's advancement, Lady Macbeth sees in the king's visit a chance "to catch the nearest way" (line 16). She starts Macbeth's treacherous purposes into a course of immediate action, and 'this night's great business' (line 66) is outlined ominously. The nervous tension of her soliloquy (lines 36–42) prepares for the effects of the reaction as revealed in V, 1.

Act I, Scene vi. Dramatic irony and the irony of situation (cf. note, I, iv, 13–14) prevail in this brief scene (cf. notes, lines 1–3, 20). The castle, with its air of peace and security, is a death trap ; the gracious mistress is an instigator of treason and murder.

Act I, Scene vii. Macbeth's soliloquy, with its vision of the evil consequences of the bloody deed, foreshadows all that comes in the falling action of the play. His faltering calls forth the energy and spirit of Lady Macbeth, who nerves him to the deed.

Act II, Scene i. The scene opens in an atmosphere of agitation and dread. Banquo's anxiety expresses itself in short, tense sentences relating to the time of night (cf. *Hamlet*, I, i, 1–14). In a few words with Macbeth he shows that his suspicions are awakened. Left alone, Macbeth has a vision of a bloody dagger, and then the bell, Lady Macbeth's signal for the murder, sounds.

Act II, Scene ii. As often in Greek tragedy, the murder is not presented on the stage, but it is suggested with all the accessories of horror in Lady Macbeth's soliloquy and her comments to Macbeth when he returns. Her strength of mind and her self-control come not from heartlessness but from a will steeled to help her husband. Before the scene closes the guilty pair are startled by a knocking at the gate ; and it is dramatically effective that one of the men knocking is the destined instrument of vengeance (cf. note, line 57).

Act II, Scene iii. The humorous soliloquy in prose with which the scene opens is a notable example of dramatic contrast. The realism and verisimilitude suggest how abnormal the conditions are through which the action has been passing. In the mechanism of stage production this interlude allows Macbeth and Lady Macbeth time to prepare for the discovery of the murder. When Macduff raises the alarm, Macbeth rushes in and rashly murders the drugged grooms, who were to be charged with the king's death, and thus he ruins the original plan made by Lady Macbeth. She swoons when she hears what he has done (cf. note, line 112). The king's sons suspect Macbeth and take refuge in flight.

Act II, Scene iv. After the rush of tragic incident this calm scene gives relief and perspective. In quiet talk, as in a Chorus speech, the immediate after effects of the occurrences are revealed. The flight of the king's sons has put " upon them suspicion of the deed " (lines 26–27) ; Macbeth has " gone to Scone to be invested " (lines 31–32) as king.

Act III, Scene i. In an opening soliloquy Banquo makes clear the menace he is to Macbeth and thus motives his own death. He holds the threads which connect Macbeth with the murder of Duncan ; the Witches prophesied that his own offspring should sit on the throne. Macbeth reveals his uneasiness, and, to end the torture of suspense, hastily arranges for the ' taking off ' of Banquo and his son.

Act III, Scene ii. Lady Macbeth begins to feel remorse. " Nought 's had, all 's spent " (line 4) is a note of deepest melancholy. Her husband is less with her than before ; the copartnership of guilt is breaking up. She conceals her feelings when Macbeth appears, flushed with his new scheme of murder. He hints of a ' deed of dreadful note ' (line 44) that is to be done that night. This half confidence enables her to play her part in the crisis of the banquet scene.

III. The Climax, Crisis, or Turning Point (the Knot Tied)

Act III, Scene iii, 1–18. Banquo is murdered, and this murder marks the height of Macbeth's success. From the entrance of the exciting force in his interview with the Witches until now the action has been a steady rise for him in power and reach.

IV. The Resolution, Falling Action, or Consequence (the Untying of the Knot)

Act III, Scene iii, 19–22. With the escape of Fleance begins the falling action of the drama. Though he is not used again as an agent, his escape symbolizes the turn of Macbeth's fortune. Macbeth's doom now darkens down, scene by scene, to the dénouement.

Act III, Scene iv. 'That Fleance is scap'd' is told to Macbeth as the banquet scene opens. He is uneasy, and for him at the feast the apparition of murdered Banquo becomes the handwriting on the wall. Superstitious terrors entangle him; he "will tomorrow . . . to the weird sisters" (lines 133–134). Macduff's absence from the banquet is referred to as significant.

Act III, Scene v. In the rising action Macbeth entered into alliance with the Witches and profited by their patronage; in the falling action, under Hecate, they contrive his ruin.

Act III, Scene vi. This quiet side-scene, like a Chorus speech (cf. II, iv), supplies comment and bridges an interval of time. Macbeth's conduct as king is making him suspected and detested in Scotland. Macduff has fled to England.

Act IV, Scene i. Macbeth meets the Witches for the second time. As before, they act as an exciting force. The repetition suggests the inevitableness of destiny. The suggestions and ambiguous oracles of the Witches first soothe Macbeth and then irritate him. His rapid moral deterioration is shown in the purposeless savagery of his scheme to massacre Macduff's wife and family.

Act IV, Scene ii. The scene has dramatic relief in the sweetness, humour, and pathos of the dialogue between Lady Macduff and her little son. The domestic calm is broken in on by the murderers. This wanton crime becomes the exciting cause of the dramatic catastrophe. It causes revolt in Scotland; it awakes Malcolm and Macduff to immediate revenge.

Act IV, Scene iii. This long scene has been censured for its 'dragging' tendency; but the slow movement represents the steady gathering of the forces, moral and material, which are about to overwhelm Macbeth. It marks the pause before the storm. When the news of his loss comes to Macduff, the emotion of tenderness and pathos, touched in the preceding scene, is intensified. For an explanation of the seemingly irrelevant passage on 'the evil,' see note, lines 146–159.

Act V, Scene i. Lady Macbeth's brooding remorse (cf. III, ii) has deepened into the melancholy of a disordered brain. In her delirium she reproduces the murder of Duncan, and though she has drifted apart from her husband into a solitude of guilty fears, she mingles his actions with her own, as she lays bare her soul. Her memories and imaginings are eating away her life; her death 'by self and violent hands' (V, viii, 70) is foreshadowed.

Act V, Scene ii. The action of the drama now oscillates between the opposing forces and Macbeth. In this scene the Scottish nobles and their followers gather to join Malcolm and the English army. They "march towards Birnam" (line 31).

Act V, Scene iii. Macbeth learns of the forces arrayed against him, and he is told that Lady Macbeth is ill. As he expresses his sense of utter loneliness, he awakens the pity due to a hero of tragedy, without disturbance of the principles of justice and moral retribution. Then his old personal courage blazes up in the presence of pressing danger.

V. Dénouement, Catastrophe, or Conclusion (the Knot Untied)

Act V, Scene iv. As the Scottish and English soldiers march through Birnam wood, they lop boughs and carry them to confuse the enemy. Thus begins the fulfilment of a prediction deemed by Macbeth impossible (IV, i, 92–100).

Act V, Scene v. Macbeth learns that Birnam wood is moving to Dunsinane, and 'the cry of women' (line 8) tells him that Lady Macbeth is dead. Again the pathos and the poetry of his intensely human cry awaken pity without interfering with the rigorous requirements of moral law.

Act V, Scene vi. This prelude to the battle reveals the spirit of the opposing forces. Battle representations were popular in the

Elizabethan theatre, and the stage conditions account in great measure for such short, typical scenes as this and the two which follow.

Act V, Scene vii. Macbeth, with hope in the prediction that " none of woman born shall harm " him (IV, i, 80–81), fights bravely against desperate odds (cf. note, line 2).

Act V, Scene viii. Despising a temptation to commit suicide, Macbeth fights on. The discovery that he has been tricked a second time by an ambiguous oracle of the ' juggling fiends ' (line 19), and that they have paltered with him ' in a double sense ' (line 20), unnerves him for a moment, but he recovers himself and goes to his doom with a speech that rings of heroic freedom and satisfies the demands of high tragedy.

VII. MANAGEMENT OF TIME AND PLACE

The historic succession of events comprised in *Macbeth* covers nearly twenty years. This period includes the time of " the warres that Duncane had with forrayne enemies in the seventh yeare of his raigne," the year of Duncan's death and Macbeth's coronation, and the seventeen years of Macbeth's reign from his accession in 1040 to his defeat and death in 1057 at the hands of Malcolm, " probably in open fight at Lumphanan in Aberdeenshire." — Hume Brown. These historic happenings are represented in the stage action as the occurrences of nine days, separated by uncertain intervals of time of not more than a few months at most ; [1] but, as we read or listen, it seems all only a matter of a few hours. In the second scene of the first act four battles recorded by Holinshed are rolled into one. Everywhere

[1] P. A. Daniel's time-analysis is : 1st day, I, i–iii. 2d day, I, iv–vii. 3d day, II, i–iv. Interval of about two weeks. 4th day, III, i–v. (III, vi, an impossible time.) 5th day, IV, i. 6th day, IV, ii. Interval (Ross's journey to England). 7th day, IV, iii; V, i. Interval (Malcolm's return to Scotland). 8th day, V, ii–iii. 9th day, V, iv–viii.

there is similar compression and dramatic economy. So with place ; the scene may shift from Forres to Inverness, from Macduff's castle to England, and from England to Dunsinane and the north again, but the unity and the continuity of perfect verisimilitude are secured in a convincing, effective plot. The genius of the great dramatist breaks down the barriers of mere locality. With him the years are as one day ; he is in the divine secret of time and of space.

VIII. THE CHARACTERS

The Weird Sisters [1]

" The Weird Sisters," says Coleridge, " are as true a creation of Shakespeare's as his Ariel and Caliban, — fates, furies, and materializing witches being the elements. They are wholly different from any representation of witches in the contemporary writers, and yet presented a sufficient external resemblance to the creatures of vulgar prejudice to act immediately on the audience." Charles Lamb, also, referring to the witches of Rowley and of Dekker says : " They are the plain, traditional, old-woman witches of our ancestors, — poor, deformed, and ignorant, the terror of villages, — themselves amenable to a justice. That should be a hardy sheriff, with the power of the county at his heels, that should lay hands on the Weird Sisters. They are of another jurisdiction."

[1] An interesting analysis of the Weird Sisters is in Professor Tolman's ' Studies in Macbeth ' in *The Views about Hamlet and other Essays*. There he says, " Strangely enough the word ' weird ' has come into modern English entirely from its use in *Macbeth*." Cf. note, page 13, line 32.

The old witches of superstition were foul, ugly, mischievous beings, generally actuated by vulgar envy or hate ; not so much wicked as mean, and more apt to excite disgust than to inspire terror or awe ; who could inflict injury, but not guilt ; and could work men's temporal ruin, but not win them to work their own spiritual ruin. The Weird Sisters are cast in quite another mould, and are beholden to those old witches for little if anything more than the drapery of the representation. Resembling old women, save that they have long beards, they bubble up in human shape, but own no human relations ; are without age, or sex, or kin ; without birth or death ; passionless and motiveless. A combination of the terrible and the grotesque, unlike the Furies of the Greek drama they are petrific, not to the senses, but to the thoughts. At first, indeed, on merely looking at them, we can scarce help laughing, so uncouth and grotesque is their appearance ; but afterwards, on looking into them, we find them terrible beyond description : and the more we look, the more terrible do they become, the blood almost curdling in our veins as, dancing, and singing their infernal glees over embryo murders, they unfold to our thoughts the cold, passionless, inexhaustible malignity and deformity of their nature. Towards Macbeth they have nothing of personal hatred or revenge ; their malice is of a higher strain, and savours as little of any such human ranklings as the thunderstorms and elemental perturbations amidst which they come and go. Coleridge describes their character as "consisting in the imaginative disconnected from the good" ; but with all their essential wickedness, the Weird Sisters have nothing gross or vulgar or sensual about them. "Fair is foul, and foul is fair," to them, by constitution of nature ;

darkness is their light, storms their sunshine, tumults, terrors, hideous rites, and Satanic liturgies their religion. They are indeed the very purity of sin incarnate ; the vestal virgins, so to speak, of hell ; in whom everything is reversed ; whose ascent is downwards ; whose proper eucharist is a sacrament of evil ; and the law of whose being is violation of law !

But is there anything of permanent truth in the matter of the Weird Sisters ? and, if so, what ? These are questions that may fairly claim to be considered in any attempt to interpret the drama.

Probably no form of superstition ever prevailed to much extent but that it had a ground and principle of truth. The old system of witchcraft was an embodiment of some natural law, a local and temporary outgrowth from something as general and permanent as human nature. Our moral being must breathe ; and therefore, in default of other provision, it puts forth some such arrangement of breathing-organs spontaneously, just as a tree puts forth leaves. The point of art then, in the case before us, was to raise and transfigure the literal into the symbolical ; to take the body, so brittle and perishable in itself, and endow it with immortality ; which could be done only by filling and animating it with the efficacy of imperishable truth. Accordingly Shakespeare took enough of current and traditionary matter to enlist old credulity in behalf of agents suited to his peculiar purpose ; he represented to the age its own thoughts, and at the same time informed that representation with a moral significance suited to all ages alike. In *The Witch* of Middleton we have the literal form of a transient superstition ; in *Macbeth* that form is made the transparent vehicle of a truth coeval and coextensive with the workings of human guilt. In their literal character the Weird Sisters answer to something that was, and is not ; in their symbolical character they answer to something that was, and is, and will abide ; for they represent the mysterious action and reaction between the evil mind and external nature.

For the external world serves in some sort as a looking-glass wherein we behold the image of our inner man ; and the evil suggestions, which seem to us written in the face or speaking from the mouth of outward objects and occasions, are in reality but projections from our own evil hearts. In a moral sense, the world around us only gives us back ourselves ; its aspect is but a reflection of what we bring to it ; so that, if the things we look on seem inviting us to crime, it is only because our depraved lusts and most frail affections construe their innocent meanings into wicked invitations.

In the spirit and virtue of this principle the Weird Sisters symbolize the inward moral history of each and every man ; and therefore they may be expected to live in the faith of reason so long as the present moral order or disorder of things shall last. They may be aptly enough described as poetical or mythical impersonations of evil influences. They body forth in living forms the fearful echo which the natural world gives back to the evil that speaks out from the human heart. And the secret of their power over Macbeth lies mainly in that they present to him his embryo wishes and half-formed thoughts. At one time they harp his fear aright, at another his hope, — and this, too, before his hope and fear have distinctly reported themselves in his consciousness, — and, by thus harping them, nurse them into purpose and draw them into act ; as men often know they would something, yet know not clearly what they would, till an articulation of it, or what seems such, comes to them from without. For so we are naturally made conscious of what is within us by the shadow it casts in the light of occasion ; and therefore it is that trials and opportunities have such an effect in revealing us to ourselves.

The Weird Sisters and Macbeth

The office of the Weird Sisters is not so much to deprave as to develop the characters whereon they act. They do not create the evil heart ; they only untie the evil hands. They put nothing into Macbeth's mind, but merely draw out what was already there ; breathing fructification upon his indwelling germs of sin, and thus acting as mediators between the secret upspringing purpose and the final accomplishment of crime. He was already minded to act as he does, only something was needed to " trammel up the consequence " ; which, in his apprehension, is just what the Weird Sisters do.

Accordingly it well appears in the course of the play that the thought of murdering Duncan is by no means new to Macbeth. As the Scottish crown was elective in a certain line, Macbeth's claim to it was legally as good as Duncan's till the vote was declared ; while his consciousness of superior fitness for the office might naturally have filled him with high expectations. At all events, it is plain enough that he has more than dallied with the purpose of retrieving that disappointment by crime ; he has entertained it seriously, and has had talks with his wife about it, she no doubt encouraging him in it with all her fiery vehemence of spirit. In his boldness of imagination he was even then ready to make an opportunity for the deed ; and it is a profound stroke of nature that, when the opportunity makes itself to his hands, its effect is to unman him. This is evident from his wife's stinging reproaches when at last his resolution falters and breaks down : " Was the hope drunk wherein you dress'd yourself ? " (I, vii, 35–36) — " When you durst do it, then you were a man " (I, vii, 49) ; and, " Nor time nor place Did then adhere, and yet you would make both " (I, vii, 51–52). These plainly refer to conversations they have had on the subject.

So that in the salutation of the Weird Sisters Macbeth just meets with an external temptation to that which he has been inwardly tempted or instigated to before. Yet he cannot all at once rest secure in the thoughts which at that prophetic greeting spring up within him ; and therefore it is that he " burns in desire to question them further." Fears and scruples as to the consequence still shake him ; a general pledge of security is not enough ; he craves to know further how and whence the means of safety are to come, his faith in the Weird promise not being strong enough at first to silence the warnings of experience, re-enforced as these are by the instinctive apprehensions of conscience :

> But in these cases
> We still have judgment here, that we but teach
> Bloody instructions, which, being taught, return
> To plague th' inventor : this even-handed justice
> Commends th' ingredients of our poison'd chalice
> To our own lips. [I, vii, 7–12.]

It is wisely ordered that the Weird Sisters meet Macbeth " in the day of success," when the exultations of victory would naturally prompt such a mind as his to catch at ambitious hopes. And " the early birth-date of his guilt " appears in that, on hearing the first Weird salutation, he is instantly seized with a kind of mental delirium. This comes out in what Banquo says :

> Good sir, why do you start, and seem to fear
> Things that do sound so fair ? — I' the name of truth,
> Are ye fantastical, or that indeed
> Which outwardly ye show ? My noble partner
> You greet with present grace and great prediction
> Of noble having and of royal hope,
> That he seems rapt withal ; to me you speak not.
> If you can look into the seeds of time,
> And say which grain will grow and which will not,
> Speak, then, to me, who neither beg nor fear
> Your favours nor your hate. [I, iii, 51–61.]

Macbeth's behaviour as here indicated is profoundly symptomatic of his moral predispositions. It is a full revelation of his criminal aptitudes that so startles and surprises him into a rapture of meditation. The Weird greeting is as a spark to a magazine of wickedness in him, and he is at once seized with a trance of terror at the result :

> Between the acting of a dreadful thing
> And the first motion, all the interim is
> Like a phantasma or a hideous dream:
> The Genius and the mortal instruments
> Are then in council ; and the state of a man,
> Like to a little kingdom, suffers then
> The nature of an insurrection.
> [*Julius Caesar*, II, i, 63–69.]

" So surely," says Coleridge, " is the guilt in its germ anterior to the supposed cause and immediate temptation." Whether the Weird Sisters " look into the seeds of time " or not, they manifestly look into the seeds of Macbeth's character; and they drop just the right stuff on them to make them sprout, as is evident from the fact that they instantly do sprout. And it was their insight of the unhatched eggs of evil within him, that drew them to him. It seems then clear that in Shakespeare's idea Macbeth already had the will, and that what he wanted further was but an earnest and assurance of success. The ordering of things so as to meet that want, and the tracing of the mental processes and the subtle workings of evil consequent thereon, — this it is that renders the drama such a paragon of ethical meaning organized into art. The Weird Sisters rightly strike the key-note and lead off the terrible chorus, because they embody and realize to us, and even to the hero himself, that secret preparation of evil within him out of which the whole action proceeds. In their fantastical and unearthly aspect, awakening mingled emotions of terror and mirth; in their mysterious reserve and oracular brevity of speech, so fitted at once to sharpen curiosity and awe down skepticism; in the circumstances of their prophetic greeting, — a blasted heath, with the elements wrangling over it, as if Nature were at odds with herself, and in love with desolation; — in all this we may discern a peculiar aptness to generate, even in strong minds, a belief in what they utter.

Macbeth and Banquo

The contrast in the behaviour of Macbeth and Banquo after the interview with the Weird Sisters is deeply significant. Belief takes hold of them both alike, for aught that appears. Yet, while Macbeth is beside himself with excitement, and transported with guilty thoughts and imaginations,

Banquo remains calm, unexcited, and perfectly self-poised. His intellectual forces are indeed stimulated by the preternatural address, but stimulated only to moralize the occasion and to draw arguments in support of his better mind. He hears the speakers with simple wonder ; shows no interest in them but that of an honest and rational curiosity ; his mind is absorbed in the matter before him ; and because he sees nothing of himself in them, and has no germs of wickedness for them to work upon, therefore he " neither begs nor fears their favours nor their hate." Macbeth, on the contrary, as we have seen, goes off in a trance or meditation, and loses what is before him in a stress of introversion : roused from this, he is eager and impatient to have them speak further, and his heart leaps forth to catch their words ; and again, when his ear is saluted with a partial fulfilment of their promise, a still more violent fit of abstraction seizes him, his very senses being palsied by the horrid suggestion which at once charms and terrifies him, and which makes him shudder simply because it reveals an answering spirit and purpose within him. That which so entrances and appalls him is but the image of his moral self, as he beholds it in the mirror of his newly-awakened consciousness. It is indeed a fearful transpiration of character !

Macbeth himself never thinks of making the Weird Sisters anywise responsible for what he does. The workings of his mind throughout manifestly infer that he feels just as free in his actions as if no supernatural soliciting had come near him. He therefore never offers to soothe his conscience or satisfy his reason on the score of his being under any fatal charm or fascination of evil. For, in truth, the promise of the throne is no more an instigation to murder for it than a promise of wealth in like sort would be to steal. To a truly honest man, such a promise, in so far as he believed it, would preclude the motives to theft. His thought would be, "Wealth is coming; I have but to work, and let it come." If, however, he were already a thief at heart, and kept from stealing only by fear of the consequences, he would be apt to construe the promise of wealth into a promise of impunity in theft, — which just marks the difference between Banquo and Macbeth. What with the one precludes the motive to crime, with the other itself becomes the motive to crime.

Banquo's moral reason, indeed, grows more vigilant and discerning for the temptations laid before him; his virtue, instead of being staggered by them, is rendered more circumspective and firm; he disarms or repels them by prayer; and the more they press upon him, the more he prays for help against them. For so we find that the having merely dreamed of the Weird Sisters moves him to exclaim, "Merciful powers, Restrain in me the cursed thoughts that nature Gives way to in repose!" (II, i, 7–9). And when Macbeth, on hearing of the dream, tries to draw him into his counsels, telling him "it shall make honour for him," he gives the prompt reply:

> So I lose none
> In seeking to augment it, but still keep
> My bosom franchis'd, and allegiance clear,
> I shall be counsell'd. [II, i, 26–29.]

Nothing could better approve his firmness of moral tone.

Macbeth

Macbeth's falterings and misgivings spring from the peculiar structure of his intellect as inflamed with the poison of meditated guilt. His understanding and imagination rush into irregular, convulsive action ; conscience being indeed the main cause of that action, yet hiding itself in the agitations of mind which it stirs up. Thus a strange, fearful hallucination, all begotten of guilt, takes possession of him. Hence his long and fatal course of self-delusion. He has done the greatest possible violence to his moral nature, and thereby " put rancours in the vessel of his peace " ; but the agonies thence resulting he still misderives from external causes, and keeps mistranslating them into the warnings of prudence, the forecastings of reason, and the threatenings of danger. His strong and excitable imagination, set on fire of conscience, fascinates and spellbinds his other faculties, and so gives objectiveness to its internal workings. His moral forces even usurp his eyes and ears, turning them into " miraculous organs," so that he cannot choose but see and hear things that are not ; as in case of " the air-drawn dagger " which leads him to Duncan, and the cry that haunts him, " Sleep no more ! Macbeth does murder sleep." Thus his conscience, instead of acting directly in the form of remorse, comes to act through imaginary terrors, which in turn react on his conscience, as fire is made hotter by the current of air which itself generates.

It is probably from oversight of this that some have set Macbeth down as a timid, cautious, remorseless villain, withheld from crime only by a shrinking, selfish apprehensiveness. He does indeed seem strangely dead to the guilt, and morbidly alive to the dangers, of his enterprise ; free from remorses of conscience, and filled with imaginary fears ; but whence his uncontrollable irritability of imagination ? how comes it that his mind so swarms with horrible imaginings, but that his imagination itself is set on fire of hell ?

Such "paintings of fear," it scarce need be said, are not the offspring of a mind in which the moral sense is weak or dead; rather they attest a peculiar strength and quickness in that sense. Call it insanity, if you will; but it is an insanity full of moral inspiration. And what a lesson does it read us of the secret possibilities of evil, ay, and of punishment too, wrapped up in the moral constitution of man!

It is a natural result of an imagination so redundant and excitable as Macbeth's that the agonies of remorse should project and embody themselves in imaginary terrors, and so spur him on to further crimes for security against those terrors. To give himself peace, he must still keep using his dagger; and yet every thrust he makes with it stabs a new wound in his own soul. Such is the dreadful madness which guilt engenders in him! His moral forces, indeed, turn to a downright fury and venom of infatuation, insomuch that he boldly enters the lists against the very powers in which he trusted.

All this comes out in his interview with Lady Macbeth on the eve of Banquo's murder:

> We have scotch'd the snake, not kill'd it:
> She 'll close and be herself, whilst our poor malice
> Remains in danger of her former tooth.
> But let the frame of things disjoint, both the worlds suffer,
> Ere we will eat our meal in fear, and sleep
> In the affliction of these terrible dreams
> That shake us nightly: better be with the dead,
> Whom we, to gain our place, have sent to peace,
> Than on the torture of the mind to lie
> In restless ecstasy. Duncan is in his grave;
> After life's fitful fever he sleeps well;
> Treason has done his worst: nor steel, nor poison,
> Malice domestic, foreign levy, nothing,
> Can touch him further. [III, ii, 13–26.]

Here we see that crime has filled his mind with scorpions, and still he thinks of no way to clear them out but by crime. And the thought of Duncan instantly charms him into a feverish brooding over the dangers which he seems to have invited against himself by murdering him. And it is well worth noting how, in this speech, as in several others, he goes on kindling more and more with his theme, till he fairly loses himself in a trance of moral and imaginative thought. The inward burnings of guilt act as a sort of inspiration to him. For the preternatural illumination of mind, which so often transports him, marks the insurgent stress of moral forces.

Lady Macbeth

In the structure and working of her mind and moral frame, Lady Macbeth is the opposite of her husband, and therefore all the fitter to countervail his infirmity of purpose; that is, she differs from him in just the right way to supplement him. Of a firm, sharp, wiry, matter-of-fact intellect, doubly charged with energy of will, she has little in common with him save a red-hot ambition : hence, while the Weird disclosures act on her will just as on his, and she jumps forthwith into the same purpose, the effect on her mind is wholly different. Without his irritability of understanding and imagination, she is therefore subject to no such involuntary transports of thought. Accordingly she never loses herself in any raptures of meditation ; no illusions born of guilty fear get the mastery of her ; at least, not when her will is in exercise : in her waking moments her senses are always so thoroughly in her keeping that she hears and sees things just as they are. As conscience draws no visions before her eyes, and shapes no voices in her hearing, so, while he is shaken and quite unmanned with fantastical terrors, she remains externally calm, collected, and cool. Her presence of mind indeed seems firmest when his trances of illusion run highest ; so that, instead of being at all infected with his agitations, her forces then move in the aptest order to recover him from them. Which shows that her sympathy with his ambition, intense as it is, has no power to make her sympathize with his mental workings. It may almost be said, indeed, that what stimulates his imagination stifles hers.

There was strong dramatic reason why Lady Macbeth should have such a mind and temper as to be moved and impressed, when awake, by nothing but facts. She ought to be, as indeed she is, so constituted that the evil which has struck its roots so deep within never comes back to her in the elements and aspects of nature, either to mature the guilty purpose or to obstruct the guilty act. It is remarkable that she does not once recur to the Weird Sisters, nor make any use of their salutations ; they seem to have no weight with her but for the impression they have wrought on her husband. That this impression may grow to the desired effect, she refrains from meddling with it, and seeks only to fortify it with impressions of another sort. And what could better approve her shrewdness and tact than that, instead of overstraining this one motive, and so weakening it, she thus lets it alone and labours to strengthen it by mixing others with it ? For in truth the Weird Sisters represent, in most appalling sort, the wickedness of the purpose they suggest : so that Macbeth's fears as well as his hopes are stimulated, and his fears even more than his hopes, by the recollection of their greetings : the instant he reverts to them, his imagination springs into action, — an organ of which ambition works the bellows indeed, but conscience still governs the stops and keys. The very thought of them, indeed, seems to put him at once under a fascination of terror. All this does not escape his wife ; who therefore judges it best rather to draw his thoughts off from that matter, and fix them on other inducements. He had thought of the murder, when as yet he could see no opportunities for doing it. When those opportunities come, *they* are the arguments that tell with her ; and she therefore makes it her business to urge them upon him, invoking his former manhood withal, to redintegrate and shame him out of his present weakness :

> Nor time nor place
> Did then adhere, and yet you would make both :
> They have made themselves, and that their fitness now
> Does unmake you. [I, vii, 51–54.]

Coleridge justly remarks upon her adroit boldness in first pressing those very considerations which most stagger her husband's purpose. That Duncan has cast himself unreservedly on their loyalty and hospitality, this she puts forth as the strongest argument for murdering him ! An awful stroke of character indeed, and therefore awful, because natural. By thus anticipating his greatest drawbacks, and urging them as the chief incentives, she forecloses all debate. Which is just what she wants ; for she knows full well that the thing will not stand the tests of reason a moment ; it must be done first, and discussed afterwards. And throughout this wrestling-match she surveys the whole ground, and darts upon the strongest points with the quickness and sureness of instinct ; the sharpness of the exigency being to her a sort of practical inspiration. The finishing stroke in this part of the work is when, her husband's resolution being all in a totter, she boldly cuts the sinews of retreat, casting the thing into a personal controversy and making it a theme of domestic war :

> LADY MACBETH. Art thou afeard
> To be the same in thine own act and valour
> As thou art in desire ? Wouldst thou have that
> Which thou esteem'st the ornament of life,
> And live a coward in thine own esteem,
> Letting ' I dare not ' wait upon ' I would,'
> Like the poor cat i' the adage ?
> MACBETH. Prithee, peace :
> I dare do all that may become a man ;
> Who dares do more is none.
> LADY MACBETH. What beast was 't, then,
> That made you break this enterprise to me ?
> [I, vii, 39–48.]

The virtues and affections of the husband are now drawn up against the conscience of the man. For, to be scorned and baited as a coward by the woman he loves, and by whom he is loved, is the last thing a soldier can bear : death is nothing to it. Macbeth, accordingly, goes about the deed, and goes through it, with an assumed ferocity caught from his wife.

Nor is that ferocity native to her own breast : surely, on her part too, it is assumed ; for though in her intense overheat of expectant passion it is temporarily fused into her character, it is disengaged and thrown off as soon as that heat passes away, — as men, in the ardour of successful effort, sometimes pass for a while into a character which they undertake to play. Lady Macbeth begins with acting a part which is really foreign to her, but which, notwithstanding, such is her energy of will, she braves out to issues so overwhelming that her husband and many others believe it to be her own. Take, for example, the speech beginning, "I have given suck, and know how tender 't is to love the babe that milks me." Mrs. Siddons used to utter the closing words of that speech in a scream, as though scared from her propriety by the audacity of her own tongue. It is not hard to conceive how a spasmodic action of fear might lend to such a woman as Lady Macbeth an appearance of superhuman or inhuman boldness. At all events, it seems clear enough that in this case her fierce vehemence of purpose rasps her woman's feelings to the quick; and the pang thence resulting might well utter itself in a scream.

Lady Macbeth is indeed a great bad woman, whom we fear and pity; but neither so great nor so bad as is commonly supposed. She has closely studied her husband, and penetrated far into the heart of his mystery, yet she knows him rather as he is to her than as he is in himself: hence in describing his character she interprets her own. She has indeed the ambition to wish herself unsexed, but not the power to unsex herself except in words. For, though she invokes the "murdering ministers" to "come to her woman's breasts, and take her milk for gall," still she cannot make them come, and her milk, in spite of her invocation, continues to be milk. Verplanck describes her as "a woman of high intellect, bold spirit, and lofty desires, who is mastered by a fiery thirst of power, and that for her husband as well as herself."

Two characters, however, may easily be made out for Lady Macbeth, according as we lay the chief stress on what she says or what she does. No one can fail to remark that the anticipation raised by her earlier speeches is by no means sustained in her subsequent acts. When she looks upon the face of the sleeping Duncan, and sees the murderous thought passing, as it were, into a *fact* before her, a gush of womanly feeling or of native tenderness suddenly stays her hand. "Had he not resembled My father as he slept, I had done 't" (II, ii, 12–13). That such a real or fancied resemblance should thus rise up and unsinew her purpose in the moment of action, is a rare touch of nature indeed, and shows that conscience works even more effectually through the feelings in her case than through the imagination in that of her husband. And the difference of imagination and feeling in this point is, that the one acts most at a distance, the other on the spot. The towering audacity of her earlier speeches arises, at least in part, from an overstrained endeavour to school herself into a firmness and fierceness of which she feels the want.

Her whole after course favours this view. For instance, when she hears from Macbeth how he has murdered the two grooms also, she sinks down at the tale. That is not a counterfeit swoon. The thing takes her by surprise, and her iron-ribbed self-control for once gives way. The announcement of Duncan's murder had no such effect upon her, for she was prepared for that; and that was when she would have counterfeited fainting, if at all. So bold of tongue, she could indeed say, "the sleeping and the dead Are but as pictures; 't is the eye of childhood That fears a painted devil" (II, ii, 53-55); but the sequel proves her to have been better than she was aware. In truth, she has undertaken too much: in her efforts to screw her own and her husband's courage to the sticking-place, there was exerted a force of will which answered the end indeed, but at the same time flawed the core of her being.

Accordingly she gives no waking sign of the dreadful work that is doing within : the unmitigable corrodings of her rooted sorrow, even when busiest in destruction, do not once betray her, except when her self-rule is dissolved in sleep. But the truth comes out, with an awful mingling of pathos and terror, in the scene where her conscience, sleepless amidst the sleep of nature, nay, most restless even then when all other cares are at rest, drives her forth, open-eyed yet sightless, to sigh and groan over spots on her hands that are visible to none but herself, nor even to herself save when she is blind to everything else, — a living automaton worked by the agonies of remorse ! How perfectly her senses are then dominated by the conscience is shown with supreme effect in " Here 's the smell of blood still " ; which has been aptly noted as the only instance in modern times where the sense of smell has been successfully employed in high tragic expression.[1] An awful mystery, too, hangs over her death. We know not, the poet himself seems not to know, whether the gnawings of the undying worm drive her to suicidal violence, or themselves cut asunder the cords of her life : all we know is, that the death of her body springs somehow from the inextinguishable life and the immedicable wound of her soul. What a history of her woman's heart is written in her thus sinking, sinking away where imagination shrinks from following her, under the violence of an invisible yet unmistakable disease, which still sharpens its inflictions and at the same time quickens her sensibilities !

[1] See quotation from Verplanck illustrating V, i, 48–49.

Lady Macbeth dies before her husband. This is one of the most judicious points of the drama. Her death touches Macbeth in the only spot where he seems to retain the feelings of a man, and draws from him some deeply-solemn, soothing, elegiac tones :

> MACBETH. Wherefore was that cry ?
> SEYTON. The queen, my lord, is dead.
> MACBETH. She should have died hereafter ;
> There would have been a time for such a word.
> To-morrow, and to-morrow, and to-morrow,
> Creeps in this petty pace from day to day,
> To the last syllable of recorded time ;
> And all our yesterdays have lighted fools
> The way to dusty death. Out, out, brief candle !
> Life 's but a walking shadow ; a poor player
> That struts and frets his hour upon the stage
> And then is heard no more. It is a tale
> Told by an idiot, full of sound and fury,
> Signifying nothing. [V, v, 15-28.]

IX. GENERAL CHARACTERISTICS

Dr. Johnson observes, with singular infelicity, that this play "has no nice discriminations of character." In respect of characterization, Macbeth and Lady Macbeth are equalled only by Shakespeare's other masterpieces, — by Shylock, Hamlet, Lear, and Iago ; while the Weird Sisters, so seemingly akin (though whether as mothers or sisters or daughters we cannot tell) to the thunderstorms that come and go with them, occupy the summit of his preternatural creations. Nevertheless, it must be owned that the grandeur of the dramatic combination somewhat overshadows the individual characters ; insomuch that something of special effort is required to keep the delicate limning of the agents from being lost sight of in the magnitude, the manifold unity and thought-like rapidity of the action.

The style of this great drama is pitched in the same high tragic key as the action. Throughout we have an explosion, as of purpose into act, so also of thought into speech, both literally kindling with their own swiftness. No sooner thought than said, no sooner said than done, is the law of the piece. Therewithal thoughts and images come crowding and jostling each other in such quick succession as to prevent a full utterance. Nowhere is there greater concentration of expression. The least touching of the ear sends vibrations through all the chambers of the mind. Hence the large, manifold suggestiveness which lurks in the words : they seem instinct with something which the speakers cannot stay to unfold. And between these invitations to linger, and the continual drawings onward, the reader's mind is kindled to an almost preternatural activity. All which might at length grow wearisome, but that the play is throughout a conflict of antagonist elements and opposite extremes, which are so managed as to brace up the interest on every side : so that the effect of the whole is to refresh, not exhaust the powers, the mind being sustained in its long and lofty flight by the wings that grow forth as of their own accord from its superadded life. The lyrical element, instead of being interspersed here and there in the form of musical lulls and pauses, is thoroughly interfused with the dramatic ; while the ethical sense underlies them both, and is forced up through them by their own pressure. The whole drama, indeed, may be described as a tempest set to music

X. STAGE HISTORY

The strong dramatic interest of *Macbeth* has made its popularity as an acting play among Shakespeare's tragedies almost as great as that of *Hamlet*. The red shadow of murder and the gloom of disaster hang over it from first to last; with the exception of the opening of the scene after the murder of Duncan, there is an almost total lack of comic relief; but the vigorous style, the rapid action, the playwright's structural methods, the spectacular stage effects, and the superb opportunity afforded for the interpretation of a notable heroine as well as for that of a great hero, have made it a strong favourite with actors and audiences.

The Seventeenth Century

The evidence for the date of composition (see pages xxvi-xxvii) attests the popularity of the play before Shakespeare's death, and the theory of interpolations by Middleton (see pages xxxi-xxxiii) would indicate that with or without alterations it held the stage up to the time of the closing of the theatres. Richard Burbage (Burbidge, Burbadge), the famous member of the company to which Shakespeare belonged, was undoubtedly the first stage Macbeth. Though short and stout, he had a musical voice, and Overbury speaks of "his full and significant action of body." In the theatre of the Restoration, in such adaptations as are represented by the Quartos of 1673 and 1674 (see page xxx), it was one of the most popular of the Shakespearian revivals, Thomas Betterton, the great Shakespeare actor of the time, taking the leading part and Mrs. Betterton playing Lady Macbeth.

Pepys has eight distinct references to performances at " the Duke's house " (the theatre at Lincoln's Inn Fields) between 1666 and 1669. The description under the date, January 7, 1667, is significant: " To the Duke's house and saw *Macbeth*, which though I saw it lately, yet appears a most excellent play in all respects, but especially in divertisement, though it be a deep tragedy; which is a strange perfection in a tragedy, it being most proper here and suitable." The " divertisement " probably has reference to such " alterations, amendments, additions, and new songs " as are mentioned on the title-page of the D'Avenant Quarto (see page xxxi). After the opening of the theatres methods of opera were applied to some of Shakespeare's plays, and none suffered more in this respect than *Macbeth* and *The Tempest*. The accompanying music to *Macbeth* is now known to have been by Matthew Locke (Lock), one of the earliest English composers to write for the stage.[1] Among other changes and deformations in D'Avenant's version [2] are the abbreviation of the blank verse speeches, the use of rhymed heroics in the dialogue between Macduff and his wife, and the modernization of the diction. The matter of the Witches offered an opportunity for display too good to be neglected, and the Weird Sisters as conceived by Shakespeare, with their solemn suggestion of the Destinies of the Greek and Roman mythology and the Norns of the Scandinavian, gave place to semi-comic furies, now flying and now participating in spectacular dances.

[1] A controversy has raged over the authorship of the original *Macbeth* music, some claiming that Purcell wrote it. As a matter of fact the music appeared when Purcell was only fourteen years old.

[2] See Furness's *A New Variorum. Macbeth*, pages 507–543.

The Eighteenth Century

The D'Avenant version was popular on the stage until Garrick appeared as Macbeth at Drury Lane in 1744. Garrick professed to give "*Macbeth* as written by Shakespeare," and though he retained the operatic business in the Witch scenes and Locke's music, he was on the whole faithful to the original text except at the close of the play. In Garrick's version Macbeth is represented on the stage to the last, and he dies with this most un-Shakespearian speech on his lips :[1]

> 'T is done ! the scene of life will quickly close.
> Ambition's vain delusive dreams are fled,
> And now I wake to darkness, guilt, and horror. —
> I cannot rise : — I dare not ask for mercy —
> It is too late ; hell drags me down ; — I sink,
> I sink ; — my soul is lost for ever ! Oh ! — Oh !

In Garrick's later revivals Lady Macbeth was played by Mrs Pritchard, one of the great interpreters of the part in the traditions of the stage.

Garrick played Macbeth in scarlet coat, gold lace and powdered tiewig, the full court dress of the time of George II. It had been suggested to him that he should appear in Highland costume, but he replied naïvely : "You forget that the Pretender was here only thirty years ago, and, egad ! I should be pelted off the stage with orange-peel."

The first time [2] that a stage Macbeth appeared in tartan and kilt was when "rough honest old" Macklin took the

[1] This arrangement with these added lines was continued in Kemble's version of the play.

[2] Steevens pointed out that in IV, iii, 160, there may be an indication that appropriate Scottish dress was used in Shakespeare's day.

part at Covent Garden in 1773. All the characters were in Scottish costumes, and one of his detractors described Macklin as an "old Scotch piper stumping along at the head of his army." In his later revivals he abandoned the Highland dress and acted the part in conventional costume.

On April 21, 1794, a notable performance took place at the opening of new Drury Lane, when John Philip Kemble played Macbeth, his sister, Mrs. Siddons, acted Lady Macbeth, and the younger brother, Charles Kemble, appeared as Malcolm. Kemble was singularly impressive in the banquet scene, and this was the first time that it was given without a visible ghost.[1] "Mrs. Siddons," writes Doran, "imagined Lady Macbeth, the heroine of the most tragic of tragedies, to be a delicate blonde, who ruled by her intellect, and subdued by her beauty, but with whom no one feeling of common general nature was congenial, a woman prompt for wickedness, but swiftly possessed by remorse."

The Nineteenth Century

Kemble's Macbeth with its dignity and poetry dominated the stage until Edmund Kean appeared in the part, November 5, 1814. Kean was peculiarly effective in the murder scene. "As a lesson of common humanity," says Hazlitt, "it was heart-rending. The hesitation, the bewildered look, the coming to himself when he sees his hands bloody; the manner in which his voice clung to his throat and choked his utterance; his agony and tears; the force of nature overcome by passion — beggared description." To Kean

[1] Macready, Booth, and Irving followed Kemble in this; Edmund Kean, Forrest, and Charles Kean adhered to the old tradition of a visible ghost.

belongs the credit of having swept away the last of the comic business that had clung to the Witch scenes from the time of the Restoration. From his day to the beginning of the twentieth century the stage history of *Macbeth* is a history of noteworthy performances by the great actors of the modern world. Macready, Forrest, Phelps, Charles Kean, Booth, Irving, and Salvini are names that will ever be associated with the title rôle ; and Helen Faucit (Lady Martin), Ellen Terry, and Charlotte Cushman have widened in a remarkable and varied way the conception of what is involved in the dramatic interpretation of the heroine.

AUTHORITIES

(With the more important abbreviations used in the notes.)

F_1 = First Folio, 1623.
F_2 = Second Folio, 1632.
F_3 = Third Folio, 1664.
F_4 = Fourth Folio, 1685.
Ff = all the seventeenth century Folios.
D'Avenant = D'Avenant's version, 1674.
Rowe = Rowe's editions, 1709, 1714.
Pope = Pope's editions, 1723, 1728.
Theobald = Theobald's editions, 1733, 1740.
Hanmer = Hanmer's edition, 1744.
Johnson = Johnson's edition, 1765.
Capell = Capell's edition, 1768.
Malone = Malone's edition, 1790.
Steevens = Steevens's edition, 1793.
Globe = Globe edition (Clark and Wright), 1864.
Clar = Clarendon Press (second) edition (Clark and Wright), 1869.
Dyce = Dyce's (third) edition, 1875.
Delius = Delius's (fifth) edition, 1882.
Camb = Cambridge (third) edition (W. A. Wright), 1891.
Libby = M. F. Libby's *Some New Notes on Macbeth*, 1893.
Manly = J. M. Manly's edition, Longmans' English Classics, 1896.
Verity = A. W. Verity's edition, Pitt Press, 1902.
Furness = H. H. Furness's *A New Variorum. Macbeth* (revised edition), 1903.
Liddell = M. H. Liddell's edition, Doubleday, Page & Co., 1903.
Herford = C. H. Herford's *The Eversley Shakespeare*, 1903.
Abbott = E. A. Abbott's *A Shakespearian Grammar*.
Cotgrave = Cotgrave's *Dictionarie of the French and English Tongues*, 1611.
Schmidt = Schmidt's *Shakespeare Lexicon*.
Skeat = Skeat's *An Etymological Dictionary*.
Murray = *A New English Dictionary* (*The Oxford Dictionary*).
Century = *The Century Dictionary*.
Holinshed = Raphael Holinshed's *Chronicles of England, Ireland, and Scotland* (second edition), 1586–1587.
Scot = Reginald Scot's *The Discoverie of Witchcraft*, 1584.

CHRONOLOGICAL CHART

Except in the case of Shakespeare's plays (see note) the literature dates refer to first publication.

Year	Shakespeare: Biography; Poems	Shakespeare: Plays	British and Foreign Literature	History and Biography
1564	Birth. Baptism, April 26, Stratford-on-Avon	Note. The plays in the columns below are arranged in the probable, though purely conjectural, order of composition. Dates appended to plays are those of first publication. Where no date is given, the play was first published in the First Folio (1623). M signifies that the play was mentioned by Meres in the **Palladis Tamia** (1598)	**Quart livre de Pantagruel**	Michelangelo died. Calvin died. Marlowe born. Galileo born.
1565	Father became alderman		Sackville and Norton's **Gorboduc** printed	Philip II of Spain gave his name to Philippine Islands
1566	Brother Gilbert born		Udall's **Roister Doister** printed ?	Murder of Rizzio
1568	Father, as bailiff of Stratford, entertained Queen's and Earl of Worcestor's actors		The Bishops Bible. La Taille's **Saülle Furieux**. R. Grafton's **Chronicle**	Mary of Scots a prisoner in England. Ascham died. Coverdale died. Netherlands War of Liberation
1572			Camoens' **Os Lusiadas** (The Lusiads)	Knox died. Massacre of St. Bartholomew
1573			Tasso's **Aminta**	Ben Jonson born? Donne born
1574	Brother Richard born		**Mirror for Magistrates** (third edition)	Earl of Leicester's players licensed
1575			**Gammer Gurton's Needle.** Golding's Ovid (complete)	Queen Elizabeth at Kenilworth. Palissy lectured on Natural History
1576			**The Paradise of Dainty Devices.** Gascoigne's **Steel Glass**	"The Theatre" opened in Finsbury Fields, London, followed by "The Curtain." Hans Sachs died
1577	Father in financial difficulties		Holinshed's **Chronicles**	Drake sailed to circumnavigate globe

		Comedies	Histories	Tragedies		
1579	Sister Ann died (aged eight)				Gosson's **School of Abuse.** North's Plutarch. Lyly's **Euphues** (pt. 1). Spenser's **Shepherd's Calendar**	**Union of Utrecht.** Tasso put in confinement at Ferrara
1580	Brother Edmund born				Montaigne's **Essais** (first edition)	Brown founded Separatists. Camoens died
1581					Tasso's **Gerusalemme Liberata**	Dutch Declaration of Independence
1582	Married Anne Hathaway				The Rheims New Testament	Accademia della Crusca founded
1583	Daughter Susanna born				Garnier's **Les Juives**	Sir Humphrey Gilbert drowned
1584					Lyly's **Campaspe.** Peele's **Arraignment of Paris**	William the Silent assassinated. Ivan the Terrible died
1585	Twin children (Hamnet, Judith) born				Guarini's **Pastor Fido** (1590)	Ronsard died
1586	Probably went to London				Camden's **Britannia**	Sir Philip Sidney killed
1587					Hakluyt's **Four Voyages. Faustbuch** (Spiess, Frankfort)	Execution of Mary of Scots
1588					**Martin Marprelate: The Epistle**	Defeat of Spanish Armada
1589					Puttenham's **Art of English Poesie**	Henry of Navarre, King of France. Palissy died in Bastille
1590		**Love's Labour's Lost** (M, 1598)			Marlowe's **Tamburlaine.** Spenser's **Faerie Queene,** I-III. Lodge's **Rosalynde.** Sidney's **Arcadia**	Battle of Ivry
1591		**Comedy of Errors** (M)	**1 Henry VI** **2 Henry VI**		Sidney's **Astrophel and Stella.** Harington's tr. of **Orlando Furioso**	Herrick born

CHRONOLOGICAL CHART (CONTINUED)

YEAR	SHAKESPEARE				BRITISH AND FOREIGN LITERATURE	HISTORY AND BIOGRAPHY
	BIOGRAPHY; POEMS	PLAYS (see note above)				
1592	Greene's attack in **Groatsworth of Wit**	**Two Gentlemen of Verona** (M)	**Richard III** (M, 1597). **3 Henry VI**	**Romeo and Juliet** (M, 1597)	Daniel's **Delia.** Lyly's **Gallathea (Galatea)**	Greene died. Montaigne died. London theatres closed through plague
1593	**Venus and Adonis** (seven editions, 1593–1602)		**King John** (M). **Richard II** (M, 1597)	**Titus Andronicus** (M, 1594)	Peele's **Edward I.** Barnes's **Sonnets**	Marlowe died. Herbert born
1594	**Lucrece** (five editions, 1594–1616)	**A Midsummer Night's Dream** (M, 1600)			Rinuccini's **Dafne. Satire Ménipée**	Palestrina ("Princeps Musicæ") died
1595	Valuable contemporary references to Shakespeare	**All 's Well that Ends Well. Taming of the Shrew**			Peele's **Old Wives' Tale.** Spenser's **Epithalamion**	Tasso died. Sir Walter Raleigh's expedition to Guiana. Sir J. Hawkins died
1596	Son Hamnet died. Family applied for coat-of-arms		**1 Henry IV** (M, 1598). **2 Henry IV** (1600)		Drayton's **Mortimeriados. Faerie Queene,** Books IV-VI	Burbage built Blackfriar's Theatre. Descartes born. Sir F. Drake died
1597	Purchased New Place, Stratford	**Merry Wives of Windsor. Merchant of Venice** (M, 1600)			Bacon's **Essays** (first edition). Hall's **Virgidemiarum**	The Tyrone rebellion
1598	Shakespeare acted in Jonson's **Every Man in His Humour**	**Much Ado About Nothing** (1600)	**Henry V** (1600)		Meres's **Palladis Tamia.** Chapman's Homer (pt. 1). Lope de Vega's **Arcadia**	Peele died. Edict of Nantes
1599	Part proprietor of Globe Theatre. Coat-of-arms granted. **The Passionate Pilgrim**	**As You Like It**			Aleman's **Guzman de Alfarache.** Peele's **David and Bethsabe**	Spenser died. Globe Theatre built. Oliver Cromwell born
1600	Won a London lawsuit	**Twelfth Night**			**England's Helicon**	Calderon born. Bruno died

1601	Father died. **The Phœnix and Turtle**			**Julius Cæsar**	Jonson's **Poetaster**	The Essex plot. Rivalry between London adult and boy actors
1602	Purchased more Stratford real estate			**Hamlet** (1603)	Dekker's **Satiromastix**	Bodleian Library founded
1603	His company acted before the Queen	**Troilus and Cressida** (1609)			Jonson's **Sejanus**	Queen Elizabeth died. Millenary Petition
1604	Sued Rogers at Stratford	**Measure for Measure**		**Othello**	Marlowe's **Faustus** (1588-1589)	Hampton Court Conference
1605	Godfather to William D'Avenant			**Macbeth**	**Don Quixote** (pt. 1)	Gunpowder plot. Sir Thomas Browne born
1606	**King Lear** given before Court			**King Lear** (1608)	Chapman's **Monsieur D'Olive**	Lyly died. Corneille born
1607	Daughter Susanna married Dr. Hall			**Timon of Athens**	Dekker and Webster's **Westward Ho !**	Settlement of Jamestown
1608	Birth of granddaughter, Elizabeth Hall. Death of mother (Mary Arden)	**Pericles** (1609)		**Antony and Cleopatra**	Captain John Smith's **A True Relation.** Middleton's **A Mad World**	Milton born. Quebec founded
1609	**Sonnets. A Lover's Complaint**			**Coriolanus**	The Douai Old Testament	Separatists (Pilgrims) in Leyden
1610	Purchased more real estate	**Cymbeline**			Strachey's **Wracke and Redemption**	Henry IV (Navarre) assassinated
1611	Subscribed for better highways	**Winter's Tale** **The Tempest**			King James Bible (A.V.). Bellarmine's **Puissance du Pape**	Gustavus Adolphus, King of Sweden
1613	Invested in London house property. Brother Richard died		**Henry VIII**		Drayton's **Polyolbion**	Globe Theatre burned
1616	Made his will. Daughter Judith married Thomas Quiney. Died April 23 (May 3, New Style)				Captain John Smith's **New England.** Folio edition of Jonson's Poems. D'Aubigné's **Les Tragiques** (1577)	Cervantes died. Beaumont died. Baffin explores Baffin's Bay. Harvey lectured on the circulation of the blood

DISTRIBUTION OF CHARACTERS

In this analysis are shown the acts and scenes in which the characters (see Dramatis Personæ, page 2) appear, with the number of speeches and lines given to each.

NOTE. Parts of lines are counted as whole lines.

Character	Act, Scene	No. of Speeches	No. of Lines
MACBETH	I, iii	13	50
	I, iv	3	16
	I, v	3	4
	I, vii	7	48
	II, i	6	45
	II, ii	14	39
	II, iii	13	33
	III, i	15	114
	III, ii	5	41
	III, iv	25	110
	IV, i	16	75
	V, iii	10	55
	V, v	6	44
	V, vi	5	10
	V, viii	5	26
		146	710
MALCOLM	I, ii	2	6
	I, iv	1	10
	II, iii	5	14
	IV, iii	23	139
	V, iv	3	11
	V, vi	1	6
	V, vii	1	2
	V, viii	4	20
		40	208
MACDUFF	II, iii	15	37
	II, iv	7	14
	IV, iii	28	91
	V, iv	1	3
	V, vi	1	2
	V, vii	1	10
	V, viii	5	19
		58	176
ROSS	I, ii	4	18
	I, iii	2	16
	II, iv	10	26
	III, iv	3	5
	IV, ii	4	19
	IV, iii	13	41
	V, viii	3	9
		39	134
BANQUO	I, iii	12	42
	I, iv	1	2
	I, vi	1	8
	II, i	8	24
	II, iii	2	11
	III, i	6	20
	III, iii	3	4
		33	111
LENNOX	I, ii	1	2
	II, iii	7	20
	III, iv	4	5
	III, vi	3	32
	IV, i	5	6
	V, ii	2	7
		22	72
DUNCAN	I, ii	8	14
	I, iv	6	36
	I, vi	4	18
		18	68
SCOTCH DOCTOR	V, i	15	34
	V, iii	4	9
		19	43
PORTER	II, iii	3	24
CAPTAIN	I, ii	3	35
1 MURDERER	III, i	7	10
	III, iii	7	11
	III, iv	4	7
	IV, ii	3	4
		21	32
OLD SIWARD	V, iv	3	10
	V, vi	1	3
	V, vii	2	6
	V, viii	5	11
		11	30

		NO. OF SPEECHES	NO. OF LINES
All (Witches)	I, i	1	3
	I, iii	1	6
	IV, i	8	13
		10	22
All (Lords)	II, iii	2	2
	V, viii	1	1
		3	3
Lord	III, vi	3	21
Lords	III, iv	3	3
Messenger	I, v	2	5
	IV, ii	1	9
	V, v	3	9
		6	23
Angus	I, iii	2	12
	V, ii	2	9
		4	21
Son	IV, ii	14	20
2 Murderer	III, i	4	8
	III, iii	4	9
		8	17
Menteith	V, ii	3	10
	V, iv	2	2
		5	12
Old Man	II, iv	4	11
Caithness	V, ii	3	11
Donalbain	II, iii	3	9
3 Murderer	III, iii	6	8
Young Siward	V, vii	4	7
Servant	III, ii	2	2
	V, iii	3	3
		5	5
3 Apparition	IV, i	1	5

		NO. OF SPEECHES	NO. OF LINES
English Doctor	IV, iii	1	5
Seyton	V, iii	3	3
	V, v	2	2
		5	5
2 Apparition	IV, i	2	4
1 Apparition	IV, i	1	2
Fleance	II, i	2	2
Attendant	III, i	1	1
Lady Macbeth	I, v	6	68
	I, vi	2	11
	I, vii	6	43
	II, ii	14	46
	II, iii	3	6
	III, i	1	3
	III, ii	7	18
	III, iv	14	40
	V, i	6	20
		59	255
1 Witch	I, i	3	4
	I, iii	9	28
	III, v	2	2
	IV, i	9	27
		23	61
2 Witch	I, i	2	3
	I, iii	6	6
	IV, i	6	17
		14	26
3 Witch	I, i	2	2
	I, iii	6	8
	IV, i	4	16
		12	26
Lady Macduff	IV, ii	19	41
Hecate	III, v	1	34
	IV, i	1	5
		2	39
Gentlewoman	V, i	11	23

THE TRAGEDY OF MACBETH

F

DRAMATIS PERSONÆ [1]

DUNCAN,[2] King of Scotland.
MALCOLM, DONALBAIN, } his sons.
MACBETH, BANQUO,[3] } generals of the King's army.
MACDUFF, LENNOX, ROSS, MENTEITH, ANGUS, CAITHNESS,[4] } noblemen of Scotland.
FLEANCE, son to Banquo.
SIWARD, earl of Northumberland, general of the English forces.
Young SIWARD, his son.
SEYTON, an officer attending on Macbeth.
Boy, son to Macduff.
An English Doctor.
A Scotch Doctor.
A Captain.
A Porter.
An Old Man.

Lady MACBETH.
Lady MACDUFF.
Gentlewoman [5] attending on Lady Macbeth.
HECATE.
Three Witches.
Apparitions.

Lords, Gentlemen, Officers, Soldiers, Murderers, Attendants, and Messengers.

SCENE: *Scotland; England.*

[1] In D'Avenant's version of the play (1674) is a list of 'The Persons Names,' but Rowe was the first editor to give the Dramatis Personæ in essentially the modern form. Capell expanded Rowe's list. That given here is substantially Dyce's.

[2] The names of all the leading characters are from Holinshed.

[3] BANQUO. The name and title as given by Holinshed is 'Banquho the thane of Lochquhaber.' For an interesting discussion of the pronunciation, see Furness.

[4] "Malcolme . . . created manie earles. . . . Manie of them that before were thanes, were at this time made earles, as Fife, Menteth, Atholl, Leuenox, Murrey, Cathnes, Rosse, and Angus. These were the first earles that haue beene heard of amongst Scotishmen." — Holinshed.

[5] **Gentlewoman** . . . Capell | Gentlewomen . . . Rowe.

ACT I

SCENE I. *A desert place*

Thunder and lightning. Enter three WITCHES

1 WITCH. When shall we three meet again
In thunder, lightning, or in rain ?
2 WITCH. When the hurlyburly 's done,
When the battle 's lost and won.
3 WITCH. That will be ere the set of sun. 5
1 WITCH. Where the place ?
2 WITCH. Upon the heath.
3 WITCH. There to meet with Macbeth.

A desert place Camb | Ff omit. 1. again Hanmer | againe ? Ff.

ACT I. SCENE I. The division into acts and scenes in this edition is that given with Latin nomenclature in the First Folio, except in the case of the fifth act, where *Scena Septima* of the Folio is subdivided into scenes vii and viii.

A desert place. Line 6 indicates that this is not ' the heath.'

Enter three WITCHES. " The true reason for the first appearance of the Witches is to strike the key-note of the character of the whole drama." — Coleridge.

1-2. The question concerns time, not weather. ' Or ' emphasizes the difference in the three elements. " In Stormes of Haile, or Snowe, Wind, Tempest, or Lightning, is accounted amongst magicians, a Tyme for Conjuring at an easie rate." — Scot.

3. hurlyburly : tumult. This onomatopoetic word was used in a dignified sense in the sixteenth century. See Murray.

7. A strong pause after ' meet ' heightens the metrical effect.

1 WITCH. I come, Graymalkin.
ALL. Paddock calls : — Anon !
Fair is foul, and foul is fair ; 10
Hover through the fog and filthy air.
[*Exeunt*]

9. ALL. Paddock calls : — Anon !| ALL. Padock calls anon : Ff. **9–10. Paddock . . . fair ;** | one line in Ff.

8. Graymalkin : gray cat, cat. In Scotland ' malkin ' (' mawkin ') is ' hare.' Cf. ' puss ' for ' hare ' in sportsmen's slang. In the old witchcraft lore witches are represented as having attendants, called familiars, in the guise of animals. " They can keep the Divils and Spirits in the likenesse of Todes and Cats." — Scot.

9-10. Some modern editors, including Clark and Wright (Clar, Globe), follow Hunter's conjecture and distribute the dialogue among the witches thus : " 2 WITCH. Paddock calls. 3 WITCH. Anon. ALL. Fair is foul," etc. In the D'Avenant version the arrangement is that of the Folios. This probably indicates the stage tradition. — **Paddock** : toad. The word (often pronounced ' padda,' cf. Middle English *padde*, Icelandic *padda*) is still used in Scotland and provincial England for ' frog.' In the Western Highlands ' padock ' is the name sometimes given to a malevolent spirit. — **Anon** : immediately. The usual inn-waiter's reply to a call. Cf. *1 Henry IV*, II, iv, 36, 72, 109, etc. Here the toad serving as familiar is supposed to make a sign for the witches to leave, and ' Anon ! ' is the reply. — **Fair is foul, and foul is fair.** Cf. Spenser, *The Faerie Queene*, I, ii, 38. Farmer also quotes Spenser's " Then faire grew foule and foule grew faire," to show the proverbial character of this phrase. But the expression probably signifies the moral confusion or inversion which the witches represent.

11. filthy : murky. See Murray. Gloom is the background of the play.

SCENE II. *A camp near Forres*

Alarum within. Enter DUNCAN, MALCOLM, DONALBAIN, LENNOX, *with* Attendants, *meeting a bleeding* CAPTAIN

DUNCAN. What bloody man is that? He can report,
As seemeth by his plight, of the revolt
The newest state.

MALCOLM. This is the sergeant
Who like a good and hardy soldier fought
'Gainst my captivity. Hail, brave friend! 5
Say to the king thy knowledge of the broil
As thou didst leave it.

CAPTAIN. Doubtful it stood,
As two spent swimmers that do cling together
And choke their art. The merciless Macdonwald —
Worthy to be a rebel, for to that 10

A camp . . . Capell | Ff omit. — DUNCAN, Capell | King Ff. — *bleeding* CAPTAIN Ff | bleeding Sergeant Globe Dyce Camb.

1. DUNCAN | King Ff (so elsewhere).

5. **Hail** | Haile F_1 | Haile: haile F_2 | Haile, haile F_3F_4.

7. CAPTAIN | Cap. Ff | Sergeant Globe Dyce Camb.

9. Macdonwald F_1 | Macdonnell $F_2F_3F_4$.

SCENE II. This scene is regarded by many modern editors as not Shakespeare's. The reasons given are slovenly diction, bombastic style, alleged inconsistencies, and the absurdity of sending news of victory by a wounded soldier. Daniel notes that the sergeant was not formally sent but was merely a straggler.

3. **sergeant.** Probably trisyllabic. In the fourteenth century sergeants held lands by tenure of military service. "The offendors were sent for by a sergeant at armes." — Holinshed.

5. **Hail.** Probably dissyllabic, but see Abbott, §§ 480-482.

9. **Macdonwald.** "Manie slanderous words also, and railing tants this Macdowald vttered against his prince." — Holinshed.

10. **to that**: to that end, for that purpose. See Abbott, § 186.

The multiplying villainies of nature
Do swarm upon him — from the western isles
Of kerns and gallowglasses is supplied ;
And fortune, on his damned quarry smiling,
Show'd like a rebel's whore : but all 's too weak ; 15
For brave Macbeth — well he deserves that name —
Disdaining fortune, with his brandish'd steel,
Which smok'd with bloody execution,
Like valour's minion carv'd out his passage
Till he fac'd the slave ; 20

13. gallowglasses Steevens | Gallowgrosses F_1 | Gallow glasses F_2F_3 F_4. — is Ff | was Pope.

14. quarry | Quarry Ff | quarrel Hanmer (Warburton Johnson conj.) Globe Camb.

13. **Of**: with. See Abbott, § 171. — **kerns**: light-armed Erse infantry. Cf. *Richard II*, II, i, 156. See Skeat. — **gallowglasses** : heavy-armed Erse infantry. Cf. *2 Henry VI*, IV, ix, 26. See Murray. "For out of the westerne Iles there came vnto him a great multitude of people, offering themselves to assist him in that rebellious quarell, and out of Ireland in hope of the spoile came no small number of Kernes and Galloglasses, offering gladlie to serve vnder him, whither it should please him to lead them." — Holinshed.

14. **damned quarry** : doomed prey. 'His' may refer to 'fortune' or to 'Macdonwald.' The Warburton-Johnson suggestion that 'quarrel' (cf. 'rebellious quarell' in the quotation from Holinshed just given) should be read here is adopted by most modern editors. In IV, iii, 206, 'quarry' means 'heap of slain.' Cf. *Coriolanus*, I, i, 202. Other Elizabethan writers use 'quarry' in the sense of 'square-headed bolt of a crossbow.'

15. **all 's**. Unless this be a contraction of 'all was,' it is an example of mixing up historical present and past tenses. Pope omitted 's, interpreting 'all too weak.' Cf. 'is supplied,' line 13.

18. **execution**. The termination '-ion' is frequently pronounced as two syllables at the end of a line, and occasionally in the middle of a line. See Abbott, § 479.

19. **minion** : favourite. In a good sense, as in *1 Henry IV*, I, i, 83

Which ne'er shook hands, nor bade farewell to him,
Till he unseam'd him from the nave to th' chops,
And fix'd his head upon our battlements.

DUNCAN. O valiant cousin! worthy gentleman!

CAPTAIN. As whence the sun 'gins his reflection 25
Shipwrecking storms and direful thunders,
So from that spring whence comfort seem'd to come
Discomfort swells. Mark, king of Scotland, mark:
No sooner justice had, with valour arm'd,
Compell'd these skipping kerns to trust their heels, 30

21. **ne'er** Knight | nev'r $F_1F_2F_3$ | never F_4. — **bade** Steevens | bad Ff.
26. **Shipwrecking** | Shipwracking Ff. — **thunders,** | Thunders: F_1 | Thunders breaking $F_2F_3F_4$ | thunders break Pope Camb.

21. **Which.** The antecedent is Macbeth. See Abbott, § 265. — **shook hands.** In the sixteenth and seventeenth centuries 'to shake hands with' a thing was a picturesque phrase for 'to leave.' "I have shaken hands with delight in my warm blood and canicular days; I perceive I do anticipate the vices of age." — Browne, *Religio Medici.* But there may be an allusion to the formal handshaking before a duel. "The shaking of handes was with sharp weapons." — Sidney, *Arcadia.*

22. **nave**: navel. Hanmer read 'nape,' as 'nave' occurs nowhere else, and such a sword-stroke as that described seems ridiculous. Steevens quotes from Nash's *Dido, Queen of Carthage* (1594), II, 256: "Then from the navel to the throat at once He ripp'd old Priam." — **chops**: jaws. Another form of 'chaps.'

23. "Makbeth entring into the castell by the gates . . . found the carcasse of Makdowald lieng dead . . . he caused the head to be cut off, and set upon a pole's end (and so sent it as a present to the king). . . . The headlesse trunke he commanded to be hoong up upon an high paire of gallowes." — Holinshed.

25.-28. As from the east, the region of quiet dawn and fair promise, come fiercest storms, so from a victory that brought joy spring fresh dangers and alarms. — There seems no valid reason for adding 'break' to line 26, as many editors do, for with ideas of motion the verb is often omitted, and the irregular verse is characteristic of *Macbeth* and onomatopoetically effective. See Liddell.

But the Norweyan lord, surveying vantage,
With furbish'd arms and new supplies of men,
Began a fresh assault.

DUNCAN. Dismay'd not this
Our captains, Macbeth and Banquo ?

CAPTAIN. Yes ;
As sparrows eagles, or the hare the lion. 35
If I say sooth, I must report they were
As cannons overcharg'd with double cracks ;
So they doubly redoubled strokes upon the foe :
Except they meant to bathe in reeking wounds,
Or memorize another Golgotha, 40
I cannot tell —
But I am faint, my gashes cry for help.

32. furbish'd | furbusht Ff.
33–34. Dismay'd . . . Banquo Pope | one line in Ff.
34–35. Yes . . . lion Pope | two lines in Ff, ending **eagles, lion.**
38. So they | separate line in Steevens Camb.
42. I . . . help Rowe | two lines in Ff, first ending **faint.**

31. **surveying vantage** : perceiving a favourable opportunity. " Immediatlie whereupon woord came that Sueno king of Norway was arrived in Fife with a puissant armie, to subdue the whole realme of Scotland." — Holinshed.

34. **captains**. Probably trisyllabic. ' Capitains ' is a common sixteenth century form of the word. This pronunciation is still heard in dialect. Cf. *3 Henry VI*, IV, vii, 30.

36. **sooth** : truth. ' Sooth ' (Middle English ' sōth,' Anglo-Saxon *sóð*) is both adjective and substantive, the adjectival sense being the older. The root idea is ' being.' See Skeat.

37. By a well-known figure of speech, ' crack ' is here put for that which makes the ' crack.' Cf. *Antony and Cleopatra*, V, i, 14, 15.

39-41. Unless they meant to bathe in reeking wounds and make the place as memorable as Golgotha, I cannot tell what they intended. Golgotha, " the place of a skull " (*Matthew*, xxvii, 33 ; *Mark*, xv, 22), i.e. of slaughter, is here referred to.

DUNCAN. So well thy words become thee as thy wounds ;
They smack of honour both. Go get him surgeons.
[*Exit* CAPTAIN, *attended*]

Enter ROSS *and* ANGUS

Who comes here ?
MALCOLM. The worthy thane of Ross. 45
LENNOX. What a haste looks through his eyes ! So should he look
That seems to speak things strange.
ROSS. God save the king !
DUNCAN. Whence cam'st thou, worthy thane ?
ROSS. From Fife, great king ;
Where the Norweyan banners flout the sky
And fan our people cold. 50
Norway himself, with terrible numbers,
Assisted by that most disloyal traitor,
The thane of Cawdor, began a dismal conflict ;
Till that Bellona's bridegroom, lapp'd in proof,

44. [*Exit* . . . | Ff omit.
46. a haste F_1 | hast $F_2F_3F_4$.
46–47. So . . . strange Hanmer | one line in Ff.

45. *Enter* ROSS *and* ANGUS. This is the First Folio stage direction. Most modern editors omit 'and Angus,' as Angus does not speak and is not addressed. But in the next scene Ross and Angus together bring to Macbeth the news of his promotion.

47. **seems to** : is about to. " 'Seem' in Early English often connotes an immediate or near futurity." — Liddell. The D'Avenant version reads 'comes.' Johnson suggested 'teems.'

49-50. The Norwegian banners proudly reared aloft and fluttering in the wind seemed to mock or insult the Scottish sky, and the sight of them struck chills of dismay into our countrymen. 'Flout' and 'fan' are examples of the historic present. See note, line 15.

54. **Bellona's bridegroom.** Steevens sneered at Shakespeare's ignorance in making Bellona, the old Roman goddess of war (*bellum*),

Confronted him with self-comparisons, 55
Point against point, rebellious arm 'gainst arm,
Curbing his lavish spirit ; and, to conclude,
The victory fell on us.
DUNCAN. Great happiness !
ROSS That now
Sweno, the Norways' king, craves composition ;
Nor would we deign him burial of his men 60
Till he disbursed, at Saint Colme's inch,
Ten thousand dollars to our general use.
DUNCAN. No more that thane of Cawdor shall deceive

58-59. **That . . . composition** Steevens | two lines in Ff, the first one ending **king.**

61. **Colme's inch** | Colmes ynch F_1 | Colmes-hill $F_2F_3F_4$ | Colmes-kill-isle Pope.

the wife of Mars, but Shakespeare poetically makes her the bride of Macbeth. — **lapp'd in proof** : clad in impenetrable armour. Cf. 'armed in proof' in *Richard III*, V, iii, 219.

55. Met him in every respect upon equal terms.

56. The punctuation is that of the First Folio. Many editors put the comma after 'rebellious.' "If the old punctuation be right, 'rebellious,' being applied to the arm of the loyal combatant, must be taken to mean 'opposing, resisting assault.'" — Clar.

57. **Curbing his lavish spirit** : checking his reckless daring.

58. **That** : so that. 'That' often expresses result. See Abbott, § 283. 'That' is an overworked word in Elizabethan English.

59. **composition** : terms of peace. Cf. the phrase 'composed a quarrel.' Cf. *Measure for Measure*, I, ii, 2.

61. **Saint Colme's inch** : the island of Inchcolm. It is in the Firth of Forth and on it was a monastery dedicated to St. Columba. 'Inch' is from the Gaelic *innis*, 'island,' or 'land by a river.' "They . . . obteined of Makbeth for a great summe of gold, that such of their friends as were slaine at this last bickering, might be buried in saint Colmes Inch." — Holinshed.

62. A characteristic Shakespearian anachronism. Dollars were first coined in the sixteenth century.

Our bosom interest. Go pronounce his present death,
And with his former title greet Macbeth. 65
 Ross. I 'll see it done.
 DUNCAN. What he hath lost, noble Macbeth hath won.
[*Exeunt*]

SCENE III. *A heath*

Thunder. Enter the three WITCHES

 1 WITCH. Where hast thou been, sister?
 2 WITCH. Killing swine.
 3 WITCH. Sister, where thou?
 1 WITCH. A sailor's wife had chestnuts in her lap,
And munch'd, and munch'd, and munch'd. 'Give me,'
 quoth I: 5
'Aroint thee, witch!' the rump-fed ronyon cries.
Her husband 's to Aleppo gone, master o' the Tiger:
 But in a sieve I 'll thither sail,

A heath Capell | A heath near Forres Globe | Ff omit.
5. **munch'd** | mouncht Ff. — **Give** . . . I | separate line in Ff Globe.
6. **Aroint** | Aroynt F_1F_2 | Anoynt F_3F_4.

2. "Finallie she said she would be even with me: and soone after my child, my cow, my sow . . . died, or was strangelie taken." — Scot.

6. 'Aroint thee!' is probably an old exorcism against witches. Cf. *King Lear*, III, iv, 129. The etymology is uncertain. — **rump-fed**. Either 'offal-fed' or 'pampered.'— **ronyon**: mangy creature. A general term of abuse. See Century. So in *The Merry Wives of Windsor*, IV, ii, 195. Cf. 'roynish clown,' *As You Like It*, II, ii, 8.

7. **Tiger**. A common name for a ship. Cf. *Twelfth Night*, V, i, 65. In Hakluyt's *Voyages* is an account of a ship of this name that went to Tripolis with cargo for Aleppo in 1583.

8. Witches were believed to go to sea in sieves. "They can go in and out at awger holes, and saile in an egge shelle, a cockle or muscle shell, through and under the tempestuous seas." — Scot.

And, like a rat without a tail,
I 'll do, I 'll do, and I 'll do. 10

2 WITCH. I 'll give thee a wind.

1 WITCH. Thou 'rt kind.

3 WITCH. And I another.

1 WITCH. I myself have all the other;
And the very points they blow, 15
All the quarters that they know
I' the shipman's card.
I 'll drain him dry as hay.
Sleep shall neither night nor day
Hang upon his pent-house lid; 20
He shall live a man forbid:
Weary se'nnights nine times nine
Shall he dwindle, peak, and pine:

12. **Thou 'rt** Capell | Th' art Ff. 18. **I'll** | Ile F_1 | I will Pope. 22. **se'nnights** | Seu'nights Ff | seven-nights Steevens.

9. Whatever animal form the witch might assume, there would always be some defect. Cf. the 'devil's limp,' 'the cloven foot,' etc.

10. **do**: work him mischief. The vagueness adds impressiveness.

11-12. This free gift of a wind is to be taken as an act of sisterly kindness, witches being thought to have the power of selling winds.

17. **shipman's card**. Either the mariner's compass, i.e. the circular card marked with the points of the compass, or a 'chart' showing the points of the compass.

20. **pent-house lid**: eyelid. A 'pent-house' is a shed or 'lean-to' sloping down from a main building. Drayton and Tennyson use 'pent-house' to describe the eyebrow.

21. **forbid**. Either 'under a curse,' or 'excommunicated.'

22. **se'nnights**: seven-nights, weeks. Cf. 'fortnight' (for 'fourteen-night'). 'Sennet' (sennit) is still heard in English dialect.

23. **peak**: grow thin. Usually in the expression 'peak and pine.' See Murray. Holinshed, describing the means used for destroying King Duff, says that the witches were found "rosting . . . an image

Though his bark cannot be lost,
Yet it shall be tempest-tost. 25
Look what I have.

2 WITCH. Show me, show me.

1 WITCH. Here I have a pilot's thumb,
Wreck'd as homeward he did come.
[*Drum within*]

3 WITCH. A drum, a drum! 30
Macbeth doth come.

ALL. The weird sisters, hand in hand,
Posters of the sea and land,
Thus do go about, about:
Thrice to thine, and thrice to mine, 35
And thrice again, to make up nine.
Peace! the charm 's wound up.

29. Wreck'd | Wrackt Ff. 32. weird Theobald | weyward Ff.

of wax at the fier, resembling in each feature the kings person . . . so that as the wax euer melted so did the kings flesh."

32. weird. The Folios spell the word 'weyward,' but Holinshed has 'weird': "These women were either the weird sisters, that is (as ye would say) the goddesses of destinie, or else some nymphs or feiries indued with knowledge of prophesie by their necromantical science, bicause euery thing came to passe as they had spoken." Probably the Folio spelling represents a southern pronunciation of the word. According to Skeat 'weird' as an adjective here means 'subservient to destiny.' The Anglo-Saxon *wyrd* means 'fate,' 'destiny,' also one of the Norns, or Fates. Gavin Douglas translates *Parcae* in the *Æneid*, III, 379, by 'weird sisteris.'

33. Posters: messengers, rapid travellers. Cf. 'post-haste.'

36. Here the witches perform a sort of incantation by joining hands and dancing round in a ring, three rounds for each. Odd numbers and multiples of odd numbers, especially three and nine, were thought to have great magical power in thus winding up a charm.

Enter MACBETH *and* BANQUO

MACBETH. So foul and fair a day I have not seen.
BANQUO. How far is 't call'd to Forres? What are these
So wither'd, and so wild in their attire, 40
That look not like th' inhabitants o' the earth,
And yet are on 't? Live you? or are you aught
That man may question? You seem to understand me,
By each at once her choppy finger laying
Upon her skinny lips: you should be women 45
And yet your beards forbid me to interpret
That you are so.
MACBETH. Speak, if you can: what are you?
1 WITCH. All hail, Macbeth! hail to thee, thane of Glamis!
2 WITCH. All hail, Macbeth! hail to thee, thane of Cawdor!
3 WITCH. All hail, Macbeth, that shall be king hereafter! 50

38. Scene IV Pope. 39. Forres | Foris Pope | Soris Ff.

38. Macbeth's first words may refer only to the symbolical sunshine and storm of the day, or to a day fouled with storm but brightened with victory. Dowden reads here a deeper meaning: "Observe that the last words of the witches in the opening scene of the play are the first words which Macbeth himself utters: 'Fair is foul, and foul is fair.' Shakespeare intimates by this that, although Macbeth has not yet set eyes upon these hags, the connection is already established between his soul and them. Their spells have already wrought upon his blood."

40. "Three women in strange and wild apparell." — Holinshed.

48–50. "The first of them spake and said: 'All haile Makbeth, thane of Glammis' (for he had latelie entered into that dignitie and office by the death of his father Sinell). The second of them said:

BANQUO. Good sir, why do you start, and seem to fear
Things that do sound so fair ? — I' the name of truth,
Are ye fantastical, or that indeed
Which outwardly ye show ? My noble partner
You greet with present grace and great prediction 55
Of noble having and of royal hope,
That he seems rapt withal ; to me you speak not.
If you can look into the seeds of time,
And say which grain will grow and which will not,

57. **rapt** Pope | wrapt Ff.

' Haile Makbeth thane of Cawder.' But the third said : ' All haile Makbeth that heereafter shalt be king of Scotland.' " — Holinshed.

53. **fantastical** : imaginary. Cf. line 139 ; *Richard II*, I, iii, 299. Holinshed has " vaine fantasticall illusion."

55. An example of ' respective construction.' ' Present grace ' refers to ' noble having ' (i.e. ' possession ') and ' great prediction ' to ' royal hope.' Similarly in lines 60–61, ' beg ' refers to ' favours ' and ' fear ' to ' hate.'

57. **That** : so that. Cf. I, ii, 58. — **withal** therewith, with it. Here ' withal ' is an adverb (cf. German *damit*) not, as often in Shakespeare, the emphatic form of ' with,' used after the object, generally a relative, at the end of a sentence. Macbeth's rapture or trance of thought on this occasion is deeply significant of his moral predispositions. Coleridge remarks upon the passage as follows :

> How truly Shakespearian is the opening of Macbeth's character given in the *unpossessedness* of Banquo's mind, wholly present to the present object ; an unsullied, unscarified mirror ! And how strictly true to nature it is that Banquo, and not Macbeth himself, directs our notice to the effect produced on Macbeth's mind, rendered temptable by previous dalliance of the fancy with ambitious thoughts. . . Banquo's questions are those of natural curiosity, such as a girl would put after hearing a gipsy tell her school-fellow's fortune : — all perfectly general, or rather planless. But Macbeth, lost in thought, raises himself to speech only by the witches being about to depart, . . . and all that follows is reasoning on a problem already discussed in his mind, — on a hope which he welcomes, and the doubts concerning the attainment of which he wishes to have cleared up

Speak, then, to me, who neither beg nor fear 60
Your favours nor your hate.
1 WITCH. Hail!
2 WITCH. Hail!
3 WITCH. Hail!
1 WITCH. Lesser than Macbeth, and greater. 65
2 WITCH. Not so happy, yet much happier.
3 WITCH. Thou shalt get kings, though thou be none:
So all hail, Macbeth and Banquo!
1 WITCH. Banquo and Macbeth, all hail!
MACBETH. Stay, you imperfect speakers, tell me more: 70
By Sinel's death I know I am thane of Glamis;
But how of Cawdor? the thane of Cawdor lives,
A prosperous gentleman; and to be king
Stands not within the prospect of belief
No more than to be Cawdor. Say from whence 75
You owe this strange intelligence? or why
Upon this blasted heath you stop our way
With such prophetic greeting? Speak, I charge you.
[WITCHES *vanish*]

78. Two lines in Ff.

73. A prosperous gentleman. There is seemingly a strange discrepancy here. In the preceding scene, Macbeth is said to have met Cawdor face to face in the ranks of Norway: he must therefore have known him to be a rebel and traitor.

74. prospect of belief. Cf. 'prospect of his soul,' *Much Ado about Nothing*, IV, i, 231; 'prospect of my hopes,' *Twelfth Night*, III, iv, 90. "Elizabethan thinking was full of such metaphors for the perceptive powers of the mind." — Liddell.

76. owe: have, possess. This, the original meaning of the word, is common in Shakespeare, as in *King John*, II, i, 247–248. From 'to possess another's property' comes the meaning 'to be in debt for.'

BANQUO. The earth hath bubbles as the water has,
And these are of them. Whither are they vanish'd? 80
MACBETH. Into the air; and what seem'd corporal melted
As breath into the wind. Would they had stay'd!
BANQUO. Were such things here as we do speak about?
Or have we eaten on the insane root
That takes the reason prisoner? 85
MACBETH. Your children shall be kings.
BANQUO. You shall be king.
MACBETH. And thane of Cawdor too: went it not so?
BANQUO. To th' selfsame tune and words. Who 's here?

Enter ROSS *and* ANGUS

ROSS. The king hath happily receiv'd, Macbeth,
The news of thy success: and, when he reads 90
Thy personal venture in the rebels' fight,
His wonders and his praises do contend
Which should be thine or his: silenc'd with that,

81–82. Three lines in Ff, ending corporal, wind, stay'd.
84. on $F_1F_2F_3$ | of F_4.
89. Scene V Pope.
91. rebels' Theobald | rebels Ff.

81. corporal: corporeal. Shakespeare never uses the latter form.

84. on: of. Cf. 'on 's' in V, i, 61. — **the insane root.** This is usually taken to mean hemlock or henbane, but it is probable that Shakespeare had in mind this passage from North's Plutarch: "They were compelled to live of herbs and roots . . . among the which there was one that . . . made them out of their wits. For he that had once eaten of it, his memory was gone from him." — *The Life of Marcus Antonius*. With this causal use of 'insane,' cf. 'oblivious' in V, iii, 43. For the pronunciation 'in′sane' see Abbott, § 492. Cf. 'ob′scure,' II, iii, 45.

92–93. The construction is involved (cf. 'respective construction,' line 55), but the meaning seems to be, He knows not whether to

In viewing o'er the rest o' the selfsame day,
He finds thee in the stout Norweyan ranks, 95
Nothing afeard of what thyself didst make,
Strange images of death. As thick as tale
Came post with post ; and every one did bear
Thy praises in his kingdom's great defence,
And pour'd them down before him.

ANGUS. We are sent 100
To give thee from our royal master thanks ;
Only to herald thee into his sight,
Not pay thee.

ROSS. And, for an earnest of a greater honour,
He bade me, from him, call thee thane of Cawdor ; 105
In which addition, hail, most worthy thane !
For it is thine.

97. tale Ff | hail Rowe Globe Camb | bale Becket conj.
98. Came Rowe | Can Ff | Ran Delius conj.
102. herald F_4 | harrold F_1 | herrald F_2F_3.
105. bade Theobald | bad Ff.

express his own wonder at these achievements or to sound your praises.

96. Nothing : not at all. This adverbial use is common in Shakespeare. — **afeard.** The past participle of 'afear' (Anglo-Saxon *áfæ'ran*) ; 'afraid' is the participle of 'affray' (Low Lat. *ex-fridare*). See Murray. 'Afeard' (''feard') is still heard in dialect.

97. Strange images : unusual forms. This refers to the heaps of slain. In *2 Henry VI*, I, iii, 179, is 'Image of pride' ; in *King Lear*, II, iv, 91, 'images of revolt.' Cf. 'picture of health.' — **thick as tale** : fast as could be counted. " A phrase peculiarly Shakespearian in its pregnant condensation . . . transformed into bald commonplace by the substitution of 'thick as hail.' " — Churton Collins. 'Thick' for 'fast' occurs in *2 Henry IV*, II, iii, 24 ; 'tell' for 'count' occurs often. Cf. 'keep tally,' also 'tale' in *Exodus*, v, 8.

106. addition : title. Something added to a man's name to show his rank. Cf. III, i, 99 ; *Hamlet*, I, iv, 20.

BANQUO. [*Aside*] What, can the devil speak true?
MACBETH. The thane of Cawdor lives: why do you dress me
In borrow'd robes?
ANGUS. Who was the thane lives yet;
But under heavy judgment bears that life 110
Which he deserves to lose. Whether he was combin'd
With those of Norway, or did line the rebel
With hidden help and vantage, or that with both
He labour'd in his country's wreck, I know not;
But treasons capital, confess'd and prov'd, 115
Have overthrown him.
MACBETH. [*Aside*] Glamis, and thane of Cawdor!
The greatest is behind. [*To* ROSS *and* ANGUS] Thanks for your pains.
[*To* BANQUO] Do you not hope your children shall be kings,
When those that gave the thane of Cawdor to me
Promis'd no less to them?
BANQUO. That trusted home 120
Might yet enkindle you unto the crown,
Besides the thane of Cawdor. But 't is strange;
And oftentimes, to win us to our harm,

107, 116. [*Aside*] Ff omit.
108–109. **why . . . robes** Capell | one line in Ff.
111–114. **Which . . . know not** Malone | five lines in Ff, ending **loose, Norway, help, labour'd, not.**
117. [*To* ROSS . . .] Ff omit.
118. [*To* BANQUO] Ff. omit.

112. **line**: strengthen, reënforce. So in *1 Henry IV*, II, iii, 86.
120. **home**: thoroughly. Cf. *Measure for Measure*, IV, iii, 148; *Cymbeline*, III, v, 92; *King Lear*, III, iii, 13.
123–126. It is nowise likely that Shakespeare was a reader of Livy, but in these lines, which give, as Professor Corson says, the entire moral of the tragedy, is a striking resemblance to a passage in Book xxviii, 42, 4: "An Syphaci Numidisque credis? satis sit semel

The instruments of darkness tell us truths,
Win us with honest trifles, to betray 's 125
In deepest consequence.
Cousins, a word, I pray you.

MACBETH. [*Aside*] Two truths are told,
As happy prologues to the swelling act
Of the imperial theme. — I thank you, gentlemen. —
[*Aside*] This supernatural soliciting 130
Cannot be ill; cannot be good: if ill,
Why hath it given me earnest of success,
Commencing in a truth? I am thane of Cawdor:
If good, why do I yield to that suggestion
Whose horrid image doth unfix my hair 135
And make my seated heart knock at my ribs,
Against the use of nature? Present fears
Are less than horrible imaginings.
My thought, whose murder yet is but fantastical,
Shakes so my single state of man that function 140

127, 130. [*Aside*] Ff omit.
131–132. **if . . . success** | one ne in Ff.
135. **hair** Rowe | heire $F_1F_2F_3$.
140–142. **that . . . not** | two lines in Ff.

creditum: non semper temeritas est felix, et fraus fidem in parvis sibi praestruit ut, quum operae pretium sit, cum mercede magna fallit."

128–129. The image is of the stage, with an august drama of kingly state to be performed; the inspiring prologue has been spoken, and the glorious action is about to begin. — **imperial theme**: theme of empire. Cf. 'sterile curse,' *Julius Cæsar*, I, ii, 9, and 'slanderous loads,' *Julius Cæsar*, IV, i, 20. "In such phrases the adjective defines the sphere or character of the noun." — A. W. Verity.

134. **suggestion**: temptation. Cf. *The Tempest*, II, i, 288.

137. **use**: custom. — **fears**: dangers, terrors. Effect for cause.

139-141. My thought, though it is only of a murder in imagination, so disturbs my feeble human condition that the power of action is

Is smother'd in surmise, and nothing is
But what is not.

BANQUO. Look, how our partner's rapt.

MACBETH. [*Aside*] If chance will have me king, why, chance may crown me,
Without my stir.

BANQUO. New honours come upon him,
Like our strange garments, cleave not to their mould 145
But with the aid of use.

MACBETH. [*Aside*] Come what come may,
Time and the hour runs through the roughest day.

BANQUO. Worthy Macbeth, we stay upon your leisure.

142. **Look . . . rapt** | separate line in Ff.

143. Two lines in Ff.

143, 146. [*Aside*] Ff omit.

lost in speculation. Shakespeare often uses 'single' in the sense of 'weak,' as in I, vi, 16. Staunton quotes as a parallel passage *Julius Cæsar*, II, i, 63–69, and interprets 'state' as 'kingdom.'

141–142. **nothing is But what is not.** Facts are lost sight of; he sees nothing but what is unreal, nothing but the spectres of his own fancy. Macbeth's conscience here acts through his imagination, sets it all on fire, and he is terror-stricken, and lost to the things before him, as the elements of evil within him gather and fashion themselves into the wicked purpose. Of this wonderful development of character Coleridge says: "So surely is the guilt in its germ anterior to the supposed cause and immediate temptation." And again: "Every word of his soliloquy shows the early birth-date of his guilt. He wishes the end, but is irresolute as to the means; conscience distinctly warns him, and he lulls it imperfectly."

147. **Time and the hour.** A reduplicate phrase like 'time and tide,' probably proverbial. 'Il tempo e l' ore' occurs in one of Michelangelo's sonnets. The sense of the line in the text is thus explained by Heath: "The advantage of time and of seizing the favourable hour, whenever it shall present itself, will enable me to make my way through all obstruction and opposition. Every one knows the Spanish proverb, — 'Time and I against any two.'"

MACBETH. Give me your favour: my dull brain was wrought
With things forgotten. Kind gentlemen, your pains 150
Are register'd where every day I turn
The leaf to read them. Let us toward the king.
Think upon what hath chanc'd; and, at more time,
The interim having weigh'd it, let us speak
Our free hearts each to other.
BANQUO. Very gladly. 155
MACBETH. Till then, enough. Come, friends. [*Exeunt*]

SCENE IV. *Forres. The palace*

Flourish. Enter DUNCAN, MALCOLM, DONALBAIN, LENNOX, *and* Attendants

DUNCAN. Is execution done on Cawdor? Are not
Those in commission yet return'd?

156. Two lines in Ff.
SCENE IV | Scene VI Pope.
Enter DUNCAN... LENNOX | Enter King, Lenox, Malcolme, Donalbaine Ff.

1. DUNCAN Capell | King Ff (and throughout the scene). — **Is . . . Cawdor** | one line in Ff. — **Are** $F_2F_3F_4$ | Or F_1.

149. **favour**: indulgence. — **wrought**: agitated, worked up. Cf. *The Winter's Tale*, V, iii, 58. Macbeth puts forth a pretext to hide the true cause of his trance of guilty thought.

151. **register'd**: noted on the table of memory. Cf. *Hamlet*, I, v, 98.

154. **The interim having weigh'd it**: the lapse of time having enabled us to see it in its true light. But Abbott, § 202, would construe this as a case of the omission of the preposition in adverbial expressions of time.

SCENE IV. This scene takes place the day after the previous scenes, which may be regarded as happening on one day. "The behaviour of the thane of Cawdor corresponds in almost every circumstance with that of the unfortunate Earl of Essex, as related by Stowe." — Steevens. The execution of the Earl of Essex took place in 1601.

MALCOLM. My liege,
They are not yet come back. But I have spoke
With one that saw him die; who did report
That very frankly he confess'd his treasons, 5
Implor'd your highness' pardon, and set forth
A deep repentance: nothing in his life
Became him like the leaving it; he died
As one that had been studied in his death
To throw away the dearest thing he ow'd, 10
As 't were a careless trifle.

DUNCAN. There 's no art
To find the mind's construction in the face:
He was a gentleman on whom I built
An absolute trust.

Enter MACBETH, BANQUO, ROSS, *and* ANGUS

O worthiest cousin!
The sin of my ingratitude even now 15
Was heavy on me. Thou art so far before,

2–8. **My . . . died** | seven lines in Ff, ending **back, die, he, pardon, repentance, him, died.**
10. **ow'd** Ff | own'd Warburton.

9. studied in his death: well instructed in the art of dying.
10. ow'd: owned. So in I, iii, 76. See note.
11. careless: uncared for. So 'sightless,' I, vii, 23. See Abbott, § 3.
13–14. Duncan's words spoken as Macbeth enters are often quoted as a splendid example of that 'tragic irony' (when a speaker unconsciously uses words that have a double meaning to his hearers) which pervades the whole of this scene. "Duncan's childlike spirit makes a moment's pause of wonder at the act of treachery, and then flings itself, like Gloucester in *King Lear*, with still more absolute trust and still more want of reflection, into the toils of a far deeper and darker treason." — Moberly.

That swiftest wing of recompense is slow
To overtake thee. Would thou hadst less deserv'd,
That the proportion both of thanks and payment
Might have been mine! Only I have left to say, 20
More is thy due than more than all can pay.

MACBETH. The service and the loyalty I owe,
In doing it, pays itself. Your highness' part
Is to receive our duties; and our duties
Are to your throne and state children and servants; 25
Which do but what they should, by doing every thing
Safe toward your love and honour.

DUNCAN. Welcome hither:
I have begun to plant thee, and will labour
To make thee full of growing. Noble Banquo,
That hast no less deserv'd, nor must be known 30
No less to have done so, let me infold thee
And hold thee to my heart.

23–27. **Your . . . honour** | five lines in Ff, ending **receive our duties, state, should, love, honour.**
27. **Safe** Ff | Shap'd Hanmer.

19–20. That my return of thanks and payment might have been in the right proportion to thy deserts, or in the due relation to them.

24–25. 'Duties' is here put, apparently, for the faculties and labours of duty; the meaning being, All our works and forces of duty are children and servants to your throne and state. Hypocrisy and hyperbole are apt to go together; and so here Macbeth overacts the part of loyalty, and tries how high he can strain up his expression of it. We have a parallel instance in Goneril's and Regan's finely worded professions of love. Such high-pressure rhetoric is the right vernacular of hollowness.

27. **Safe toward your love and honour.** One of the many condensed, elliptical expressions in the play. The meaning may be, With a firm and sure purpose to have you loved and honoured; or, So as to merit and secure love and honour from you. It may mean both.

BANQUO. There if I grow,
The harvest is your own.
DUNCAN. My plenteous joys,
Wanton in fulness, seek to hide themselves
In drops of sorrow. Sons, kinsmen, thanes, 35
And you whose places are the nearest, know,
We will establish our estate upon
Our eldest, Malcolm, whom we name hereafter
The Prince of Cumberland; which honour must
Not unaccompanied invest him only, 40
But signs of nobleness, like stars, shall shine
On all deservers. From hence to Inverness,
And bind us further to you.
MACBETH. The rest is labour, which is not us'd for you.
I 'll be myself the harbinger, and make joyful 45

35. **kinsmen** F_1 | kinsman $F_2F_3F_4$.
42. **Inverness** Pope | Envernes Ff.
45. **harbinger** Rowe | Herbenger $F_1F_2F_3$ | Harbenger F_4.

33–35. Cf. *Much Ado about Nothing*, I, i, 22; *Romeo and Juliet*, III, ii, 102–104; *The Winter's Tale*, V, ii, 50. — **Wanton**: unrestrained, undisciplined (the original sense of the word).

38–39. "King Duncane, hauing two sonnes by his wife which was the daughter of Siward earle of Northumberland, he made the elder of them called Malcolme prince of Cumberland, as it were thereby to appoint him his successor in the kingdome, immediatelie after his deceasse. Mackbeth sore troubled herewith . . . he began to take counsell how he might vsurpe the kingdome by force, hauing a iust quarell so to doo (as he tooke the matter) for that Duncane did what in him lay to defraud him." — Holinshed.

44. Even the repose, which is not taken for your sake or spent in your service, is a labour to me.

45. **harbinger**: an officer who goes in advance to make provision for the night's shelter. The Middle English form is *herbergeour* and is found in Chaucer, *The Man of Lawes Tale*, 997: "herbergeours that wenten him biforn."

The hearing of my wife with your approach;
So humbly take my leave.

DUNCAN. My worthy Cawdor!

MACBETH. [*Aside*] The Prince of Cumberland! that is a step
On which I must fall down, or else o'erleap,
For in my way it lies. Stars, hide your fires; 50
Let not light see my black and deep desires;
The eye wink at the hand; yet let that be
Which the eye fears, when it is done, to see. [*Exit*]

DUNCAN. True, worthy Banquo; he is full so valiant,
And in his commendations I am fed; 55
It is a banquet to me. Let 's after him,
Whose care is gone before to bid us welcome.
It is a peerless kinsman. [*Flourish. Exeunt*]

SCENE V. *Inverness.* MACBETH'S *castle*

Enter LADY MACBETH, *alone, with a letter*

LADY MACBETH. [*Reads*] They met me in the day of success; and I have learn'd by the perfect'st report, they have

48. [*Aside*] Ff omit.
SCENE V | Scene VII Pope. — *Inverness . . . castle* | Ff omit.
LADY MACBETH | Macbeth's Wife Ff.
1. LADY MACBETH | Lady Ff.

50. **Stars, hide your fires.** We are not to understand from this that the present scene takes place at night. Macbeth is evidently contemplating night as the time when the murder is to be done.

52. **The eye wink at**: Let the eye refuse to see. 'Wink at' sometimes means 'encourage' or 'prompt,' but is used here literally.

54. **True, worthy Banquo.** Duncan and Banquo have been speaking about Macbeth during his soliloquy. The beginning of Duncan's speech refers to something Banquo has said in praise of Macbeth.

more in them than mortal knowledge. When I burn'd in desire to question them further, they made themselves air, into which they vanish'd. Whiles I stood rapt in the wonder of it, came missives from the King, who all-hail'd me 'Thane of Cawdor'; by which title, before, these weird sisters saluted me, and referr'd me to the coming on of time, with 'Hail, king that shalt be!' This have I thought good to deliver thee, my dearest partner of greatness, that thou mightst not lose the dues of rejoicing, by being ignorant of what greatness is promis'd thee. Lay it to thy heart, and farewell. 12

Glamis thou art, and Cawdor, and shalt be
What thou art promis'd. Yet do I fear thy nature;
It is too full o' the milk of human kindness
To catch the nearest way: thou wouldst be great;
Art not without ambition, but without
The illness should attend it: what thou wouldst highly,
That wouldst thou holily; wouldst not play false, 19
And yet wouldst wrongly win: thou 'ldst have, great Glamis,

20-21. **And . . .** it Pope | three lines in Ff, ending **win, cries, it.**

6. **missives**: messengers. So in *Antony and Cleopatra*, II, ii, 74.

15. **human kindness.** "'Humankind' is still an expression for human nature, and the sense of the passage . . . would be more obvious if the whole phrase were printed as one word, not 'human kindness' but 'humankind-ness': — that shrinking from what is not natural. . . . 'Milk of humankind-ness' suggests absence of hardness but it equally connotes natural, inherited traditional feelings, imbibed at the mother's breast." — R. G. Moulton.

18. **illness**: unscrupulousness. See Murray. "Macbeth is described by Lady Macbeth so as at the same time to reveal her own character. Could he have every thing he wanted, he would rather have it innocently; — ignorant, as, alas, how many of us are! that he who wishes a temporal end for itself does in truth will the means; and hence the danger of indulging fancies." — Coleridge.

That which cries, 'Thus thou must do,' if thou have it ; 21
And that which rather thou dost fear to do
Than wishest should be undone. Hie thee hither,
That I may pour my spirits in thine ear,
And chastise with the valour of my tongue 25
All that impedes thee from the golden round
Which fate and metaphysical aid doth seem
To have thee crown'd withal.

Enter a MESSENGER

What is your tidings ?

MESSENGER. The king comes here to-night.

LADY MACBETH. Thou 'rt mad to say it :

26. impedes thee | impeides thee F_1 | thee hinders $F_2F_3F_4$.

27. seem | seek Johnson conj.

28. Two lines in Ff.

21–23. A passage involved and obscure. Does 'That which' of line 21 refer to the crown personified, or to the murder of Duncan ? In the Folios are no inverted commas, and in some modern editions (Clar) they are put at the end of line 21 ; in others (Globe Camb) Pope is followed and they are put after 'undone.' In previous editions of Hudson's Shakespeare, 'An act which' was substituted for 'And that which' in line 22, 'that which' being supposed to have crept in by mistake from the preceding line. If the crown is the thing which Glamis would have, and if the crown is here represented as crying out to him "Thus thou must do, if thou have," there appears no way of getting the sense but by substituting 'me' for 'it.' If we suppose only the words "Thus thou must do" to be spoken by the crown, and the following words to be spoken by Lady Macbeth in her own person, then 'it' is right ; and this is probably the way the passage ought to be understood and printed. Johnson saw the difficulty, and proposed to read "if thou have me."

26. **golden round** : crown. Cf. IV, i, 88 ; *Richard II*, III, ii, 160–161.

27. **metaphysical** : supernatural. — **seem**. See note, I, ii, 47.

Is not thy master with him? who, were 't so, 30
Would have inform'd for preparation.

MESSENGER. So please you, it is true; our thane is coming.
One of my fellows had the speed of him,
Who, almost dead for breath, had scarcely more
Than would make up his message.

LADY MACBETH. Give him tending; 35
He brings great news. [*Exit* MESSENGER]
The raven himself is hoarse
That croaks the fatal entrance of Duncan
Under my battlements. Come, you spirits
That tend on mortal thoughts, unsex me here;
And fill me from the crown to the toe top-full 40
Of direst cruelty! make thick my blood;
Stop up th' access and passage to remorse,
That no compunctious visitings of nature
Shake my fell purpose, nor keep peace between

36. Two lines in Ff.

36–38. The raven has made himself hoarse with croaking, or has croaked so loud and long as to become hoarse, over the fatal entrance, etc. The ominousness of the raven's croak is implied elsewhere in Shakespeare. Cf. *Othello*, IV, i, 21; *Hamlet*, III, ii, 264; *2 Henry VI*, III, ii, 40. 'Entrance' is here trisyllabic. See Abbott, § 477.

39. mortal: deadly. So in III, iv, 81; IV, iii, 3.

42. remorse: pity, compassion. So in *As You Like It*, I, iii, 72; *The Tempest*, V, i, 76.

43. compunctious visitings of nature: natural feelings of compunction. A common Shakespearian construction.

44–45. keep peace between The effect and it: come as peacemaker between the purpose and the effect. Another elliptical expression. In previous editions of Hudson's Shakespeare 'break' was substituted for 'keep.

The effect and it! Come to my woman's breasts, 45
And take my milk for gall, you murd'ring ministers,
Wherever in your sightless substances
You wait on nature's mischief! Come, thick night,
And pall thee in the dunnest smoke of hell,
That my keen knife see not the wound it makes, 50
Nor heaven peep through the blanket of the dark,
To cry, 'Hold, hold!'

Enter MACBETH

Great Glamis! worthy Cawdor!
Greater than both, by the all-hail hereafter!
Thy letters have transported me beyond

45. it F_3F_4 | hit F_1F_2.

46. **take my milk for gall.** Either, Take away my milk and give me gall instead (Johnson); or, Change my milk into gall by your malignant power (Schmidt). In support of Schmidt's interpretation, Manly quotes *Merry Wives of Windsor*, IV, iv, 33; *Hamlet*, I, i, 163; *King Lear*, II, iv, 166; III, iv, 60. In her fiery thirst for power, Lady Macbeth feels that her woman's heart is unequal to the calls of her ambition, and she would fain exchange her "milk of human kindness" for a fiercer infusion.

47. **sightless**: invisible. See note on 'careless,' I, iv, 11.

49. **pall**: shroud, wrap as in a pall (Lat. *pallium*, 'cloak'). — **dunnest smoke.** Cf. Milton's "dun shades," *Comus*, 127; "dun air," *Paradise Lost*, III, 72.

51. The metaphor of darkness being a blanket wrapped round the world, so as to keep the Divine Eye from seeing the deed which Lady Macbeth longs and expects to have done, is just such as it was fitting for the boldest of poets to put into the mouth of the boldest of women. But the expressions 'peep' and 'blanket' have seemed undignified to many commentators, and some strange substitutes have been suggested. Coleridge proposed 'blank height' for 'blanket'! In *Romeo and Juliet*, III, ii, 5, we have "Spread thy

This ignorant present, and I feel now 55
The future in the instant.
MACBETH. My dearest love,
Duncan comes here to-night.
LADY MACBETH. And when goes hence?
MACBETH. To-morrow, as he purposes.
LADY MACBETH. O, never
Shall sun that morrow see!
Your face, my thane, is as a book where men 60
May read strange matters. To beguile the time,
Look like the time; bear welcome in your eye,
Your hand, your tongue; look like the innocent flower,
But be the serpent under 't. He that 's coming
Must be provided for; and you shall put 65
This night's great business into my dispatch,
Which shall to all our nights and days to come
Give solely sovereign sway and masterdom.
MACBETH. We will speak further.

61. matters. To . . . time, Theobald | matters, to . . . time. Ff.

close curtain, love-performing night." Cf. *The Faerie Queene*, I, iv, 44: "darkesome night displayd Her coleblack curtein." Malone quotes from Drayton's *Mortimeriados*: "sullen night in mistie rugge is wrapp'd."

56. **instant**: present. The enthusiasm of her newly-kindled expectation quickens the dull present with the spirit of the future, and gives to hope the life and substance of fruition.

59. Abbott, § 511, in a suggestive note on "single lines with two or three accents interspersed amid the ordinary verses of five accents," says that in this broken line is indicated the way in which Lady Macbeth pauses to watch the effect of her words.

62. 'Time' is here put for its contents, or what occurs in time. It is a time of full-hearted welcome and hospitality; and such are the looks which Macbeth is urged to counterfeit.

LADY MACBETH. Only look up clear;
To alter favour ever is to fear. 70
Leave all the rest to me. [*Exeunt*]

SCENE VI. *Before* MACBETH'S *castle*

Hautboys and torches. Enter DUNCAN, MALCOLM, DONALBAIN, BANQUO, LENNOX, MACDUFF, ROSS, ANGUS, *and* Attendants

DUNCAN. This castle hath a pleasant seat; the air
Nimbly and sweetly recommends itself
Unto our gentle senses.
BANQUO. This guest of summer,
The temple-haunting martlet, does approve,

SCENE VI | Scene VIII Pope. — *Before . . . castle* | Ff omit. — *Enter* DUNCAN | Enter King Ff.

1-2. the air . . . itself | one line in Ff.
4. martlet Rowe | Barlet Ff.

70. favour: countenance. Lady Macbeth is here mad, or inspired, with a kind of extemporized ferocity, so that she feels herself able to perform without flinching the crime she has conceived, if her husband will only keep his face from telling any tales of their purpose. As Coleridge says, "Hers is the mock fortitude of a mind deluded by ambition: she shames her husband with a superhuman audacity of fancy which she cannot support, but sinks in the season of remorse, and dies in suicidal agony."

1-3. The air, by its purity and sweetness, attempers our senses to its own state, and so makes them gentle, or sweetens them into gentleness. A proleptical form of speech.

The subject of this quiet and easy conversation gives that repose so necessary to the mind after the tumultuous bustle of the preceding scenes, and perfectly contrasts the scene of horror that immediately succeeds. . . . This also is frequently the practice of Homer, who, from the midst of battles and horrors, relieves and refreshes the mind of the reader, by introducing some quiet rural image or picture of familiar domestic life. — Sir J. Reynolds.

4. approve: prove, make evident. So in *2 Corinthians*, vii, 11.

By his lov'd mansionry, that the heaven's breath 5
Smells wooingly here: no jutty, frieze,
Buttress, nor coign of vantage, but this bird
Hath made his pendent bed and procreant cradle:
Where they most breed and haunt, I have observ'd
The air is delicate.

Enter LADY MACBETH

DUNCAN. See, see, our honour'd hostess! 10
The love that follows us sometime is our trouble,
Which still we thank as love. Herein I teach you
How you shall bid God 'ild us for your pains,
And thank us for your trouble.

LADY MACBETH. All our service
In every point twice done and then done double 15
Were poor and single business to contend
Against those honours deep and broad wherewith

5. **mansionry** Theobald | Mansonry Ff | masonry Pope.
9. **most** Rowe | must Ff.
10. *Enter* . . . | Enter Lady Ff.
13. **God 'ild** | God-eyld Ff.
17–20. **Against . . . hermits** | four lines in Ff, ending **broad, house, dignities, hermits.**

6. **jutty**: projection. The Folios read 'jutty frieze.' See Murray.

7. **coign of vantage**: convenient corner. A 'coign' ('quoin') is 'a projecting corner,' or 'a corner-stone at the exterior angle of a building.' So in *Coriolanus*, V, iv, i: "See you yon coign o' the Capitol, yon corner-stone?" See Murray.

11. **sometime**: sometimes. Shakespeare and Milton use both forms.

13. **bid God 'ild**: pray God repay. The kind-hearted monarch means that his love is what puts him upon troubling them thus, and therefore they will be grateful for the pains he causes them. 'God 'ild' ('God 'ield,' 'God dild,' etc.) is a common Elizabethan corruption of 'God yield,' i.e. 'God reward.'

16. **single**: weak. Contrasted with 'double' in preceding line.

Your majesty loads our house: for those of old,
And the late dignities heap'd up to them,
We rest your hermits.

DUNCAN. Where 's the thane of Cawdor? 20
We cours'd him at the heels, and had a purpose
To be his purveyor: but he rides well,
And his great love, sharp as his spur, hath holp him
To his home before us. Fair and noble hostess,
We are your guest to-night.

LADY MACBETH. Your servants ever 25
Have theirs, themselves, and what is theirs, in compt,
To make their audit at your highness' pleasure,
Still to return your own.

DUNCAN. Give me your hand;
Conduct me to mine host: we love him highly,
And shall continue our graces towards him. 30
By your leave, hostess. [*Exeunt*]

20. **We rest your hermits**: we remain as beadsmen to pray for you. "The lyrical movement with which this scene opens, and the free and unengaged mind of Banquo, loving Nature, and rewarded in the love itself, form a highly dramatic contrast with the laboured rhythm and hypocritical over-much of Lady Macbeth's welcome, in which you cannot detect a ray of personal feeling, but all is thrown upon the 'dignities,' the general duty." — Coleridge. — **thane of Cawdor.** "How gracious the mention here of Macbeth's new title, how poignant the irony!" — Verity.

22. **purveyor**: forerunner. Literally 'one sent in advance to provide (Fr. *pourvoir*) food.' The word is here accented on the first syllable. Cf. 'harbinger,' I, iv, 45.

23. **holp.** The old preterite of 'help' used as a past participle.

26. **in compt**: subject to account, reckoning. So in *Othello*, V, ii, 273: "When we shall meet at compt," i.e. at the judgment-day.

31. **By your leave.** "Here Duncan gives his hand to Lady Macbeth, and leads her into the castle." — Clar.

SCENE VII. MACBETH'S *castle*

Hautboys and torches. Enter a Sewer, *and divers* Servants *with dishes and service, over the stage. Then enter* MACBETH

MACBETH. If it were done when 't is done, then 't were well
It were done quickly : if th' assassination
Could trammel up the consequence, and catch
With his surcease success ; that but this blow

SCENE VII | Scene IX Pope. — MACBETH'S *castle* | Ff omit. — *Hautboys . . .* MACBETH Ff.
1–2. well It | well, It Ff.

Sewer. An officer in a noble household whose duty was to arrange the dishes on the table. Cf. " sewers and seneschals " in *Paradise Lost*, IX, 38. ' Sewer ' is not connected etymologically with Fr. *essayeur*, ' a taster,' but probably with Fr. *asseour*, ' one who sets the table.'

1–2. The punctuation is similar to that of the Folios. Some editors put a period, or colon, at the end of line 1. The meaning is, If all were done when the murder is done, or if the mere doing of the deed were sure to finish the matter, then the quicker it were done the better. Macbeth then goes on to amplify and intensify the same thought in other language.

2–4. if th' assassination . . . success. That is, If the assassination could foreclose or shut off all sequent issues, and end with itself. ' His ' for ' its ' refers undoubtedly to ' assassination.' So ' his ' is commonly used in Elizabethan literature. ' To trammel up ' is ' to entangle ' as in a net. So Spenser has the noun in *The Faerie Queene*, III, ix, 20 : " Her golden locks, that were in tramells gay Upbounden." ' Surcease ' is properly a legal term, meaning the arrest or stay of a suit. So in Bacon's essay *Of Church Controversies* : " It is more than time that there were an end and surcease made of this immodest and deformed manner of writing," etc. ' Success ' probably has the sense of ' sequel,' ' succession,' or ' succeeding events.' So that ' to catch success ' is to arrest and stop off all further outcome, or all entail of danger.

Might be the be-all and the end-all here, 5
But here, upon this bank and shoal of time,
We 'd jump the life to come. But in these cases
We still have judgment here, that we but teach
Bloody instructions, which, being taught, return
To plague th' inventor : this even-handed justice 10
Commends th' ingredients of our poison'd chalice
To our own lips. He 's here in double trust :
First, as I am his kinsman and his subject,
Strong both against the deed ; then, as his host,
Who should against his murderer shut the door, 15
Not bear the knife myself. Besides, this Duncan
Hath borne his faculties so meek, hath been
So clear in his great office, that his virtues
Will plead like angels, trumpet-tongu'd, against
The deep damnation of his taking-off ; 20
And pity, like a naked new-born babe
Striding the blast, or heaven's cherubin hors'd

5. be-all Pope | be all Ff. — end-all here Hanmer | end all. Heere F_1F_2.

6. shoal Theobald | Schoole F_1F_2 | School F_3F_4 | shelve Warburton.

6. But : only. — **bank and shoal**. Theobald's brilliant emendation is generally accepted by modern editors. The metaphor, bringing out the contrast between the shallows of time and the abysses of eternity, is thoroughly Shakespearian. For a defence of the Folio text, see Furness, Liddell, and Porter and Clarke's ' First Folio ' *Macbeth*.

7. jump : risk, hazard. Cf. *Cymbeline*, V, iv, 188. In *Antony and Cleopatra*, III, viii, 6, ' jump ' in this sense is a noun.

8. still : always. — **that** : so that. So in line 25. Cf. I, iii, 57.

17. faculties : honours, dignities, prerogatives. Cf. *Henry VIII*, I, ii, 73. " The essential idea of ' faculty ' is ' power of doing ' (Lat. *facere*, ' to do ') and a common meaning formerly was ' power, liberty, right of doing.' " — Verity.

22. Cf. *Psalms*, xviii, 10 : " he rode upon a cherub and did fly."

Upon the sightless couriers of the air,
Shall blow the horrid deed in every eye,
That tears shall drown the wind. I have no spur 25
To prick the sides of my intent, but only
Vaulting ambition, which o'erleaps itself
And falls on th' other.

Enter LADY MACBETH

How now! what news?

LADY MACBETH. He has almost supp'd: why have you left the chamber? 29

MACBETH. Hath he ask'd for me?

LADY MACBETH. Know you not he has?

MACBETH. We will proceed no further in this business:
He hath honour'd me of late; and I have bought
Golden opinions from all sorts of people,
Which would be worn now in their newest gloss,
Not cast aside so soon.

LADY MACBETH. Was the hope drunk 35
Wherein you dress'd yourself? hath it slept since?

23. couriers Pope | Curriors Ff.
28. th' other. Ff | th' other —. Rowe | th' other side. Hanmer. — Scene X Pope.

23. **sightless couriers of the air**. Cf. 'viewless winds,' *Measure for Measure*, III, i, 124; 'posting winds,' *Cymbeline*, III, iv, 38.

25. **tears shall drown the wind.** The metaphor is common in Shakespeare. Cf. *Troilus and Cressida*, IV, iv, 55, and *Lucrece*, 1790. — **I have no spur**, etc. As Malone pointed out, this passage contains two distinct metaphors. Both are taken from horsemanship, and they follow naturally the figure in lines 22–23.

36. Though it seems natural to take 'dress'd' as carrying on the metaphor in line 34, it here means something more. 'Dress' and 'address' are used by Elizabethan writers in the sense of 'prepare'

And wakes it now, to look so green and pale
At what it did so freely? From this time
Such I account thy love. Art thou afeard
To be the same in thine own act and valour 40
As thou art in desire? Wouldst thou have that
Which thou esteem'st the ornament of life,
And live a coward in thine own esteem,
Letting 'I dare not' wait upon 'I would,'
Like the poor cat i' the adage?

MACBETH. Prithee, peace: 45
I dare do all that may become a man;
Who dares do more is none.

LADY MACBETH. What beast was 't, then,
That made you break this enterprise to me?
When you durst do it, then you were a man;
And, to be more than what you were, you would 50

39. love Ff | liver Bailey conj. — afeard | affear'd $F_1F_2F_3$ | afraid F_4. 45. adage? Capell | Addage. $F_1F_2F_3$. 47. do Rowe | no Ff.

or 'make ready.' The meaning here may be, Was it a drunken man's hope, in the strength of which you made yourself ready for the killing of Duncan? and does that hope now wake from its drunken sleep, to shudder and turn pale at the preparation which it made so freely? In accordance with this explanation, Lady Macbeth's next speech shows that at some former time Macbeth had been, or had fancied himself, ready to make an opportunity for the murder.

42. **ornament of life.** The 'golden opinions' of line 33.

45. The proverb is a common one. Probably the version Shakespeare was familiar with is that in Heywood's *Three Hundred Epigrammes*, 1562: "The cat would eate fyshe, but she wyll not weate her feete."

47. **beast.** The word is exceedingly well chosen here: it conveys a stinging allusion to what Macbeth has just said. If you dare do all that may become a man, then what beast was it that put this enterprise into your head?

Be so much more the man. Nor time nor place
Did then adhere, and yet you would make both :
They have made themselves, and that their fitness now
Does unmake you. I have given suck, and know
How tender 't is to love the babe that milks me ; 55
I would, while it was smiling in my face,
Have pluck'd my nipple from his boneless gums,
And dash'd the brains out, had I so sworn as you
Have done to this.

MACBETH. If we should fail ?

LADY MACBETH. We fail.

But screw your courage to the sticking-place, 60
And we 'll not fail. When Duncan is asleep —
Whereto the rather shall his day's hard journey

58. In Ff the line ends with **sworn.** — so F_1 | but so $F_2F_3F_4$.
59. should fail ? | should faile ? Ff | should fail ? — Rowe | fail, — Theobald. — **We fail.** Capell | We faile ? Ff | We fail ! Rowe.

52. **adhere** : agree, consist with the purpose. This passage seems to infer that the murdering of Duncan had been a theme of conversation between Macbeth and his wife long before the weird salutation. He was then for making a time and place for the deed ; now that they have made themselves to his hand, he is unmanned by them.

59. Probably the sense of this much-disputed passage is simply this : If we should fail, why then, to be sure, we fail, and it is all over with us. So long as there is any hope or prospect of success, Lady Macbeth is for going ahead, and she has a mind to risk all and lose all, rather than let slip any chance of being queen. And why should she not be as ready to jump the present life in such a cause as her husband is to "jump the life to come" ?

60. "A metaphor perhaps taken from the 'screwing-up' the chords of string-instruments to their proper degree of tension, when the peg remains fast in its 'sticking-place.'" — Steevens. "Lady Macbeth is thinking of the cross-bow rack or gaffle, a small detachable winch to draw the string of the bow to its 'sticking-place,' the action of which would naturally be connoted by 'screw.'" —Liddell.

Soundly invite him — his two chamberlains
Will I with wine and wassail so convince,
That memory, the warder of the brain, 65
Shall be a fume, and the receipt of reason
A limbeck only : when in swinish sleep
Their drenched natures lie as in a death,
What cannot you and I perform upon
Th' unguarded Duncan ? what not put upon 70
His spongy officers, who shall bear the guilt
Of our great quell ?

MACBETH. Bring forth men-children only ;
For thy undaunted mettle should compose
Nothing but males. Will it not be receiv'd,
When we have mark'd with blood those sleepy two 75

68. lie Pope | lyes F_1 | lye $F_2F_3F_4$.

63-64. " He got him into his priuie chamber, onelie with two of his chamberlains . . . till they had charged their stomachs with such foul gorges, that their heads were no sooner got to the pillow, but asleepe they were so fast, that a man might haue remooued the chamber ouer them, sooner than to haue awaked them out of their droonken sleepe." — Holinshed. — **wassail** : carousing. See Skeat. — **convince** : overcome. Cf. IV, iii, 142.

65-67. " By the old anatomists the brain was divided into three ventricles, in the hindermost of which they placed the memory. That this division was not unknown to Shakespeare we learn from *Love's Labour's Lost*, IV, ii, 70. . . . When the memory is converted by intoxication into a mere fume (cf. *The Tempest*, V, i, 67), then it fills the brain itself, the receipt or receptacle of reason, which thus becomes like the alembic or cap of a still." — Clar. — **limbeck** : alembic.

71. **spongy** : drunken. Cf. *The Merchant of Venice*, I, ii, 107 : " I will do any thing, Nerissa, ere I' ll be married to a sponge."

72. **quell** : slaying, slaughter. Cf. ' manqueller,' i.e. ' murderer,' in *2 Henry IV*, II, i, 58. From the same root as ' kill ' (Anglo-Saxon *cwęllan*).

Of his own chamber and us'd their very daggers,
That they have done 't?

LADY MACBETH. Who dares receive it other,
As we shall make our griefs and clamour roar
Upon his death?

MACBETH. I am settled, and bend up
Each corporal agent to this terrible feat. 80
Away, and mock the time with fairest show;
False face must hide what the false heart doth know.

[*Exeunt*]

77. other: otherwise. So in V, iv, 8; *King John*, V, ii, 58.

79. bend up. Cf. 'bend up every spirit,' in *Henry V*, III, i, 16. The figure is from stringing a bow, and this strengthens Professor Liddell's interpretation of line 60.

ACT II

SCENE I. *Inverness. Court of* MACBETH'S *castle*

Enter BANQUO, *and* FLEANCE *with a torch before him*

BANQUO. How goes the night, boy?
FLEANCE. The moon is down; I have not heard the clock.
BANQUO. And she goes down at twelve.
FLEANCE. I take 't, 't is later, sir.
BANQUO. Hold, take my sword. There 's husbandry in heaven;
Their candles are all out. Take thee that too. 5
A heavy summons lies like lead upon me,
And yet I would not sleep. Merciful powers,
Restrain in me the cursed thoughts that nature
Gives way to in repose!

Inverness . . . castle Dyce | Ff omit.
4. Two lines in Ff.
7–10. In the Ff lines end **sleep, thoughts, repose, there.**

4. **husbandry**: economy. If 'heaven' be taken as a collective noun, the grammatical construction of 'their' in the next line will be normal.

5. **candles**. Cf. *The Merchant of Venice*, V, i, 220; *Romeo and Juliet*, III, v, 9. — **thee**. See Abbott, § 212. — **that**. He hands Fleance something, a helmet, a shield, or a dagger.

7–9. From line 20 we learn that Banquo has been dreaming of the weird sisters. He understands how their greeting may act as an incentive to crime, and shrinks with horror from the poison of such evil suggestions, and seeks refuge in prayer from the invasion of

Enter MACBETH, *and a* Servant *with a torch*

Give me my sword.

Who 's there ? 10

MACBETH. A friend.

BANQUO. What, sir, not yet at rest ? The king 's a-bed :
He hath been in unusual pleasure, and
Sent forth great largess to your offices :
This diamond he greets your wife withal, 15
By the name of most kind hostess ; and shut up
In measureless content.

MACBETH. Being unprepar'd,
Our will became the servant to defect ;
Which else should free have wrought.

13. In Ff the line ends with pleasure.

16. By . . . hostess | separate line in Ff.

guilty thoughts even in his sleep. His character stands in marked contrast to that of Macbeth, whose mind is inviting wicked thoughts, and catching eagerly at temptation, and revolving how he may work the guilty suggestions through into act.

14. " Comming foorth, he called such afore him as had faithfullie serued him in pursute and apprehension of the rebels, and giuing them heartie thanks, he bestowed sundrie honourable gifts amongst them, of the which number Donwald was one, as he that had been euer accounted a most faithful seruant to the king." — Holinshed. — **offices** : the apartments of those in charge of the various branches of household work. ' Officers ' has been suggested as an emendation, but no change is needed.

16. **shut up**. A difficult expression. It may mean ' composed himself to rest ' ; or here may be a participle in an elliptical construction, and the whole passage will mean, He is wrapped in a sense of boundless satisfaction.

18. A man may be said to be the servant of that which he cannot help : and Macbeth means that his will would have made ampler preparation, but that it was fettered by want of time.

BANQUO. All 's well.
I dreamt last night of the three weird sisters : 20
To you they have show'd some truth.
MACBETH. I think not of them ;
Yet, when we can entreat an hour to serve,
We would spend it in some words upon that business,
If you would grant the time.
BANQUO. At your kind'st leisure.
MACBETH. If you shall cleave to my consent, when 't is,
It shall make honour for you.
BANQUO. So I lose none 26
In seeking to augment it, but still keep
My bosom franchis'd, and allegiance clear,
I shall be counsell'd.
MACBETH. Good repose the while !
BANQUO. Thanks, sir : the like to you ! 30
[*Exeunt* BANQUO *and* FLEANCE]
MACBETH. Go bid thy mistress, when my drink is ready,
She strike upon the bell. Get thee to bed. [*Exit* Servant]
Is this a dagger which I see before me,
The handle toward my hand ? Come, let me clutch thee.
I have thee not, and yet I see thee still. 35
Art thou not, fatal vision, sensible

24. kind'st F_1 | **kindst** F_2 | **kind** F_3F_4.
25–26. when 't is . . . you | one line in Ff.
30. [*Exeunt* BANQUO *and* FLEANCE] Exit Banquo Ff.
31. Scene II Pope.
32. [*Exit* Servant] Exit Ff.

25–26. If you will join my party (i.e. what has my consent), when the time comes (or, when the result is gained), it shall make honour for you. 'Consort,' 'contest,' 'ascent,' 'concept,' have all been suggested as emendations of the obscure 'consent' of the Folio text.

36. **sensible** : "perceptible through the bodily organs." — Century. "Capable of being perceived through the senses." — Clar.

To feeling as to sight? or art thou but
A dagger of the mind, a false creation,
Proceeding from the heat-oppressed brain?
I see thee yet, in form as palpable 40
As this which now I draw.
Thou marshall'st me the way that I was going;
And such an instrument I was to use.
Mine eyes are made the fools o' the other senses,
Or else worth all the rest: I see thee still; 45
And on thy blade and dudgeon gouts of blood,
Which was not so before. There 's no such thing:
It is the bloody business which informs
Thus to mine eyes. Now o'er the one half-world
Nature seems dead, and wicked dreams abuse 50
The curtain'd sleep; witchcraft celebrates
Pale Hecate's offerings; and wither'd murder,

44–45. 'Senses' is here used with a double reference, (1) to the bodily organs of sense, and (2) to the inward faculties of the mind. Either his eyes are deceived by his imaginative forces in being made to see that which is not, or else his other senses are at fault in not being able to find the reality which his eyes behold.

46. **dudgeon**: haft, hilt. The name of a kind of wood (probably boxwood) used by turners for the handles of knives, daggers, etc. Then, by metonymy, the handle or the dagger itself. — **gouts**: large drops. Fr. *goutte*; Lat. *gutta*.

51. "The loss of an unstressed syllable after a cæsural pause is of common occurrence in English verse." — Liddell. But may not 'witchcraft' be trisyllabic here, 'witchc(e)raft,' in accordance with the rule that 'r' and liquids in dissyllables are frequently pronounced as though an extra vowel were introduced between them and the preceding consonant. See Abbott, § 477.

51–52. **celebrates Pale Hecate's offerings**. That is, Makes offerings or sacrifices to Hecate, who was the queen of Hades, the patroness of all infernal arts, and of course the mistress of all who

Alarum'd by his sentinel, the wolf,
Whose howl 's his watch, thus with his stealthy pace,
With Tarquin's ravishing strides, towards his design 55
Moves like a ghost. Thou sure and firm-set earth,
Hear not my steps, which way they walk, for fear
Thy very stones prate of my whereabout,
And take the present horror from the time,
Which now suits with it. Whiles I threat, he lives : 60
Words to the heat of deeds too cold breath gives.
[*A bell rings*]
I go, and it is done ; the bell invites me.
Hear it not Duncan ; for it is a knell
That summons thee to heaven or to hell. [*Exit*]

55. strides Pope | sides Ff.
56. sure Capell | sowre F_1F_2 | sowr F_3 | sour F_4.
57. way they Rowe | they may Ff.

practised them ; here called 'pale,' because, under the name of Diana, she was identified with the moon. Cf. *Childe Harold*, II, 22 : " beneath pale Hecat's blaze." The name is, properly, trisyllabic, but Shakespeare always has it dissyllabic, except in *1 Henry VI*, III, ii, 64.

54. ' Watch ' is here used probably for ' signal.' The figure is of the wolf acting as the sentinel of murder, and his howl being the signal to give warning of approaching danger.

55. Steevens points out that ' strides ' (Pope's emendation for ' sides ' in the Folio text) did not necessarily carry the idea of violence or noise, but was used by Elizabethan writers in a sense coherent enough with ' stealthy pace ' :

> They passing forth kept on their readie way,
> With easie steps so soft as foot could stryde.
>
> *The Faerie Queene*, IV, viii, 37.

58. Cf. *Luke*, xix, 40.

59–60. " Macbeth would have nothing break through the universal silence that added such horror to the night, as suited well with the bloody deed he was about to perform." — Steevens.

SCENE II. *The same*

Enter LADY MACBETH

LADY MACBETH. That which hath made them drunk hath made me bold;
What hath quench'd them hath given me fire. Hark! Peace!
It was the owl that shriek'd, the fatal bellman,
Which gives the stern'st good-night. He is about it:
The doors are open; and the surfeited grooms 5
Do mock their charge with snores: I have drugg'd their possets,

SCENE II | Scene III Pope | Rowe continues scene.
2–6. In Ff the lines end **fire, shriek'd, good-night, open, charge, possets.**

1–2. Lady Macbeth has fired her courage by drinking wine; but, while she is kindled by drink, the grooms are stupefied, "their possets" having been drugged.

3. Shakespeare has more than one allusion to the supposed ominousness of the owl's note. Cf. *1 Henry VI*, IV, ii, 15; *Richard III*, IV, iv, 509; *Lucrece*, 165. Cf. "fatal fowle! As ravens, schrich-owles." — Webster's *The Duchess of Malfi*, IV, ii, 63–64. "For one will saie; I had a dreame to-night, or a crowe croked upon my house, or an owle flew by me and screeched (which augurie Lucius Silla tooke of his death)." — Scot. — **the fatal bellman.** So in *The Duchess of Malfi*, IV, ii, 179–181:

> I am the common bellman,
> That usually is sent to condemn'd persons
> The night before they suffer.

Lady Macbeth of course regards Duncan as the condemned person to whom the 'fatal bellman' gives 'the stern'st good-night.'

6. "Posset is hot milk poured on ale or sack, having sugar, grated bisket, and eggs, with other ingredients boiled in it, which all goes to a curd." — *Academy of Armourie* (1688). "Get me three hundred milch bats, to make possets to procure sleepe." — *The Duchess of Malfi*, IV, ii, 116.

That death and nature do contend about them,
Whether they live or die.

Enter MACBETH

MACBETH. Who 's there ? what, ho !
LADY MACBETH. Alack, I am afraid they have awak'd,
And 't is not done. Th' attempt and not the deed 10
Confounds us. Hark ! I laid their daggers ready ;
He could not miss 'em. Had he not resembled
My father as he slept, I had done 't. My husband !
MACBETH. I have done the deed. Didst thou not hear a noise ?
LADY MACBETH. I heard the owl scream and the crickets cry. 15
Did not you speak ?

8. *Enter* MACBETH Ff | in Globe Camb after **done 't,** line 13.
13. **My husband** | separate line in Ff.
14. Two lines in Ff.

7. **That** : so that. So in line 23. Cf. I, ii, 58 ; I, vii, 8.
8. *Enter* MACBETH. The Folio stage direction. " It may be that on the Elizabethan stage Macbeth entered here, not to the stage proper, but to the balcony above." — Manly.
10–11. The attempt without the deed destroys or ruins us.
12–13. This little touch of nature is one of Shakespeare's most pregnant hints of character, and of itself should be enough to upset the more common notion of Lady Macbeth. It tells us that, notwithstanding her appalling invocation to the " murdering ministers," her milk continues to be milk. And what a suggestive contrast it makes to the terrible audacity of thought and speech she has just displayed ! It is the tenderness of her woman's heart that causes her to see in the sleeping king an image of her father.
15. Webster imitated this in *The White Devil*, V, iv, 91–94 :

> When scritch-howles croke upon the chimney tops,
> And the strange cricket i' th' oven singes and hoppes . . . .
> Be certaine then you of a corse shall heare.

MACBETH. When?

LADY MACBETH. Now.

MACBETH. As I descended?

LADY MACBETH. Ay.

MACBETH. Hark!
Who lies i' the second chamber?

LADY MACBETH. Donalbain. 19

MACBETH. This is a sorry sight. [*Looking on his hands*]

LADY MACBETH. A foolish thought, to say a sorry sight.

MACBETH. There 's one did laugh in 's sleep, and one cried 'Murder!'
That they did wake each other: I stood and heard them:
But they did say their prayers, and address'd them
Again to sleep.

LADY MACBETH. There are two lodg'd together. 25

MACBETH. One cried 'God bless us!' and 'Amen' the other,
As they had seen me with these hangman's hands:
Listening their fear, I could not say 'Amen,'
When they did say 'God bless us!'

LADY MACBETH. Consider it not so deeply. 30

MACBETH. But wherefore could not I pronounce 'Amen'?
I had most need of blessing, and 'Amen'
Stuck in my throat.

18–19. **Hark! . . . chamber?** one line in Ff.
20. [*Looking* . . .] Ff omit.
22–25. Lines in Ff end **sleep, other, prayers, sleep.**
32–33. **I had . . . throat** | one line in Ff.

24. **address'd**: prepared. Cf. *The Merchant of Venice*, II, ix, 19.
27. **As**: as if. See Abbott, § 107. — **hangman's**: executioner's.
28. The Folio punctuation. In previous editions of Hudson's Shakespeare a comma closed the preceding line and a colon was put after 'fear,' so that 'listening' modified 'me' and not 'I.'

LADY MACBETH. These deeds must not be thought
After these ways: so, it will make us mad. 34
MACBETH. Methought I heard a voice cry 'Sleep no more!
Macbeth does murder sleep,' — the innocent sleep,
Sleep that knits up the ravell'd sleave of care,
The death of each day's life, sore labour's bath,
Balm of hurt minds, great nature's second course,
Chief nourisher in life's feast, —
LADY MACBETH. What do you mean? 40
MACBETH. Still it cried 'Sleep no more!' to all the house:
'Glamis hath murder'd sleep, and therefore Cawdor
Shall sleep no more; Macbeth shall sleep no more!'
LADY MACBETH. Who was it that thus cried? Why, worthy thane,
You do unbend your noble strength, to think 45
So brainsickly of things. Go get some water,
And wash this filthy witness from your hand.
Why did you bring these daggers from the place?

35–36. 'Sleep . . . sleep' | marked as quotation by Johnson.
37. sleave Steevens | sleeve Ff.
41. 'Sleep . . . more' | marked as quotation by Hanmer.
42–43. 'Glamis . . . more!' | marked as quotation by Hanmer.

35. "A voice was heard as he was in bed in the night time to take his rest vttering unto him these or the like woordes . . . The king with this voice being striken into great dread and terror, passed that night without anie sleepe comming in his eies." — Holinshed. The Folio printing does not indicate where the words of the 'voice' end. Hanmer extended the quotation as far as 'life's feast.'

37. ravell'd sleave: tangled skein of floss-silk. Cf. *Troilus and Cressida*, V, i, 35: "thou idle immaterial skein of sleave-silk."

39–40. In the second course at Elizabethan feasts were served the most nourishing dishes.

45–46. to think So brainsickly: in thinking so crazily. The gerundive use of the infinitive. See Abbott, § 356.

They must lie there : go carry them, and smear
The sleepy grooms with blood.
  MACBETH. I 'll go no more : 50
I am afraid to think what I have done ;
Look on 't again I dare not.
  LADY MACBETH. Infirm of purpose !
Give me the daggers : the sleeping and the dead
Are but as pictures ; 't is the eye of childhood
That fears a painted devil. If he do bleed, 55
I 'll gild the faces of the grooms withal ;
For it must seem their guilt. [*Exit. Knocking within*]
  MACBETH. Whence is that knocking ?
How is 't with me, when every noise appals me ?
What hands are here ? ha ! they pluck out mine eyes !
Will all great Neptune's ocean wash this blood 60

57. [*Knocking* . . . | Knocke . . . Ff.

52–55. With her firm self-control, this bold woman, when awake was to be moved by nothing but facts : when her powers of self-control were unknit by sleep, then was the time for her to see things that were not, save in her own conscience.

56. gild. ' Red ' is a common epithet for ' gold ' in early English literature, and ' golden blood ' occurs in II, iii, 100. Cf. *King John*, II, i, 316. " ' Gild with blood ' was an expression not uncommon in the sixteenth century." — Nares. — withal. See note, I, iii, 57.

57. guilt. The same quibble, also with tragic setting, occurs in *2 Henry IV*, IV, v, 129–130 ; and *Henry V*, Prol. II, 26. It is famous in English literature from Marlowe to Hood. — *Knocking within.* For the tragic significance of this, see De Quincey, " On the Knocking at the Gate in *Macbeth.*" It is dramatically effective that one of the men whose knocking startles the guilty pair is the destined instrument of vengeance. " The knocking here seems to show that the opening of the next scene always formed part of the play." — E. K. Chambers.

60–61. For parallel passages in Sophocles, Catullus, Lucretius, and Seneca, see Furness.

Clean from my hand? No; this my hand will rather
The multitudinous seas incarnadine,
Making the green one red.

Re-enter LADY MACBETH

LADY MACBETH. My hands are of your colour, but I shame
To wear a heart so white. [*Knocking within*] I hear a knocking 65
At the south entry: retire we to our chamber.
A little water clears us of this deed:
How easy is it, then! Your constancy
Hath left you unattended. [*Knocking within*] Hark! more knocking.
Get on your night-gown, lest occasion call us, 70
And show us to be watchers. Be not lost
So poorly in your thoughts.

MACBETH. To know my deed, 't were best not know myself. [*Knocking within*]
Wake Duncan with thy knocking! I would thou couldst!
[*Exeunt*]

63. green one red | Green one Red F_4 | Greene one, Red $F_1F_2F_3$.
64. *Re-enter* . . . | Enter Ff.
65, 69, 73. [*Knocking within*] Knocke Ff.
65–69. Seven lines in Ff, ending white, entry, chamber, deed, constancy, unattended, knocking.
73. Two lines in Ff.
74. Two lines in Ff.

63. Some editors have followed the Folio punctuation. "Converting the green into one uniform red. The comma after 'one' yields a tame, not to say ludicrous, sense." — Clar. Cf. *Hamlet*, II, ii, 479.

68–69. **Your constancy Hath left you unattended**: firmness, which was once your attendant, has deserted you.

70. **night-gown**: dressing-robe. Usual sixteenth century meaning.

73. While thinking of what I have done, it were best I should be lost to myself, or should not know myself as the doer of it.

SCENE III. *The same*

Enter a PORTER. *Knocking within*

PORTER. Here 's a knocking indeed! If a man were porter of hell-gate, he should have old turning the key. [*Knocking*] Knock, knock, knock! Who 's there, i' the name of Beelzebub? Here 's a farmer, that hang'd himself on the expectation of plenty. Come in time; have napkins

SCENE III | Scene IV Warburton (Pope) | Rowe continues scene. — *The same* Capell | Ff omit.

3, 6, etc. [*Knocking*] Knock Ff.
4. Beelzebub | Belzebub Ff.

SCENE III. This, the famous "Porter's scene," has been regarded by some critics, including Coleridge, as unauthentic. But it is thoroughly Shakespearian in conception and execution. Its broad drollery serves as a proper foil to the antecedent horrors; its very discordance with the surrounding matter imparts an air of verisimilitude to the whole. "Looking at the scene as a practical dramatist, I see that it is absolutely necessary to get Macbeth off the stage. A motive must be contrived for this. That motive is at once supplied by the sudden knocking." — Tom Taylor.

2. old: plenty of. A frequent intensive or augmentative in colloquial Elizabethan speech, and still heard in modern slang. Cf. *The Merchant of Venice*, IV, ii, 15: "We shall have old swearing."

4. Beelzebub. Perhaps the Folio trisyllabic spelling should be retained in the text as representing the popular pronunciation. The Porter proceeds to hold a dialogue with several imaginary persons at 'hell-gate' who are supposed to be knocking for admission. Too much, perhaps, has been made of supposed 'topical allusions' in this dialogue for determining the date of composition of the play. See Introduction.

4–5. That a farmer who hoarded grain against a 'lean' year should hang himself when a year of plenty came seems to have been a current Elizabethan jest. Hall and Ben Jonson both make use of it.

5. Come in time: an early arrival. — **napkins**. In Baret's *Alvearie* we have "a napkin, or handkerchiefe, wherewith wee wipe away the sweate." In Tindale's New Testament 'napkin' is used to translate σουδάριον, Lat. *sudarium*.

enough about you ; here you 'll sweat for 't. [*Knocking*] Knock, knock ! Who 's there, in the other devil's name ? Faith, here 's an equivocator that could swear in both the scales against either scale ; who committed treason enough for God's sake, yet could not equivocate to heaven. O, come in, equivocator. [*Knocking*] Knock, knock, knock ! Who 's there ? Faith, here 's an English tailor come hither for stealing out of a French hose. Come in, tailor ; here you may roast your goose. [*Knocking*] Knock, knock ; never at quiet ! What are you ? But this place is too cold for hell. I 'll devil-porter it no further : I had thought to have let in some of all professions, that go the primrose way

8. Some editors, following Malone, find here a reference to the trial of Henry Garnet in March, 1606, in connection with the Gunpowder Plot. At this trial the doctrine of ' equivocation ' was much discussed, but ' equivocation ' was " at all times so favourite a theme of invective with Protestant preachers that it could not but be familiar to the public, who in those days frequented the pulpit as assiduously as the stage." — Clar. Verity notes that " the *alias* under which Garnet often passed was ' Mr. Farmer ' . . . so that the transition (for the two must not be identified) from ' the farmer that hang'd himself ' to the ' equivocator ' was a sort of jest."

10. **equivocate to heaven** : win heaven by equivocating.

13. **hose** : trousers. " The joke consists in this, that, a French hose being very short and strait, a tailor must be master of his trade who could steal any thing from thence." — Warburton. Another view is that the allusion is to a French fashion, which made the hose very large and wide, and so with more cloth to be stolen.

14. A tailor's ' goose ' is the heavy flatiron with which he smooths and presses his work, so called because the handle bore some resemblance to the neck of a goose. The quibble is an ancient one.

17–18. **the primrose way to the everlasting bonfire**. Cf. *All's Well that Ends Well*, IV, v, 56 : " They'll be for the flowery way that leads to the broad gate and the great fire " ; *Hamlet*, I, iii, 50 : " Himself the primrose path of dalliance treads." " A bonfire at that date is

to the everlasting bonfire. [*Knocking*] Anon, anon! I pray you, remember the porter. [*Opens the gate*]

Enter MACDUFF *and* LENNOX

MACDUFF. Was it so late, friend, ere you went to bed, 20
That you do lie so late?

PORTER. Faith, sir, we were carousing till the second cock.

MACDUFF. I believe drink gave thee the lie last night.

PORTER. That it did, sir, i' the very throat on me: but I requited him for his lie; and, I think, being too strong for him, though he took up my legs sometime, yet I made a shift to cast him. 27

Enter MACBETH

MACDUFF. Is thy master stirring?
Our knocking has awak'd him; here he comes.

LENNOX. Good morrow, noble sir.

MACBETH. Good morrow, both.

MACDUFF. Is the king stirring, worthy thane?

MACBETH. Not yet.

19. [*Opens* . . .] Ff omit. 28. Scene IV Pope.

invariably given in Latin Dictionaries as equivalent to *pyra* or *rogus*; it was the fire for consuming the human body after death: and the hell-fire differed from the earth-fire only in being everlasting. This use of a word so remarkably descriptive in a double meaning is intensely Shakespearian." — Fleay. See Murray.

22. **the second cock.** Cf. *Romeo and Juliet*, IV, iv, 3–4:

> The second cock hath crow'd,
> The curfew bell hath rung, 't is three o'clock.

27. **cast him.** The quibble is between 'cast,' i.e. 'throw,' as a wrestling term, and 'cast' in the sense of 'ease my stomach of.'

MACDUFF. He did command me to call timely on him:
I have almost slipp'd the hour.
MACBETH. I 'll bring you to him.
MACDUFF. I know this is a joyful trouble to you;
But yet 't is one. 35
MACBETH. The labour we delight in physics pain.
This is the door.
MACDUFF. I 'll make so bold to call,
For 't is my limited service. [*Exit*]
LENNOX. Goes the king hence to-day?
MACBETH. He does; — he did appoint so.
LENNOX. The night has been unruly: where we lay, 40
Our chimneys were blown down; and, as they say,
Lamentings heard i' the air, strange screams of death,
And, prophesying with accents terrible
Of dire combustion and confus'd events
New hatch'd to th' woeful time, the obscure bird 45
Clamour'd the livelong night: some say, the earth
Was feverous and did shake.
MACBETH. 'T was a rough night.

37–38. Prose in Ff.
38. [*Exit*] Exit Macduffe Ff.
40–42. In Ff four lines, ending unruly, down, air, death.
44. combustion F_1 | combustions $F_2F_3F_4$.
45–47. New . . . shake | four lines in Ff, ending time, night, feverous, shake.

38. limited: appointed. Cf. *Timon of Athens*, IV, iii, 431.
39. Here we have a significant note of character. Macbeth catches himself in the utterance of a falsehood, which is something at odds with his nature and habitual feelings; and he starts back into a mending of his speech, as from a spontaneous impulse to be true.
44. combustion. A common Elizabethan meaning was 'tumult.'
45. obscure: darkness-haunting. Cf. *Julius Cæsar*, I, iii, 26; *Titus Andronicus*, II, iii, 97. 'Obscure' as adjective is accented on the first syllable in Shakespeare; as verb, on the second. See Abbott, § 492.

LENNOX. My young remembrance cannot parallel
A fellow to it.

Re-enter MACDUFF

MACDUFF. O horror, horror, horror! tongue nor heart
Cannot conceive nor name thee!

MACBETH. }
LENNOX. } What's the matter? 51

MACDUFF. Confusion now hath made his masterpiece!
Most sacrilegious murder hath broke ope
The Lord's anointed temple, and stole thence
The life o' the building.

MACBETH. What is 't you say? the life? 55

LENNOX. Mean you his majesty?

MACDUFF. Approach the chamber, and destroy your sight
With a new Gorgon. Do not bid me speak;
See, and then speak yourselves.

[*Exeunt* MACBETH *and* LENNOX]

Awake, awake!
Ring the alarum-bell. Murder and treason! 60
Banquo and Donalbain! Malcolm! awake!
Shake off this downy sleep, death's counterfeit,
And look on death itself! up, up, and see

50-51. tongue . . . thee | separate line in Ff.

52. Confusion: destruction. So in III, v, 29.

54. The Lord's anointed temple. Shakespeare here mixes in one metaphor "Lord's anointed," *1 Samuel*, xxiv, 10, and "temple of the living God," *2 Corinthians*, vi, 16.

57. Every one who looked on Medusa, one of the three Gorgons, was turned to stone. Cf. Milton's *Comus*, 447-449:

What was that snaky-headed Gorgon shield
That wise Minerva wore, unconquered virgin,
Wherewith she freezed her foes to congealed stone?

The great doom's image ! Malcolm ! Banquo !
As from your graves rise up, and walk like sprites 65
To countenance this horror. Ring the bell. [*Bell rings*]

Enter LADY MACBETH

LADY MACBETH. What 's the business,
That such a hideous trumpet calls to parley
The sleepers of the house ? speak, speak !
MACDUFF. O gentle lady,
'T is not for you to hear what I can speak : 70
The repetition, in a woman's ear,
Would murder as it fell.

Enter BANQUO

O Banquo, Banquo,
Our royal master 's murder'd !
LADY MACBETH. Woe, alas !
What, in our house ?
BANQUO. Too cruel anywhere.
Dear Duff, I prithee, contradict thyself, 75
And say it is not so.

65. **sprites** | sprights Ff.
66. **Ring the bell** | Theobald omits.
67. Scene V Pope.
72–73. **O . . . murder'd** | one line in Ff.

64. **great doom's image** : picture of the Judgment-day. Cf. ' image of that horror ' in *King Lear*, V, iii, 264. " The strong medial pause in the line indicates that Macduff waits a moment for their reply to his summons." — Verity.

66. **countenance** : lend countenance to, be in keeping with. ' Ring the bell ' is omitted by some editors, who regard it as a stage direction that had crept into the Folio text.

74. Lady Macbeth's first thought appears to be, that she and her husband may be suspected of the murder.

Re-enter MACBETH *and* LENNOX, *with* ROSS

MACBETH. Had I but died an hour before this chance,
I had liv'd a blessed time ; for, from this instant,
There 's nothing serious in mortality :
All is but toys ; renown and grace is dead ; 80
The wine of life is drawn, and the mere lees
Is left this vault to brag of.

Enter MALCOLM *and* DONALBAIN

DONALBAIN. What is amiss ?
MACBETH. You are, and do not know 't :
The spring, the head, the fountain of your blood
Is stopp'd, the very source of it is stopp'd. 85
MACDUFF. Your royal father 's murder'd.
MALCOLM. O ! by whom ?
LENNOX. Those of his chamber, as it seem'd, had done 't :
Their hands and faces were all badg'd with blood ;
So were their daggers, which unwip'd we found
Upon their pillows : 90
They star'd, and were distracted ; no man's life
Was to be trusted with them.
MACBETH. O, yet I do repent me of my fury,
That I did kill them.
MACDUFF. Wherefore did you so ?

91-92. In Ff lines end distracted, them.

79. mortality : human life. So in *King John*, V, vii, 5.
81-82. Observe the fine links of association in 'wine' and 'vault'; the latter having a double reference, to the wine-vault and to the firmament over-arching the world of human life.
88. badg'd : marked as with a distinctive symbol. In *2 Henry VI*, III, ii, 200, occurs "Murder's crimson badge."

MACBETH. Who can be wise, amaz'd, temperate and furious, 95
Loyal and neutral, in a moment? No man:
The expedition of my violent love
Outrun the pauser, reason. Here lay Duncan,
His silver skin lac'd with his golden blood;
And his gash'd stabs look'd like a breach in nature 100
For ruin's wasteful entrance; there, the murderers,
Steep'd in the colours of their trade, their daggers
Unmannerly breech'd with gore: who could refrain,
That had a heart to love, and in that heart
Courage to make 's love known?

LADY MACBETH. Help me hence, ho! 105

MACDUFF. Look to the lady.

MALCOLM. [*Aside to* DONALBAIN] Why do we hold our tongues,
That most may claim this argument for ours?

106, 108, 111. [*Aside* . . . | Ff omit.

97. **expedition**: haste. This meaning survives in 'expeditiously.'

99. In *Much Ado About Nothing*, III, iv, 19, is "cloth of gold, lac'd with silver." See note on II, ii, 56. "It is not improbable that Shakespeare put these forced and unnatural metaphors into the mouth of Macbeth as a mark of artifice and dissimulation, to show the difference between the studied language of hypocrisy and the natural outcries of sudden passion. The whole speech, so considered, is a remarkable instance of judgment, as it consists entirely of antithesis and metaphor." — Johnson.

100–101. The image is of a besieging army making a breach in the walls of a city, and thereby opening a way for general massacre and pillage.

103. This probably means rudely covered, dressed, with blood. "Language so forced is only appropriate in the mouth of a conscious murderer dissembling guilt." — Abbott

DONALBAIN. [*Aside to* MALCOLM] What should be spoken here, where our fate,
Hid in an auger-hole, may rush, and seize us ?
Let 's away. 110
Our tears are not yet brew'd.

MALCOLM. [*Aside to* DONALBAIN] Nor our strong sorrow
Upon the foot of motion.

BANQUO. Look to the lady ;
[LADY MACBETH *is carried out*]
And when we have our naked frailties hid,
That suffer in exposure, let us meet
And question this most bloody piece of work, 115
To know it further. Fears and scruples shake us :

109–111. In Ff lines end **here, hole, away.**

112. [LADY MACBETH . . .] Rowe | Ff omit.

108–110. Where there is no hiding-place so small but that murder may be lurking therein, ready to spring upon us at any moment. The Princes divine at once that their father has been murdered for the crown, and that the same motive means death to themselves as well.

112. LADY MACBETH *is carried out.* Some regard this swoon as feigned, others as real. The question is very material in the determining of Lady Macbeth's character. If feigned, why was it not done when the murder of Duncan was announced ? The announcement of these additional murders takes her by surprise ; she was not prepared for it ; whereas in the other case she had, by her fearful energy of will, steeled her nerves up to it beforehand. "For dreadful deeds anticipated and resolved upon, she has strength ; but the surprise of a novel horror, on which she has not counted, deprives her suddenly of consciousness: when Macbeth announces his butchery of Duncan's grooms, the lady swoons, — not in feigning but in fact, — and is borne away insensible." — Dowden.

113. Banquo and the others who slept in the castle have rushed forth undressed. This is what he refers to in 'our naked frailties.'

In the great hand of God I stand, and thence
Against the undivulg'd pretence I fight
Of treasonous malice.

MACDUFF. And so do I.

ALL. So all.

MACBETH. Let 's briefly put on manly readiness, 120
And meet i' the hall together.

ALL. Well contented.

[*Exeunt all but* MALCOLM *and* DONALBAIN]

MALCOLM. What will you do? Let 's not consort with them:
To show an unfelt sorrow is an office
Which the false man does easy. I 'll to England.

DONALBAIN. To Ireland I; our separated fortune 125
Shall keep us both the safer: where we are,
There 's daggers in men's smiles: the near in blood,
The nearer bloody.

121. [*Exeunt all* . . . | Exeunt Ff.
122. Two lines in Ff.
124. Two lines in Ff.
125–128. To . . . bloody | in Ff lines end I, safer, smiles, bloody.

117–119. The natural construction is, 'and thence I fight against the undivulg'd pretence of treasonous malice.' 'Pretence' here means 'intention' or 'purpose.' A frequent usage. Cf. the verb, II, iv, 24.

120. briefly: quickly. So in *Cymbeline*, V, v, 106. — manly readiness: man's equipment. The expression suggests preparation for fight. It is in marked contrast to 'naked frailties.'

124. easy. In Elizabethan literature adjectives are often used as adverbs. See Abbott, § 1. — I 'll to England. "Malcolme Cammore and Donald Bane the sons of King Duncane, for feare of their liues . . . fled into Cumberland, where Malcolme remained . . . but Donald passed over into Ireland." — Holinshed.

127. near: nearer. 'Near' is really an old comparative, as may be seen in *Richard II*, V, i, 88. Donalbain suspects Macbeth, who is next in blood or of kin.

MALCOLM. This murderous shaft that 's shot
Hath not yet lighted ; and our safest way
Is to avoid the aim. Therefore, to horse ; 130
And let us not be dainty of leave-taking,
But shift away : there 's warrant in that theft
Which steals itself, when there 's no mercy left. [*Exeunt*]

SCENE IV. *Outside* MACBETH'S *castle*

Enter ROSS *and an* OLD MAN

OLD MAN. Threescore-and-ten I can remember well :
Within the volume of which time I have seen
Hours dreadful and things strange ; but this sore night
Hath trifl'd former knowings.
ROSS. Ah, good father,
Thou see'st the heavens, as troubl'd with man's act, 5
Threatens his bloody stage : by th' clock 't is day,
And yet dark night strangles the travelling lamp.
Is 't night's predominance, or the day's shame
That darkness does the face of earth entomb,
When living light should kiss it ?

SCENE IV | Scene VI Pope.
4. Ah Rowe | Ha Ff.
7. travelling F_3F_4 | travailing F_1F_2.

129–130. Suspecting this murder to be the work of Macbeth, Malcolm thinks it could have no purpose but what himself and his brother equally stand in the way of ; that the ' murderous shaft ' must pass through them to reach its mark.

4. trifl'd former knowings : made of no importance previous experiences.

7. travelling lamp : the sun. Cf. *1 Henry IV*, I, ii, 226.

8–10. " For the space of six monethes togither, after this heinous murther was committed, there appeered no sunne by day, nor moone

OLD MAN. 'T is unnatural, 10
Even like the deed that 's done. On Tuesday last,
A falcon, tow'ring in her pride of place,
Was by a mousing owl hawk'd at and kill'd.

ROSS. And Duncan's horses — a thing most strange and certain —
Beauteous and swift, the minions of their race, 15
Turn'd wild in nature, broke their stalls, flung out,
Contending 'gainst obedience, as they would make
War on mankind.

OLD MAN. 'T is said they eat each other.

ROSS. They did so, to th' amazement of mine eyes,
That look'd upon 't.

Enter MACDUFF

Here comes the good Macduff. 20
How goes the world, sir, now?

14. Two lines in Ff.
17–18. First line in Ff ends would.
19–20. Three lines in Ff, ending so, upon 't, Macduff.

by night in anie part of the realme." — Holinshed. These and other omens and signs are described by Holinshed in connection with the murder of King Duff.

12–18. "Monstrous sights also that were seene within the Scotish Kingdome that yeere were these, horsses in Louthian, being of singular beautie and swiftnesse, did eate their owne fleshe . . . There was a sparhawke also strangled by an owle." — Holinshed.

12. tow'ring. A technical term of falconry to describe the spiral soaring of a hawk to its 'place' whence it swoops on the prey. Cf. *2 Henry VI*, II, i, 10. The word is still used by gamekeepers to describe the vertical ascent of a game-bird fatally wounded in the head.

13. mousing. "A very effective epithet, as contrasting the falcon, in her pride of place, with a bird that is accustomed to seek its prey on the ground." — Talbot.

15. minions: darlings, favourites. From Fr. *mignon*, 'dainty.'

MACDUFF. Why, see you not?
ROSS. Is 't known who did this more than bloody deed?
MACDUFF. Those that Macbeth hath slain.
ROSS. Alas, the day!
What good could they pretend?
MACDUFF. They were suborn'd:
Malcolm and Donalbain, the King's two sons, 25
Are stol'n away and fled; which puts upon them
Suspicion of the deed.
ROSS. 'Gainst nature still!
Thriftless ambition, that will ravin up
Thine own life's means! Then 't is most like
The sovereignty will fall upon Macbeth. 30
MACDUFF. He is already nam'd; and gone to Scone
To be invested.
ROSS. Where is Duncan's body?
MACDUFF. Carried to Colmekill,
The sacred storehouse of his predecessors,
And guardian of their bones.
ROSS. Will you to Scone? 35
MACDUFF. No, cousin, I 'll to Fife.
ROSS. Well, I will thither.

28. **ravin up**: completely devour. Cf. 'kill them up,' *As You Like It*, II, i, 62.

31–33. "He . . . foorthwith went vnto Scone where . . . he receiued the inuesture of the Kingdome. . . . The bodie of Duncane was . . . remoued and conueied unto Colmekill, and there laid in a sepulture amongst his predecessors." — Holinshed. Scone (pronounced *skoon*) was the place of coronation of the Scottish kings. 'The stone of destiny,' carried to Westminster by Edward I in 1296, was part of the coronation chair. Colmekill (i.e. the cell of St. Columba) is the modern Iona.

MACDUFF. Well, may you see things well done there, — adieu ! —
Lest our old robes sit easier than our new !
ROSS. Farewell, father.
OLD MAN. God's benison go with you ; and with those
That would make good of bad, and friends of foes ! 41
[*Exeunt*]

ACT III

SCENE I. *Forres. The palace*

Enter BANQUO

BANQUO. Thou hast it now : king, Cawdor, Glamis, all,
As the weird women promis'd, and, I fear,
Thou play'dst most foully for 't : yet it was said
It should not stand in thy posterity,
But that myself should be the root and father 5
Of many kings. If there come truth from them,
As upon thee, Macbeth, their speeches shine,
Why, by the verities on thee made good,
May they not be my oracles as well,
And set me up in hope ? But hush ! no more. 10

Sennet sounded. Enter MACBETH, *as king ;* LADY MACBETH, *as queen ;* LENNOX, ROSS, Lords, Ladies, *and* Attendants

MACBETH Here's our chief guest.
LADY MACBETH. If he had been forgotten,

Forres. The palace | Ff omit.
2. weird | weyard F_1 | weyward $F_2F_3F_4$.
11. . . . LADY MACBETH, *as queen* . . . Attendants Globe | Lady Lenox, Rosse, Lords, and Attendants Ff.

7. **As** : inasmuch as. — **speeches shine** : predictions cast lustre.

11. *Sennet.* A peculiar set of notes played on the trumpet, announcing the approach of royal personages. Sometimes spelled 'signate,' as though connected etymologically with 'signal.' Cf. 'signature' in musical notation.

It had been as a gap in our great feast,
And all-thing unbecoming.

MACBETH. To-night we hold a solemn supper, sir,
And I 'll request your presence.

BANQUO. Let your highness 15
Command upon me ; to the which my duties
Are with a most indissoluble tie
For ever knit.

MACBETH. Ride you this afternoon ?

BANQUO. Ay, my good lord.

MACBETH. We should have else desir'd your good advice,
Which still hath been both grave and prosperous, 21
In this day's council ; but we 'll take to-morrow.
Is 't far you ride ?

BANQUO. As far, my lord, as will fill up the time
'Twixt this and supper : go not my horse the better, 25
I must become a borrower of the night
For a dark hour or twain.

MACBETH. Fail not our feast.

BANQUO. My lord, I will not.

MACBETH. We hear, our bloody cousins are bestow'd
In England and in Ireland, not confessing 30
Their cruel parricide, filling their hearers
With strange invention : but of that to-morrow,

13. all-thing : quite, altogether, entirely. See Murray.

14. solemn : official, formal. Cf. *All's Well that Ends Well*, II, iii, 187.

15. In previous editions of Hudson's Shakespeare Rowe's reading of ' Lay ' for ' Let ' was adopted because of ' upon ' in the next line. But ' upon ' belongs to ' command ' rather than to ' me.'

21. still: always.—grave: weighty.—prosperous: turning out well.

25. **go not my horse the better** : if my horse go not fast enough.

When therewithal we shall have cause of state
Craving us jointly. Hie you to horse ; adieu,
Till you return at night. Goes Fleance with you ? 35

BANQUO. Ay, my good lord : our time does call upon 's.

MACBETH. I wish your horses swift and sure of foot ;
And so I do commend you to their backs.
Farewell. [*Exit* BANQUO]
Let every man be master of his time 40
Till seven at night ; to make society
The sweeter welcome, we will keep ourself
Till supper-time alone : while then, God be with you !
[*Exeunt all but* MACBETH *and an* ATTENDANT]
Sirrah, a word with you : attend those men
Our pleasure ? 45

ATTENDANT. They are, my lord, without the palace-gate.

MACBETH. Bring them before us. [*Exit* ATTENDANT]
To be thus is nothing,
But to be safely thus. Our fears in Banquo
Stick deep ; and in his royalty of nature
Reigns that which would be fear'd. 'T is much he dares ; 50

34–35. Three lines in Ff, ending **horse, night, you.**
42–43. Three lines in Ff, ending **welcome, alone, you.**
43. [*Exeunt* . . .] Exeunt Lords Ff.
44. Scene II Pope.
47. [*Exit* ATTENDANT] Exit Servant Ff.
47–50. To be . . . dares | Four lines in Ff, ending **thus, deep, that, dares.**

43. **while**: until. A common Elizabethan usage. Cf. *Twelfth Night*, IV, iii, 29. — **God be with you.** The full form of ' good-bye.' Sometimes written ' God-b'wy-ye,' or ' God buy you,' which is probably the pronunciation here.

48. **But** : unless, except. The sentence means, To be on the throne is nothing at all if I cannot be so in perfect security. — **in** : on account of. Cf. *Julius Cæsar*, II, i, 190 : " There is no fear in him ; let him not die."

And, to that dauntless temper of his mind,
He hath a wisdom that doth guide his valour
To act in safety. There is none but he
Whose being I do fear ; and, under him,
My Genius is rebuk'd, as, it is said, 55
Mark Antony's was by Cæsar. He chid the sisters,
When first they put the name of king upon me,
And bade them speak to him ; then prophet-like
They hail'd him father to a line of kings :
Upon my head they plac'd a fruitless crown, 60
And put a barren sceptre in my gripe,
Thence to be wrench'd with an unlineal hand,
No son of mine succeeding. If 't be so,
For Banquo's issue have I fil'd my mind ;
For them the gracious Duncan have I murder'd ; 65
Put rancours in the vessel of my peace
Only for them ; and mine eternal jewel
Given to the common enemy of man,
To make them kings, the seed of Banquo kings !

69. **seed** Pope | **Seedes** F_1F_2.

51. **to** : in addition to. Cf. *King John*, I, i, 144.

55–56. With this use of 'Genius' cf. *Troilus and Cressida*, IV, iv, 52 ; *Julius Cæsar*, II, i, 66. The 'Cæsar' referred to is Octavius. Cf. *Antony and Cleopatra*, II, iii, 15–22. "For thy demon, said he (that is to say, the good angell and spirit that keepeth thee), is afraid of his : and being couragious and high when he is alone, becommeth fearfull and timorous when he cometh near unto the other." — *Life of Marcus Antonius*, North's Plutarch.

62. **with an unlineal hand** : by the hand of one not heir to me.

64. **fil'd** : defiled. Anglo-Saxon *fýlan*, 'make foul.' Whence 'foul,' 'filth,' etc. This use of 'file' is still common in Scotland.

67. **eternal jewel** : immortal soul. Cf. *Richard II*, I, i, 180–181.

Rather than so, come, fate, into the list, 70
And champion me to th' utterance ! — Who 's there ?

Re-enter ATTENDANT, *with two* MURDERERS

Now go to th' door, and stay there till we call. —
[*Exit* ATTENDANT]
Was it not yesterday we spoke together ?
1 MURDERER. It was, so please your highness.
MACBETH. Well then, now
Have you consider'd of my speeches ? Know 75
That it was he, in the times past, which held you
So under fortune ; which you thought had been
Our innocent self : this I made good to you
In our last conference, pass'd in probation with you,
How you were borne in hand, how cross'd, the instruments,
Who wrought with them, and all things else that might 81
To half a soul and to a notion craz'd
Say, ' Thus did Banquo.'

71. Two lines in Ff.
74. 1 MURDERER | *Murth.* Ff. — now | Ff give to line 75.
75–81. Nine lines in Ff, ending speeches, past, fortune, self, conference, you, cross'd, them, might.

71. champion me : fight against me. — **to th' utterance** : to the extremity, to the death. It is the Fr. *à outrance,* often written incorrectly *à l'outrance* (*outre,* Lat. *ultra,* ' beyond '). The meaning of the passage is, Let Fate, that has decreed the throne to Banquo's issue, enter the lists in support of its own decrees, I will fight against it to the last extremity, whatever be the consequence.

79. pass'd in probation : went over the details of the proof.

80. borne in hand : deluded with false hopes (cf. Fr. *maintenir,* from late Lat. *manutenere*). — **cross'd** : thwarted. — **instruments** : agents. The general meaning of the passage is that Banquo has managed to hold up their hopes, while secretly preventing fruition ; thus using them as tools, and cheating them out of their pay.

82. notion : understanding, judgment. Cf. *King Lear,* I, iv, 248

1 MURDERER. You made it known to us.
MACBETH. I did so, and went further, which is now
Our point of second meeting. Do you find 85
Your patience so predominant in your nature
That you can let this go? Are you so gospell'd,
To pray for this good man and for his issue,
Whose heavy hand hath bow'd you to the grave
And beggar'd yours for ever?
1 MURDERER. We are men, my liege. 90
MACBETH. Ay, in the catalogue ye go for men;
As hounds and greyhounds, mongrels, spaniels, curs,
Shoughs, water-rugs, and demi-wolves, are clept
All by the name of dogs: the valued file
Distinguishes the swift, the slow, the subtle, 95
The housekeeper, the hunter, every one
According to the gift which bounteous nature
Hath in him clos'd; whereby he does receive
Particular addition, from the bill
That writes them all alike; and so of men. 100
Now, if you have a station in the file,

84–90. Nine lines in Ff, ending so, now, meeting, predominant, go, man, hand, beggar'd, ever.

93. Shoughs | Showghes Ff | Shocks Capell. — **clept** Capell | clipt Ff.

87. so gospell'd: so filled with the spirit of the Gospel.

92–93. Cf. *King Lear*, III, vi, 71–73. — **Shoughs**: shock dog (so called from its shaggy hair). — **water-rugs**: rough water dog (Swedish *rugg*). — **demi-wolves**: mongrels bred between dogs and wolves. — **clept**: called. Cf. *Hamlet*, I, iv, 19; *Love's Labour's Lost*, V, i, 23. In *Love's Labour's Lost*, I, i, 42, V, iii, 602, 'yclept' is the form of the participle. See Murray.

94. valued file: list where dogs are graded according to their worth.

96. housekeeper: watch-dog; one that 'keeps' ('guards') the house.

99. addition: title of distinction. Cf. I, iii, 106.

Not i' the worst rank of manhood, say 't;
And I will put that business in your bosoms,
Whose execution takes your enemy off,
Grapples you to the heart and love of us, 105
Who wear our health but sickly in his life,
Which in his death were perfect.
  2 MURDERER. I am one, my liege,
Whom the vile blows and buffets of the world
Hath so incens'd, that I am reckless what
I do to spite the world.
  1 MURDERER. And I another 110
So weary with disasters, tugg'd with fortune,
That I would set my life on any chance,
To mend it, or be rid on 't.
  MACBETH. Both of you
Know Banquo was your enemy.
  BOTH MURDERERS. True, my lord.
  MACBETH. So is he mine; and in such bloody distance,
That every minute of his being thrusts 116
Against my near'st of life; and though I could
With barefac'd power sweep him from my sight

109–110. **Hath . . . do** Rowe | one line in Ff.
113–114. **Both . . . enemy** Rowe | one line in Ff.
114. BOTH MURDERERS | *Murth.* Ff.

111. **tugg'd with fortune**: "buffeted by misfortune." — Liddell.
115. 'Distance' (Old Fr. *distance*, Lat. *distantia*, 'standing apart') originally meant 'discord,' 'dispute.' Here it probably is the fencing term, meaning the definite interval of space to be observed between two antagonists. When men are in a hot mortal encounter with swords, they stand at just the right distance apart for the bloodiest strokes or thrusts. Cf. *Romeo and Juliet*, II, iv, 21.
117. **near'st of life.** Either 'most vital parts' or 'inmost soul.'

And bid my will avouch it, yet I must not,
For certain friends that are both his and mine, 120
Whose loves I may not drop, but wail his fall
Who I myself struck down; and thence it is,
That I to your assistance do make love,
Masking the business from the common eye
For sundry weighty reasons.

2 MURDERER. We shall, my lord, 125
Perform what you command us.

1 MURDERER. Though our lives —

MACBETH. Your spirits shine through you. Within this hour at most
I will advise you where to plant yourselves;
Acquaint you with the perfect spy o' the time,

127. Two lines in Ff.

119. **avouch it**: to take responsibility for the deed.

120. **For**: on account of. A common Elizabethan use. See Abbott, 150.

122. **Who**: whom. So in III, iv, 42. See Abbott, 274.

128. "He willed therefore the same Banquho with his sonne named Fleance, to come to a supper that he had prepared for them, which was in deed, as he had deuised, present[1] death at the hands of certeine murderers, whom he hired to execute that deed, appointing them to meete with the same Banquho and his son without[2] the palace, as they returned to their lodgings, and there to slea them." — Holinshed.

129. A much-disputed passage. Johnson proposed 'a' for 'the,' and made the line refer to the third murderer. More probably the meaning is, Will furnish you with an exact and sure note or signal of the time when to strike; which is probably done by or through the third murderer, who joins them just before the murder is done. The success of the undertaking depends on the assault being rightly timed. So that 'the perfect spy of the time' may be 'the sure means of spying or knowing the time.'

[1] immediate. [2] outside.

The moment on 't ; for 't must be done to-night, 130
And something from the palace ; always thought
That I require a clearness : and with him —
To leave no rubs nor botches in the work —
Fleance his son, that keeps him company,
Whose absence is no less material to me 135
Than is his father's, must embrace the fate
Of that dark hour. Resolve yourselves apart ;
I 'll come to you anon.

BOTH MURDERERS. We are resolv'd, my lord.

MACBETH. I 'll call upon you straight : abide within.

[*Exeunt* MURDERERS]

It is concluded : Banquo, thy soul's flight, 140
If it find heaven, must find it out to-night. [*Exit*]

SCENE II. *The palace*

Enter LADY MACBETH *and a* SERVANT

LADY MACBETH. Is Banquo gone from court ?

SERVANT. Ay, madam, but returns again to-night.

138. BOTH MURDERERS | Murth. Ff.
139. [*Exeunt* . . . | Ff omit.
141. [*Exit*] Rowe | Exeunt Ff.
SCENE II | Scene III Pope. — *The palace* | Ff omit.
LADY MACBETH | Macbeths Lady Ff.

131–133. It being always borne in mind that I must stand clear of blame or suspicion. " So that he would not have his house slaundered, but that in time to come he might cleare himselfe." — Holinshed. — **rubs**: roughnesses, impediments. Cf. the bowling and golfing term ' rub on the green.' The literal meaning is seen in *Henry V*, II, ii, 188, " Every rub is smoothed on our way " ; the figurative in *Hamlet*, III, i, 65, " ay, there 's the rub." — **botches**. Murray suggests that ' botch ' is probably an onomatopoetic word akin to ' patch.'

LADY MACBETH. Say to the king, I would attend his leisure
For a few words.
SERVANT. Madam, I will. [*Exit*]
LADY MACBETH. Nought 's had, all 's spent,
Where our desire is got without content : 5
'T is safer to be that which we destroy
Than by destruction dwell in doubtful joy.

Enter MACBETH

How now, my lord ! why do you keep alone,
Of sorriest fancies your companions making ;
Using those thoughts which should indeed have died 10
With them they think on ? Things without all remedy
Should be without regard : what 's done is done.
MACBETH. We have scotch'd the snake, not kill'd it :
She 'll close and be herself, whilst our poor malice
Remains in danger of her former tooth. 15
But let the frame of things disjoint, both the worlds suffer,
Ere we will eat our meal in fear, and sleep
In the affliction of these terrible dreams

13. scotch'd Theobald | scorch'd Ff. 16. Two lines in Ff.

11. without all : beyond any. 'Without' is literally 'outside of.'

13. scotch'd : cut, slashed. "Made narrow incisions, as with a 'scutcher' or riding whip."—Herford. See 'hop-scotch' in Murray. 'Close' in the next line shows this to be the meaning. Cf. *Coriolanus*, IV, v, 198 : "he scotch'd him and he notch'd him like a carbonado," where 'carbonado' means a piece of meat slashed across for broiling. Liddell defends the Folio reading on the ground that "'scorch' is a derivative verb from 'score' and means 'to hack.'"

18–19. What 'these terrible dreams' are, is shown in Lady Macbeth's sleep-walking agonies. It is of her state of mind, not of his own, that Macbeth is here thinking. "No witches have given her

That shake us nightly: better be with the dead,
Whom we, to gain our peace, have sent to peace, 20
Than on the torture of the mind to lie
In restless ecstasy. Duncan is in his grave;
After life's fitful fever he sleeps well;
Treason has done his worst: nor steel, nor poison,
Malice domestic, foreign levy, nothing, 25
Can touch him further.

LADY MACBETH. Come on;
Gentle my lord, sleek o'er your rugged looks;
Be bright and jovial among your guests to-night.

MACBETH. So shall I, love; and so, I pray, be you:
Let your remembrance apply to Banquo; 30
Present him eminence, both with eye and tongue:

20. peace F_1 | place $F_2F_3F_4$. 22. Two lines in Ff.

'hail'; no airy dagger marshals her the way she is going; nor is she afterwards haunted by the terrible vision of Banquo's gory head. As long as her will remains her own she can throw herself upon external facts, and maintain herself in relation with the definite, actual surroundings; it is in her sleep, when the will is incapable of action, that she is persecuted by the past which perpetually renews itself, not in ghostly shapes, but by the imagined recurrence of real and terrible incidents." — Dowden.

21. The reference is to the torture of the rack. Cf. *The Merchant of Venice*, III, ii, 24–27.

22. **ecstasy.** In its general sense the word describes any violent mental disturbance. Cf. *The Tempest*, III, iii, 108.

27. **Gentle my lord.** This common inversion is probably for emphasis.

30. **remembrance apply to**: consideration attach itself to.

31. **Present him eminence**: treat him as eminent. In lines 30–31 the language is strained and obscure. Is Macbeth ironical, or is he wishing to keep his wife ignorant and innocent of the new crime on foot?

Unsafe the while, that we
Must lave our honours in these flattering streams,
And make our faces vizards to our hearts,
Disguising what they are.

LADY MACBETH. You must leave this. 35

MACBETH. O, full of scorpions is my mind, dear wife!
Thou know'st that Banquo and his Fleance lives.

LADY MACBETH. But in them nature's copy 's not eterne.

MACBETH. There 's comfort yet; they are assailable;
Then be thou jocund: ere the bat hath flown 40
His cloister'd flight; ere to black Hecate's summons
The shard-borne beetle with his drowsy hums
Hath rung night's yawning peal, there shall be done
A deed of dreadful note.

LADY MACBETH. What 's to be done?

MACBETH. Be innocent of the knowledge, dearest chuck,

32–33. In Ff lines end **lave**, **streams**.
37. **Fleance** Rowe | Fleans F_1F_3 F_4 | Feans F_2.
42. **shard-borne** F_1F_2 | shard-born F_3F_4 | sharp-brow'd D'Avenant.
43–44. In Ff first line ends **peal**.

32–35. The very fact of our being obliged thus to use the arts of hypocrisy and dissimulation proves that we are not safe in our seats, not secure in the tenure of our honours: we can retain them only by making our life, even in social intercourse, a studied, continuous lie. — **flattering streams**: streams of flattery.

38. **copy**. "Probably for 'copyhold,' a form of land tenure which differed from freehold in being terminable." — Herford.

41. **cloister'd**. "The bats wheeling round the dim cloisters of Queen's College, Cambridge, have frequently impressed on me the singular propriety of this original epithet." — Steevens.

42. **shard-borne**: borne through the air on scaly wings. Cf. *Antony and Cleopatra*, III, ii, 20; *Cymbeline*, III, iii, 20. Some editors follow the spelling of the later Folios and interpret as 'born in refuse.'

43. **yawning**: drowsy. — **peal**. The curfew bell is suggested.

45. **chuck**. A term of endearment. Cf. *Othello*, III, iv, 49.

Till thou applaud the deed. Come, seeling night, 46
Scarf up the tender eye of pitiful day,
And with thy bloody and invisible hand
Cancel and tear to pieces that great bond
Which keeps me pale! Light thickens, and the crow 50
Makes wing to th' rooky wood:
Good things of day begin to droop and drowse,
Whiles night's black agents to their preys do rouse.
Thou marvell'st at my words, but hold thee still;
Things bad begun make strong themselves by ill. 55
So, prithee, go with me. [*Exeunt*]

50–51. and the crow . . . wood | one line in Ff.

46. seeling night: night that closes up the eyes. 'Seeling' is a term of falconry often used figuratively in Elizabethan literature. To tame hawks their eyelids were drawn together by a thread of fine silk. Fr. *ciller* (*siller*), Lat. *cilium*.

49. that great bond. Probably, as Mr. E. K. Chambers suggests, "the bond between destiny and the house of Banquo, made known in the prophecy of the weird sisters."

50. Light thickens. Cf. 'lustre thickens' in *Antony and Cleopatra*, II, iii, 27. So in Spenser, *The Shepheards Calender*, *March*, 115–116:

> But see, the Welkin thicks apace,
> And stouping Phebus steepes his face.

51. rooky: rook-haunted. 'Crow' and 'rook' were used of the same bird, 'crow' being generic and 'rook' specific. "The passage simply means, 'the rook hastens its evening flight to the wood where its fellows are already assembled,' and to our mind 'the rooky wood' is a lively and natural picture." — Mitford (quoted by Furness). But some editors interpret 'rooky' as 'misty,' 'gloomy,' connecting it etymologically with Anglo-Saxon *réc*, Dutch *rook*, German *Rauch*, etc. Cf. Scottish and dialectic 'reek,' as in *Coriolanus*, III, iii, 121.

52. "A motto of the entire tragedy . . . It is the tragedy of the twilight and the setting-in of thick darkness." — Dowden.

53–55. A covert allusion to the exploit which Macbeth's murderers are going about. He seems to want that his wife should suspect the

SCENE III. *A park near the palace*

Enter three MURDERERS

1 MURDERER. But who did bid thee join with us?
3 MURDERER. Macbeth.
2 MURDERER. He needs not our mistrust; since he delivers
Our offices, and what we have to do,
To the direction just.
1 MURDERER. Then stand with us.
The west yet glimmers with some streaks of day: 5
Now spurs the lated traveller apace
To gain the timely inn; and near approaches
The subject of our watch.
3 MURDERER. Hark! I hear horses.

SCENE III | Scene IV Pope | Scene II Rowe. — *A park . . .* | Ff omit.

new crime he has in hand, while he shrinks from telling her of it distinctly. And the purpose of his dark hints is probably to prepare her, as far as may be, for a further strain upon her moral forces, which he sees to be already overstrained. For he fears that, if she has full knowledge beforehand of the intended murder, she may oppose it, and that if she has no suspicion of it the shock may be too much for her.

Enter three MURDERERS. See Furness for a full statement of the ingenious theory that Macbeth himself is the Third Murderer, advanced by Mr. A. P. Paton (*Macbeth*, Hamnet edition, 1877). A strong point against this view is the way in which Macbeth is affected on hearing of Fleance's escape (III, iv, 21). Mr. Libby holds that Ross is the Third Murderer, and says that "because Shakespeare is dealing with the spy-system, he refuses to give the name of this villain."

2. **He needs not our mistrust**: we need not mistrust him.

6. **lated**: belated. Not from 'belated,' but a participial adjective in -ed from 'late.' Cf. *Antony and Cleopatra*, III, xi, 3.

BANQUO. [*Within*] Give us a light there, ho!
2 MURDERER. Then 't is he: the rest
That are within the note of expectation 10
Already are i' the court.
1 MURDERER. His horses go about.
3 MURDERER. Almost a mile: but he does usually,
So all men do, from hence to th' palace gate
Make it their walk.

Enter BANQUO, *and* FLEANCE *with a torch*

2 MURDERER. A light, a light!
3 MURDERER. 'T is he.
1 MURDERER. Stand to 't. 15
BANQUO. It will be rain to-night.
1 MURDERER. Let it come down.
[*They set upon* BANQUO]
BANQUO. O, treachery! Fly, good Fleance, fly, fly, fly!
Thou mayst revenge. O slave! [*Dies*. FLEANCE *escapes*]

16. [*They set upon* . . . | Ff omit.
17. **O . . . fly!** | two lines in Ff.
18. [*Dies . . . escapes*] Pope | Dies Rowe | Ff omit.

10. **note of expectation**: list of those guests who are expected.
17–18. "It chanced yet by the benefit of the darke night, that though the father were slaine, the sonne yet . . . escaped that danger: and afterwards hauing some inkeling . . . how his life was sought no lesse than his fathers, who was slaine not by chance-medlie [1] (as by the handling of the matter Makbeth would have had it to appeare) but euen vpon a prepensed [2] deuise: wherevpon to auoid further perill he fled into Wales." — Holinshed. Doubtless Shakespeare accepted the Stuart tradition that Fleance married a daughter of the Prince of Wales and had a son who afterwards became Lord High Steward of Scotland; from thence he assumed the name of Walter Steward (Stuart). "From him, in a direct line,

[1] accident. [2] premeditated.

3 MURDERER. Who did strike out the light?
1 MURDERER. Was 't not the way?
3 MURDERER. There 's but one down; the son is fled.
2 MURDERER. We have lost
Best half of our affair. 21
1 MURDERER. Well, let 's away, and say how much is done. [*Exeunt*]

SCENE IV. *Hall in the palace*

A banquet prepared. Enter MACBETH, LADY MACBETH, ROSS, LENNOX, LORDS, *and* Attendants

MACBETH. You know your own degrees; sit down: at first
And last the hearty welcome.
LORDS. Thanks to your majesty.
MACBETH. Ourself will mingle with society,
And play the humble host.
Our hostess keeps her state, but in best time 5
We will require her welcome.
LADY MACBETH. Pronounce it for me, sir, to all our friends,
For my heart speaks they are welcome.
[*First* MURDERER *appears at the door*]
MACBETH. See, they encounter thee with their hearts' thanks.

SCENE IV | Scene V Pope | Scene III Rowe. — *Hall in the* . . . | Ff omit.

5. best F_1 | the best $F_2F_3F_4$.
9. [*First* MURDERER . . . | Enter first Murtherer Ff.

King James I was descended, in compliment to whom our author has chosen to describe Banquo, who was equally concerned with Macbeth in the murder of Duncan, as innocent of that crime." — Malone.

5. keeps her state: remains in her chair of state.

Both sides are even : here I 'll sit 'i the midst. 10
Be large in mirth ; anon we 'll drink a measure
The table round. — [*Goes to the door*] There 's blood upon thy face.

MURDERER. 'T is Banquo's then.

MACBETH. 'T is better thee without than he within.
Is he dispatch'd ? 15

MURDERER. My lord, his throat is cut ; that I did for him.

MACBETH. Thou art the best o' the cut-throats ; yet he 's good
That did the like for Fleance : if thou didst it,
Thou art the nonpareil.

MURDERER. Most royal sir,
Fleance is scap'd. 20

MACBETH. Then comes my fit again : I had else been perfect,
Whole as the marble, founded as the rock ;
As broad and general as the casing air :
But now I am cabin'd, cribb'd, confin'd, bound in
To saucy doubts and fears. But Banquo 's safe ? 25

MURDERER. Ay, my good lord ; safe in a ditch he bides,
With twenty trenched gashes on his head,
The least a death to nature.

MACBETH. Thanks for that.
There the grown serpent lies ; the worm that 's fled

12. [*Goes* . . . | Approaching the door Grant White Globe | Ff omit.
17–19. **Thou . . . nonpareil** | in Ff lines end **cut-throats, Fleance, nonpareil.**
21. Two lines in Ff.

14. It is better on your face than in his veins.
19. **nonpareil** : one who has no equal. Cf. *Twelfth Night*, I, v, 273.
23. Having as full and free scope as the enveloping air.
29. **worm** : serpent. Cf. *A Midsummer Night's Dream*, III, ii, 71.

Hath nature that in time will venom breed, 30
No teeth for th' present. Get thee gone: to-morrow
We 'll hear 't, ourself, again. [*Exit* MURDERER]

LADY MACBETH. My royal lord,
You do not give the cheer: the feast is sold
That is not often vouch'd, while 't is a-making,
'T is given with welcome: to feed were best at home; 35
From thence the sauce to meat is ceremony;
Meeting were bare without it.

Enter the Ghost *of* BANQUO, *and sits in* MACBETH'S *place*

MACBETH. Sweet remembrancer!
Now, good digestion wait on appetite,
And health on both!

LENNOX. May 't please your highness sit.

MACBETH. Here had we now our country's honour roof'd,
Were the grac'd person of our Banquo present; 41
Who may I rather challenge for unkindness
Than pity for mischance.

ROSS. His absence, sir,
Lays blame upon his promise. Please 't your highness
To grace us with your royal company. 45

MACBETH. The table 's full!

LENNOX. Here is a place reserv'd, sir.

33–37. The feast is made or given for profit, not as a frank expression of kindness and good-will, if, during its course, it is not often declared to be given with pleasure. If merely to feed were all, that were best done at home.

37. *Enter the* Ghost . . . This is the stage direction of the Folios. Modern editors place the entry of the Ghost after line 39, and discuss the question whether, upon the stage, the Ghost should objectively appear. See note, line 89.

MACBETH. Where ?

LENNOX. Here, my good lord. What is 't that moves your highness ?

MACBETH. Which of you have done this ?

LORDS. What, my good lord ?

MACBETH. Thou canst not say I did it : never shake 50
Thy gory locks at me.

ROSS. Gentlemen, rise ; his highness is not well.

LADY MACBETH. Sit, worthy friends : my lord is often thus,
And hath been from his youth : pray you, keep seat ;
The fit is momentary ; upon a thought 55
He will again be well : if much you note him,
You shall offend him, and extend his passion :
Feed, and regard him not. [*Aside to* MACBETH] Are you a man ?

MACBETH. Ay, and a bold one, that dare look on that
Which might appal the devil.

LADY MACBETH. [*Aside to* MACBETH] O proper stuff ! 60
This is the very painting of your fear :
This is the air-drawn dagger which, you said,
Led you to Duncan. O, these flaws and starts,
Impostors to true fear, would well become
A woman's story at a winter's fire, 65
Authoriz'd by her grandam. Shame itself !

48. Two lines in Ff. 58, 60. [*Aside* . . . | Ff omit.

57. **shall** : will. — **extend his passion** : increase his agitation.

63. **flaws** : bursts of passion. Originally, 'gusts of wind.' Cf. *Coriolanus*, V, iii, 74. See Murray.

64. **to** : compared with. A common use. Cf. *Hamlet*, I, ii, 139–140.

65. Cf. *Richard II*, V, i, 40–43 ; *The Winter's Tale*, II, i, 25–26.

Why do you make such faces? When all 's done,
You look but on a stool.

MACBETH. Prithee, see there! behold! look! lo! how say you?
Why, what care I? If thou canst nod, speak too. 70
If charnel-houses and our graves must send
Those that we bury back, our monuments
Shall be the maws of kites. [Ghost *vanishes*]

LADY MACBETH. [*Aside to* MACBETH] What, quite unmann'd in folly?

MACBETH. If I stand here, I saw him!

LADY MACBETH. [*Aside to* MACBETH] Fie, for shame!

MACBETH. Blood hath been shed ere now, i' the olden time, 75
Ere humane statute purg'd the gentle weal;
Ay, and since too, murders have been perform'd
Too terrible for the ear. The time has been,
That, when the brains were out, the man would die,
And there an end; but now they rise again, 80
With twenty mortal murders on their crowns,
And push us from our stools: this is more strange
Than such a murder is.

LADY MACBETH. My worthy lord,
Your noble friends do lack you.

69. Two lines in Ff.
73. [Ghost . . .] Rowe | Exit Ghost $F_2F_3F_4$ | F_1 omits.
73, 74. [*Aside* . . . | Ff omit.
78. time has Camb | times has F_1 | times have $F_2F_3F_4$.

72–73. monuments: tombs. — maws: stomachs. Cf. *The Faerie Queene*, II, viii, 17: "But be entombed in the raven or the kight."

76. Ere humane statute made the commonwealth gentle by purging and cleansing it from the wrongs and pollutions of barbarism. 'Gentle' is here used proleptically.

MACBETH. I do forget.
Do not muse at me, my most worthy friends ; 85
I have a strange infirmity, which is nothing
To those that know me. Come, love and health to all ;
Then I 'll sit down. Give me some wine, fill full.

Re-enter the Ghost

I drink to th' general joy o' the whole table,
And to our dear friend Banquo, whom we miss ; 90
Would he were here ! to all and him we thirst,
And all to all.

LORDS. Our duties, and the pledge.

MACBETH. Avaunt ! and quit my sight ! let the earth hide thee !
Thy bones are marrowless, thy blood is cold ;

89. *Re-enter* . . . | **Enter** Ghost Ff.

85. **muse** : wonder. See Skeat. Cf. *King John*, III, i, 317.

89. *Re-enter the* **Ghost**. Much question has been made, whether there be not two several ghosts in this scene ; some maintaining that Duncan's enters here, and Banquo's before ; others, that Banquo's enters here, and Duncan's before. The question is best disposed of by referring to Forman (*Diary*, see Introduction), who, as he speaks of Banquo's ghost, would doubtless have spoken of Duncan's, had there been any such :

Next night, beinge at supper with his noble men whom he had bid to a feaste to the which also Banco should have com, he began to speak of Noble Banco, and to wish that he wer ther. And as he thus did, standing up to drincke a Carouse to him, the ghoste of Banco came and sat down in his cheier be-hind him. And he turning A-bout to sit down Again sawe the goste of banco, which fronted him so, that he fell in-to a great passion of fear and fury.

92. **all to all** : pledge all good wishes to all. An appropriate gesture would bring out the full meaning here.

Thou hast no speculation in those eyes 95
Which thou dost glare with!

LADY MACBETH. Think of this, good peers,
But as a thing of custom: 't is no other;
Only it spoils the pleasure of the time.

MACBETH. What man dare, I dare:
Approach thou like the rugged Russian bear, 100
The arm'd rhinoceros, or the Hyrcan tiger;
Take any shape but that, and my firm nerves
Shall never tremble: or be alive again,
And dare me to the desert with thy sword;
If trembling I inhabit then, protest me 105
The baby of a girl. Hence, horrible shadow!
Unreal mockery, hence! [Ghost *vanishes*]
Why, so: being gone,
I am a man again. Pray you, sit still.

LADY MACBETH. You have displac'd the mirth, broke the good meeting,
With most admir'd disorder.

101. the Hyrcan | th' Hircan F_1F_2.
105. inhabit then F_1 | inhabit, then $F_2F_3F_4$ | inhibit, then Pope | inhibit thee Malone | inhabit there Delius conj.
107. [Ghost . . . | Exit $F_2F_3F_4$ after shadow | F_1 omits. — being gone F_1F_2 | be gone F_3F_4.
109–110. broke . . . disorder | one line in Ff.

95. **speculation**: power of vision. Cf. *Othello*, I, iii, 271.

101. **arm'd**: armoured with his thick hide. — **Hyrcan**: Hyrcanian. Cf. *The Merchant of Venice*, II, vii, 41; *Hamlet*, II, ii, 472.

104–106. "Dare me to the desert with thy sword; if then I do not meet thee there; if trembling I stay in my castle, or any habitation; if I then hide my head, or dwell in any place through fear, protest me the baby of a girl." — Horne Tooke. Milton uses 'inhabit' in a similar sense, *Paradise Lost*, VII, 162: "Meanwhile inhabit lax, ye powers of heaven." Some editors take 'inhabit' in the sense of 'put on as a garment' (cf. *Psalms*, xxii, 3). — **protest me**: declare me to

MACBETH. Can such things be, 110
And overcome us like a summer's cloud,
Without our special wonder? You make me strange
Even to the disposition that I owe,
When now I think you can behold such sights,
And keep the natural ruby of your cheeks, 115
When mine is blanch'd with fear.

ROSS. What sights, my lord?

LADY MACBETH. I pray you, speak not; he grows worse and worse;
Question enrages him. At once, good night:
Stand not upon the order of your going,
But go at once.

LENNOX. Good night; and better health 120
Attend his majesty!

LADY MACBETH. A kind good night to all!

[*Exeunt all but* MACBETH *and* LADY MACBETH]

MACBETH. It will have blood; they say blood will have blood:
Stones have been known to move and trees to speak;

114. When now Ff | Now when Hanmer.
116. sights F_1 | signes F_2F_3 | signs F_4.
121. [*Exeunt* . . .] Dyce | Exit Lords Ff.
122. Two lines in Ff.

be.—baby of a girl. 'Puny offspring' and 'doll' have been suggested as the meaning here. Perhaps the expression simply means 'babyish girl.' Cf. 'wonder of a man' for 'wonderful man.'

111. Pass over us as a casual summer cloud, unregarded.

113. disposition that I owe: the bent of character I possess. 'Disposition' is used by Shakespeare "not only in its modern sense of *settled* character, ἦθος, but also in the sense of *temporary mood*, and in this latter sense we think it is used here."—Clar.

119. Stay not to go out according to order of precedence.

Augures and understood relations have
By magot-pies and choughs and rooks brought forth 125
The secret'st man of blood. What is the night?

LADY MACBETH. Almost at odds with morning, which is which.

MACBETH. How say'st thou, that Macduff denies his person
At our great bidding?

LADY MACBETH. Did you send to him, sir?

MACBETH. I hear it by the way, but I will send: 130
There 's not a one of them but in his house
I keep a servant fee'd. I will to-morrow,
And betimes I will, to the weird sisters:
More shall they speak; for now I am bent to know,
By the worst means, the worst. For mine own good 135
All causes shall give way: I am in blood
Stepp'd in so far that, should I wade no more,
Returning were as tedious as go o'er:

124. **Augures** Ff | Augurs Theobald.

133. **weird** Theobald | **weyard** F_1 | wizard $F_2F_3F_4$.

124. **Augures**: auguries, divinations.—**understood relations**: knowledge by the initiated of the secret relation between things and incidents.

125. **magot-pies**: magpies. — **choughs**. Cf. *King Lear*, IV, vi, 13.

129. By 'our great bidding' is meant, not any particular request or order to Macduff, but the general invitation implied in the very purpose of the banquet. Macbeth has heard of his refusal only 'by the way,' that is, incidentally, or through a 'servant fee'd.'

131–132. He has paid spies lurking and prowling about in the families of all the noblemen, and using the advantage of their place as servants to get information for him. The meanest and hatefullest practice of a jealous tyrant! "Makbeth had in euery noble man's house one slie fellow or other in fee with him, to reueale all that was said or doone within the same." — Holinshed.

Strange things I have in head that will to hand,
Which must be acted ere they may be scann'd. 140
LADY MACBETH. You lack the season of all natures, sleep.
MACBETH. Come, we 'll to sleep. My strange and self-abuse
Is the initiate fear that wants hard use :
We are yet but young in deed. [*Exeunt*]

SCENE V. *A heath*

Thunder. Enter the three WITCHES, *meeting* HECATE

1 WITCH. Why, how now, Hecate! you look angerly.
HECATE. Have I not reason, beldams as you are,
Saucy and overbold? How did you dare
To trade and traffic with Macbeth
In riddles and affairs of death ; 5
And I, the mistress of your charms,
The close contriver of all harms,
Was never call'd to bear my part,
Or show the glory of our art?
And, which is worse, all you have done 10

144. in deed Theobald | indeed Ff | in deeds Hanmer.

SCENE V | Scene VI Pope | Scene IV Rowe. — *A heath* | Ff omit.

141. the season : seasoning, that which preserves from decay.

142–143. self-abuse Is the initiate fear : self-delusion is the fear of the novice. Macbeth now knows that the Banquo he has just seen was but a Banquo of the mind.

SCENE V. This scene is usually regarded as an interpolation, its witches being unlike those of the earlier scenes, and their relation to Macbeth being different from what it was before.

1. angerly. "The '-ly' represents 'like.'" — Abbott, § 447.

7. close contriver : secret plotter. 'Close' often has this sense.

Hath been but for a wayward son,
Spiteful and wrathful ; who, as others do,
Loves for his own ends, not for you.
But make amends now : get you gone,
And at the pit of Acheron 15
Meet me i' the morning : thither he
Will come to know his destiny :
Your vessels and your spells provide,
Your charms, and every thing beside.
I am for th' air ; this night I 'll spend 20
Unto a dismal and a fatal end :
Great business must be wrought ere noon :
Upon the corner of the moon
There hangs a vaporous drop profound ;
I 'll catch it ere it come to ground : 25
And that distill'd by magic sleights
Shall raise such artificial sprites
As by the strength of their illusion
Shall draw him on to his confusion :
He shall spurn fate, scorn death, and bear 30
His hopes 'bove wisdom, grace, and fear ;
And you all know security
Is mortals' chiefest enemy.

[*Music, and a Song*]

26. sleights | slights Ff. 27. raise F_1 | rise F_2.

24. vaporous drop. "The *virus lunare* of the ancients, a foam which the moon was supposed to shed, when strongly solicited by enchantment." — Steevens. — **profound** : having magic qualities.

32. security: over-confidence, presumption, carelessness. Often so.

33, 35. These are the stage directions of the Folios. The song referred to is found in Middleton's *The Witch*, III, iii, and, with some

Hark! I am call'd; my little spirit, see,
Sits in a foggy cloud, and stays for me. [*Exit*]
[*Sing within*: ' Come away, come away,' etc.]

1 WITCH. Come, let 's make haste; she 'll soon be back again. [*Exeunt*]

SCENE VI. *Forres. The palace*

Enter LENNOX *and another* LORD

LENNOX. My former speeches have but hit your thoughts,
Which can interpret farther: only, I say
Things have been strangely borne. The gracious Duncan

36. Two lines in Ff.
SCENE VI | Scene VII Pope | Scene V Rowe. — *Forres* Capell | Ff omit. — *The palace* Camb | Ff omit.
1. Two lines in Ff.
3. **borne** $F_1F_2F_3$ | born F_4.

changes, in the D'Avenant Quarto of *Macbeth*. Here is the whole song, or musical dialogue, as it is in *The Witch*:

Song above.

Come away, come away,
Hecate, Hecate, come away!
Hecate. I come, I come, I come, I come,
With all the speed I may,
With all the speed I may.
Where 's Stadlin?
Voice above. Here.
Hecate. Where 's Puckle?
Voice above. Here;
And Hoppo too, and Hellwain too;
We lack but you, we lack but you:
Come away, make up the count.
Hecate. I will but 'noint, and then I mount.
[*A Spirit like a cat descends*
Voice above. There 's one come's down to fetch his dues,
A kiss, a coll, a sip of blood:
And why thou stay'st so long,
I muse, I muse,
Since the air 's so sweet and good.

Was pitied of Macbeth : marry, he was dead :
And the right-valiant Banquo walk'd too late ; 5
Whom, you may say, if 't please you, Fleance kill'd,
For Fleance fled : men must not walk too late.
Who cannot want the thought, how monstrous
It was for Malcolm and for Donalbain
To kill their gracious father ? damned fact ! 10
How it did grieve Macbeth ! did he not straight,
In pious rage, the two delinquents tear,
That were the slaves of drink and thralls of sleep ?
Was not that nobly done ? Ay, and wisely too ;
For 't would have anger'd any heart alive 15
To hear the men deny 't. So that, I say,

Hecate. O, art thou come ?
What news, what news ?
Spirit. All goes still to our delight :
Either come, or else
Refuse, refuse.
Hecate. Now I 'm furnish'd for the flight.
Fire. Hark, hark ! the cat sings a brave treble in her own language.
Hecate. [*going up*] Now I go, now I fly,
Malkin my sweet spirit and I.
O what a dainty pleasure 't is
To ride in the air
When the moon shines fair,
And sing and dance, and toy and kiss !
Over woods, high rocks, and mountains,
Over seas, our mistress' fountains,
Over steep towers, and turrets,
We fly by night, 'mongst troops of spirits:
No ring of bells to our ears sounds,
No howls of wolves, no yelps of hounds ;
No, not the noise of water's breach,
Or cannon's throat our height can reach.
Voices above. No ring of bells, etc.

8. **Who cannot want the thought** : who can fail to think.
10. In Elizabethan English ' fact ' usually means an ' evil deed.'

He has borne all things well: and I do think
That, had he Duncan's sons under his key —
As, and 't please heaven, he shall not — they should find
What 't were to kill a father; so should Fleance. 20
But, peace! for from broad words, and 'cause he fail'd
His presence at the tyrant's feast, I hear,
Macduff lives in disgrace. Sir, can you tell
Where he bestows himself?

LORD. The son of Duncan,
From whom this tyrant holds the due of birth, 25
Lives in the English court; and is receiv'd
Of the most pious Edward with such grace
That the malevolence of fortune nothing
Takes from his high respect. Thither Macduff
Is gone to pray the holy king, upon his aid 30
To wake Northumberland and warlike Siward;
That by the help of these, with Him above
To ratify the work, we may again
Give to our tables meat, sleep to our nights;
Free from our feasts and banquets bloody knives, 35
Do faithful homage and receive free honours;
All which we pine for now: and this report
Hath so exasperate the king, that he
Prepares for some attempt of war.

LENNOX. Sent he to Macduff?

24. **son** Theobald | Sonnes F_1 F_2F_3 | Sons F_4.

38. **exasperate** Ff | exasperated Rowe. — **the king** Hanmer | their king Ff.

19. **and 't**: if it. 'And,' meaning 'if,' is now usually spelled 'an.'

21. **from broad words**: on account of free outspoken words.

38. **exasperate**: exasperated. So 'articulate' in *1 Henry IV*, V, i, 72. See Abbott, § 342.

LORD. He did: and with an absolute 'Sir, not I,' 40
The cloudy messenger turns me his back,
And hums, as who should say, 'You 'll rue the time
That clogs me with this answer.'
LENNOX. And that well might
Advise him to a caution, to hold what distance
His wisdom can provide. Some holy angel 45
Fly to the court of England and unfold
His message ere he come; that a swift blessing
May soon return to this our suffering country
Under a hand accurs'd!
LORD. I 'll send my prayers with him.
[*Exeunt*]

41. cloudy: frowning. 'Foreboding,ominous.'—Delius.—**me**. The ethical dative; often used for emphasis. Cf. *Julius Cæsar*, I, ii, 267.

42. as who: like one who. Cf. *The Merchant of Venice*, I, i, 93.

43. It appears, at the close of the third scene of this act, that Macbeth did not give Macduff a special and direct invitation to the banquet; but his attendance was expected as a matter of course; and his failure to attend made him an object of distrust and suspicion to the tyrant. We are to suppose that Macbeth learned, from the paid spy and informer whom he kept in Macduff's house, that the latter had declared he would not go to the feast. So that the messenger here spoken of was probably not sent to invite Macduff, but to call him to account for his non-attendance.

48-49. The order is, "our country suffering under a hand accurs'd."

ACT IV

SCENE I. *A cavern. In the middle, a boiling cauldron*

Thunder. Enter the three WITCHES

1 WITCH. Thrice the brinded cat hath mew'd.
2 WITCH. Thrice, and once the hedge-pig whin'd.
3 WITCH. Harpier cries ; 't is time, 't is time.
1 WITCH. Round about the cauldron go ;
In the poison'd entrails throw. 5
Toad, that under cold stone
Days and nights has thirty-one
Swelter'd venom sleeping got,
Boil thou first i' the charmed pot.

ACT IV | Actus Quartus F_1 | Actus Quintus $F_2F_3F_4$. *A cavern. In the middle* . . . | Ff omit.

1. **brinded**: brindled, dark brown streaked with black. See Murray.

2. The Folio punctuation adopted in the text is faithful to the tradition that only odd numbers are magical. 'Thrice' has reference probably to the mewing of the 'brinded cat'; the 'hedge-pig' ('hedgehog') whining but once. Or 'thrice and once' may be put for 'four' to avoid the calling of unlucky even numbers.

3. **Harpier**. The name of one of the familiars. See note, I, i, 8. Steevens suggested that the word is a misprint for 'harpy.' Harpier's cry is the signal, showing that it is time to begin the mystic rites.

6. **cold**. To be so prolonged as to have the time of two syllables.

8. **Swelter'd** : sweated, exuded. — **venom**. "All manner of Toads, both of the earth and of the water, are venomous." — Topsell, *History of Serpents*, 1608. Cf. *As You Like It*, II, i, 13.

ALL. Double, double toil and trouble ; 10
Fire burn and cauldron bubble.
2 WITCH. Fillet of a fenny snake,
In the cauldron boil and bake ;
Eye of newt and toe of frog,
Wool of bat and tongue of dog, 15
Adder's fork and blind-worm's sting,
Lizard's leg and howlet's wing,
For a charm of powerful trouble,
Like a hell-broth boil and bubble.
ALL. Double, double toil and trouble ; 20
Fire burn and cauldron bubble.
3 WITCH. Scale of dragon, tooth of wolf,
Witches' mummy, maw and gulf
Of the ravin'd salt-sea shark ;
Root of hemlock digg'd i' the dark, 25
Liver of blaspheming Jew,
Gall of goat, and slips of yew

16. **fork**: forked tongue.—**blind-worm's sting**. The harmless slow-worm was regarded of old as poisonous. It is called "eyeless venom'd worm" in *Timon of Athens*, IV, iii, 182. Cf. *A Midsummer Night's Dream*, II, ii, 9–12 :

You spotted snakes with double tongue,
Thorny hedgehogs, be not seen ;
Newts and blind-worms, do no wrong,
Come not near our fairy queen.

23. Mummy was much used as medicine ; a 'witch's,' of course, had evil magic in it. "The Egyptian mummies, which Cambyses or time hath spared, avarice now consumeth. Mummie is become merchandise, Mizraim cures wounds, and Pharaoh is sold for balsams." — Sir Thomas Browne, *On Urn-burial*. — **gulf** : that which swallows up anything. Cf. *The Shepheards Calender*, *September*, 185–186 : "A wicked wolfe that with many a Lambe had glutted his gulfe."

24. **ravin'd**. Either 'ravenous' or 'glutted with prey.'

Sliver'd in the moon's eclipse,
Nose of Turk and Tartar's lips,
Finger of birth-strangled babe 30
Ditch-deliver'd by a drab,
Make the gruel thick and slab :
Add thereto a tiger's chaudron,
For th' ingredients of our cauldron.

ALL. Double, double toil and trouble ; 35
Fire burn and cauldron bubble.

2 WITCH. Cool it with a baboon's blood,
Then the charm is firm and good.

Enter HECATE *to the other three* WITCHES

HECATE. O, well done ! I commend your pains ;
And every one shall share i' th' gains : 40
And now about the cauldron sing,
Like elves and fairies in a ring,
Enchanting all that you put in.
[*Music, and a Song*, ' Black spirits,' *etc.*]
[*Exit* HECATE]

39. *Enter* HECATE *to* . . . Globe Camb | Enter Hecat, and . . . Ff.

43. [*Exit* HECATE] Dyce | Hecate retires Globe Camb | Ff omit.

28. A lunar eclipse was held to be fraught with evil magic of the highest intensity. Cf. *Paradise Lost*, I, 597–598.

32. slab : viscous, slimy. Connected etymologically with Gaelic *slaib*, ' mud.' Cf. ' slobbery ' in *Henry V*, III, v, 13.

33. chaudron : entrails, especially as used for food. See Murray.

43. *Music, and a Song*. Here is the ' Song ' as in Middleton's *The Witch*, V, ii, 68–77 :

Black spirits and white, red spirits and gray,
Mingle, mingle, mingle, you that mingle may !
Titty, Tiffin,
Keep it stiff in ;

2 WITCH. By the pricking of my thumbs,
Something wicked this way comes : 45
Open, locks,
Whoever knocks !

Enter MACBETH

MACBETH. How now, you secret, black, and midnight hags !
What is 't you do ?

ALL. A deed without a name.

MACBETH. I conjure you, by that which you profess, 50
Howe'er you come to know it, answer me :
Though you untie the winds and let them fight
Against the churches ; though the yesty waves
Confound and swallow navigation up ;
Though bladed corn be lodg'd, and trees blown down ; 55
Though castles topple on their warders' heads ;
Though palaces and pyramids do slope

46–47. One line in Ff. **48.** Scene II Pope.

Firedrake, Puckey,
Make it lucky ;
Liard, Robin,
You must bob in.
Round, around, around, about, about !
All ill come running in, all good keep out !

This is substantially as it is in the D'Avenant Quarto of *Macbeth*.

44. " It is a very ancient superstition that all sudden pains of the body which could not naturally be accounted for were presages of somewhat that was shortly to happen." — Steevens.

53. yesty : frothy, foamy. It is a variant form of 'yeasty.'

55. bladed : in the blade. — lodg'd : laid flat. Cf. *Richard II*, III, iii, 162. The word in this sense is still in common use.

Their heads to their foundations; though the treasure
Of nature's germens tumble all together,
Even till destruction sicken; answer me 60
To what I ask you.

1 WITCH. Speak.

2 WITCH. Demand.

3 WITCH. We 'll answer.

1 WITCH. Say, if thou 'dst rather hear it from our mouths,
Or from our masters?

MACBETH. Call 'em, let me see 'em.

1 WITCH. Pour in sow's blood, that hath eaten
Her nine farrow; grease that 's sweaten 65
From the murderer's gibbet throw
Into the flame.

ALL. Come, high or low;
Thyself and office deftly show!

Thunder. First APPARITION, *an armed Head*

MACBETH. Tell me, thou unknown power, —

1 WITCH. He knows thy thought:
Hear his speech, but say thou nought. 70

59. **nature's** Pope | Natures Ff. — **germens** Theobald | germaine F_1F_2.

59. **germens**: seeds, germs. Cf. *King Lear*, III, ii, 8.

65. **nine farrow**: litter of nine pigs. 'Nine' was a magic number. Cf. *King Lear*, III, iv, 126. — **sweaten.** An irregularly formed participle. See Abbott, § 344.

69. *an armed Head.* A symbolical representation of Macbeth's own head presented to Malcolm by Macduff. See V, viii, 53.

70. Silence was necessary during all incantations. Cf. *The Tempest*, IV, i, 126: "Hush and be mute, Or else our spell is marr'd."

1 APPARITION. Macbeth! Macbeth! Macbeth! beware Macduff;
Beware the thane of Fife. — Dismiss me: enough.
[*Descends*]

MACBETH. Whate'er thou art, for thy good caution, thanks;
Thou hast harp'd my fear aright: but one word more, —

1 WITCH. He will not be commanded: here 's another,
More potent than the first. 76

Thunder. Second APPARITION, *a bloody Child*

2 APPARITION. Macbeth! Macbeth! Macbeth!

MACBETH. Had I three ears, I 'd hear thee.

2 APPARITION. Be bloody, bold, and resolute; laugh to scorn
The power of man, for none of woman born 80
Shall harm Macbeth. [*Descends*]

MACBETH. Then live, Macduff: what need I fear of thee?
But yet I 'll make assurance double sure,
And take a bond of fate: thou shalt not live;
That I may tell pale-hearted fear it lies, 85
And sleep in spite of thunder.

71. Two lines in Ff.
79. Two lines in Ff.
83. assurance | assurance: Ff.
86–87. One line in Ff.

72. Spirits thus evoked were supposed to be impatient of being questioned. This line must be spoken with strong pauses. "The rhythm is full of omen." — Liddell.

77. The second Apparition represents Macduff. See V, viii, 16.

78. The stress is on 'ears,' not on 'three.' Cf. the common expression, "To listen with all one's ears."

84. **take a bond of fate**: bind fate itself to the performance of the promise. By killing Macduff he will make the promise irrevocable.

Thunder. Third APPARITION, *a Child crowned, with a tree in his hand*

What is this,
That rises like the issue of a king,
And wears upon his baby brow the round
And top of sovereignty?
ALL. Listen, but speak not to 't.
3 APPARITION. Be lion-mettl'd, proud; and take no care
Who chafes, who frets, or where conspirers are: 91
Macbeth shall never vanquish'd be until
Great Birnam wood to high Dunsinane hill
Shall come against him. [*Descends*]
MACBETH. That will never be:
Who can impress the forest; bid the tree 95
Unfix his earth-bound root? Sweet bodements! good!
Rebellion's head, rise never till the wood
Of Birnam rise, and our high-plac'd Macbeth

90. **lion-mettl'd** | Lyon metled Ff.
93. **Dunsinane** | Dunsmane F_1.
94. [*Descends*] Rowe | Descend Ff.
97. **Rebellion's head** Hanmer | Rebellious dead Ff.
98. **Birnam** F_4 | Byrnan F_1.

86. The third Apparition represents 'royal Malcolm.' See V, iv, 4.
88–89. The 'round' is that part of a crown which encircles the head: the 'top' is the ornament symbolical of sovereign power.
93. 'Dunsinane' is here rightly accented on the penult; elsewhere in the play it is accented wrongly on the last syllable. Both pronunciations occur in Wyntoun's *Cronykil* (see Introduction). Pope attempted to make the pronunciation here conformable to that in the later scenes by reading 'Dunsinane's high.' "A certeine witch, whom hee had in great trust, had told that he should neuer be slaine with man borne of anie woman, nor vanquished till the wood of Bernane came to the castell of Dunsinane." — Holinshed.
95. **impress**: force to serve as soldiers. Cf. *1 Henry IV*, I, i, 21.

Shall live the lease of nature, pay his breath
To time and mortal custom. Yet my heart 100
Throbs to know one thing : tell me, if your art
Can tell so much : shall Banquo's issue ever
Reign in this kingdom ?

ALL. Seek to know no more.

MACBETH. I will be satisfied : deny me this,
And an eternal curse fall on you ! Let me know : 105
Why sinks that cauldron ? and what noise is this ?

[*Hautboys*]

1 WITCH. Show !

2 WITCH. Show !

3 WITCH. Show !

ALL. Show his eyes, and grieve his heart ; 110
Come like shadows, so depart !

A show of eight Kings, *the last with a glass in his hand ;*
BANQUO'S Ghost *following*

MACBETH Thou art too like the spirit of Banquo ; down !
Thy crown does sear mine eyeballs. And thy hair,
Thou other gold-bound brow, is like the first :
A third is like the former. Filthy hags ! 115
Why do you show me this ? A fourth ! Start, eyes !
What, will the line stretch out to th' crack of doom ?

112. *A show . . . the last . . . Ghost following* | A shew . . . and Banquo last, with a glasse in his hand Ff. 113. **hair** | haire Ff | air Warburton.

99–100. Live the full time allotted and die a natural death.

112. The eight kings are supposed to be Robert II, Robert III, and the six Jameses. Mary Stuart, daughter of James V, is passed over, as the Witches' prediction had reference only to kings.

117. **crack of doom.** This now proverbial expression has been taken to mean specifically either the thunder-peal announcing the

Another yet! A seventh! I 'll see no more:
And yet the eighth appears, who bears a glass
Which shows me many more; and some I see 120
That twofold balls and treble sceptres carry:
Horrible sight! Now I see 't is true;
For the blood-bolter'd Banquo smiles upon me,
And points at them for his. What, is this so?

1 WITCH. Ay, sir, all this is so; but why 125
Stands Macbeth thus amazedly?
Come, sisters, cheer we up his sprites,
And show the best of our delights:
I 'll charm the air to give a sound,

119. **eighth** F_3F_4 | eight F_1F_2.

Judgment-day or the blast of the last trumpet. Why should it not connote both? See Murray.

119. A magic glass, or charmed mirror, representing and revealing future events, was and is a common method of divination. Cf. *Measure for Measure*, II, ii, 94–95. Such was the "brood mirour of glas" which the "king of Arabie and of Inde" sent to the "Tartre Cambinskan" as told by Chaucer in *The Squieres Tale*. But the most wonderful glass of this kind in literature is that which

> The great Magitien Merlin had deviz'd,
> By his deepe science and hell-dreaded might.
>
> *The Faerie Queene*, III, ii, 18.

121. This line is usually regarded as a marked compliment to James I. The two balls or globes probably symbolized the two independent crowns of England and Scotland; the three sceptres, the kingdoms of England, Scotland, and Ireland. Scott, in *Quentin Durward*, when Charles the Bold has Louis of France in his power, makes Comines say to the King: "It is his (the Duke's) purpose to close his ducal coronet with an imperial arch, and surmount it with a globe, in emblem that his dominions are independent."

123. blood-bolter'd: having hair matted with blood. "The normal forms of the word are 'baltered,' 'baultered.'" — Liddell.

While you perform your antic round ; 130
That this great king may kindly say
Our duties did his welcome pay.

[*Music. The* WITCHES *dance, and vanish with* HECATE]

MACBETH. Where are they ? Gone ? Let this pernicious hour
Stand aye accursed in the calendar !
Come in, without there !

Enter LENNOX

LENNOX. What 's your grace's will ? 135

MACBETH. Saw you the weird sisters ?

LENNOX. No, my lord.

MACBETH. Came they not by you ?

LENNOX. No, indeed, my lord.

MACBETH. Infected be the air whereon they ride,
And damn'd all those that trust them ! I did hear
The galloping of horse : who was 't came by ? 140

LENNOX. 'T is two or three, my lord, that bring you word
Macduff is fled to England.

MACBETH. Fled to England !

LENNOX. Ay, my good lord.

130. antic | antick Theobald | antique Ff.
132. *with* HECATE | Ff omit.
133. Two lines in Ff.
136. weird | weyard F_1 | wizard F_2F_3 | wizards F_4.

130. antic : quaint. The same word as ' antique ' (' old-fashioned ' and so ' quaint '). In Shakespeare the accent is invariably on the first syllable.

138–139. Cf. *Paradise Lost*, II, 662–663. Milton's indebtedness to *Richard III* and *Macbeth* is very marked. ' Macbeth ' is one of the subjects from British history which he jotted down in 1639–1640 as the theme of a possible poem. See Masson's *Life of Milton*, II, 115.

MACBETH. [*Aside*] Time, thou anticipat'st my dread exploits :
The flighty purpose never is o'ertook 145
Unless the deed go with it : from this moment
The very firstlings of my heart shall be
The firstlings of my hand. And even now,
To crown my thoughts with acts, be it thought and done :
The castle of Macduff I will surprise ; 150
Seize upon Fife ; give to the edge o' the sword
His wife, his babes, and all unfortunate souls
That trace him in his line. No boasting like a fool ;
This deed I 'll do before this purpose cool :
But no more sights ! Where are these gentlemen ? 155
Come, bring me where they are. [*Exeunt*]

SCENE II. *Fife*. MACDUFF'S *castle*

Enter LADY MACDUFF, *her* SON, *and* ROSS

LADY MACDUFF. What had he done, to make him fly the land ?

ROSS. You must have patience, madam.

144. [*Aside*] Johnson | Ff omit. SCENE II | Scene III Pope. — *Fife . . . castle* | Ff omit. LADY MACDUFF Rowe | Macduffe's Wife Ff.

144. anticipat'st : dost prevent. So in *Sonnets*, CXVIII, 9.

145. flighty : swift to take flight. The original meaning.

155. sights : visions. As ' portents ' the word is used in *Julius Cæsar*, I, iii, 138 ; II, ii, 16. Macbeth is greatly disturbed by what he has seen in the cavern.

SCENE II. " To omit this scene, as is usually the case on the stage, is to present Macbeth's character in a far more favourable light than Shakespeare intended, and to weaken the force of Macduff's

LADY MACDUFF. He had none ;
His flight was madness : when our actions do not,
Our fears do make us traitors.

ROSS. You know not
Whether it was his wisdom or his fear. 5

LADY MACDUFF. Wisdom ! to leave his wife, to leave his babes,
His mansion, and his titles, in a place
From whence himself does fly ! He loves us not ;
He wants the natural touch : for the poor wren,
The most diminutive of birds, will fight, 10
Her young ones in her nest, against the owl.
All is the fear and nothing is the love ;
As little is the wisdom, where the flight
So runs against all reason.

ROSS. My dearest coz,
I pray you, school yourself : but, for your husband, 15
He is noble, wise, judicious, and best knows
The fits o' the season. I dare not speak much further :
But cruel are the times, when we are traitors

14. **coz** Rowe | Cooz F_1F_2 | Couz F_3F_4.

cry of agony, and Lady Macbeth's heart-piercing question in the sleep-walking scene." — Bodenstedt.

4. **make us** : make us out to be. When our actions do not convict us of being traitors, our fears do. Lady Macduff is apprehensive that her husband's flight will be construed as proceeding from guilty fear.

7. **titles** : possessions. The things to which he has a 'title.'

9. **natural touch** : natural affection, sensibility of nature. Cf. 'only touch of love,' *The Two Gentlemen of Verona*, II, vii, 18 ; 'touch of nature,' *Troilus and Cressida*, III, iii, 175.

17. **fits o' the season** : exigencies, dangers, of the time.

And do not know ourselves ; when we hold rumour
From what we fear, yet know not what we fear, 20
But float upon a wild and violent sea
Each way and move. I take my leave of you ;
Shall not be long but I 'll be here again.
Things at the worst will cease, or else climb upward
To what they were before. My pretty cousin, 25
Blessing upon you !

LADY MACDUFF. Father'd he is, and yet he 's fatherless.

ROSS. I am so much a fool, should I stay longer,
It would be my disgrace and your discomfort :
I take my leave at once. [*Exit*]

LADY MACDUFF. Sirrah, your father 's dead : 30
And what will you do now ? How will you live ?

SON. As birds do, mother.

LADY MACDUFF. What, with worms and flies ?

27. Two lines in Ff. 29. [*Exit* | Exit Rosse Ff.

19–20. Fear makes us credit rumour, yet we know not what to fear, because ignorant when we offend. A condition wherein men believe the more, because they fear, and fear the more, because they cannot foresee the danger.

22. and move. An awkward expression. Upwards of twenty emendations have been suggested (see Furness and Clar), but the general meaning is obvious. ' Move ' may be either (1) a noun meaning ' direction,' or (2) a verb with the sense of ' are tossed about.'

24. The worse a disease becomes, the sooner there will be either death or recovery. The very excess of an evil often starts a reaction, and thence a return to a better state.

29. Disgrace myself and make you uncomfortable by weeping.

30. Sirrah. Often used as a form of address to inferiors, or to young people.

32. SON. A peculiar pathos attaches to all Shakespeare's portraits of children. Cf. Prince Arthur in *King John* and Mamillius in

SON. With what I get, I mean ; and so do they.

LADY MACDUFF. Poor bird ! thou 'dst never fear the net nor lime,
The pitfall nor the gin. 35

SON. Why should I, mother ? Poor birds they are not set for.
My father is not dead, for all your saying.

LADY MACDUFF. Yes, he is dead : how wilt thou do for a father ?

SON. Nay, how will you do for a husband ?

LADY MACDUFF. Why, I can buy me twenty at any market.

SON. Then you 'll buy 'em to sell again. 41

LADY MACDUFF. Thou speak'st with all thy wit ; and yet i' faith,
With wit enough for thee.

SON. Was my father a traitor, mother ?

LADY MACDUFF. Ay, that he was. 45

SON. What is a traitor ?

34, 36, 38. Two lines in Ff.
42. with all | withall F_1.
42–43. and yet . . . for thee | One line in Ff.

The Winter's Tale. His own little boy Hamnet died in 1596. Webster caught the spirit of this pathos in *The White Devil* in the scenes between Brachiano and his little son Giovanni. " This scene, dreadful as it is, is still a relief, because a variety, because domestic, and therefore soothing, as associated with the only real pleasures of life. The conversation between Lady Macduff and her child heightens the pathos, and is preparatory for the deep tragedy of their assassination." — Coleridge.

36. Traps are not set for the poor but for the rich ; not for children, but for important, grown-up men.

44. " The broken metre gradually merges into prose, here as in II, iii, used by Shakespeare for purposes of dramatic relief." — E. K. Chambers.

LADY MACDUFF. Why, one that swears and lies.

SON. And be all traitors that do so?

LADY MACDUFF. Every one that does so is a traitor, and must be hang'd. 50

SON. And must they all be hang'd that swear and lie?

LADY MACDUFF. Every one.

SON. Who must hang them?

LADY MACDUFF. Why, the honest men. 54

SON. Then the liars and swearers are fools; for there are liars and swearers enow to beat the honest men and hang up them.

LADY MACDUFF. Now, God help thee, poor monkey! But how wilt thou do for a father? 59

SON. If he were dead, you'd weep for him: if you would not, it were a good sign that I should quickly have a new father.

LADY MACDUFF. Poor prattler, how thou talk'st!

Enter a MESSENGER

MESSENGER. Bless you, fair dame! I am not to you known,
Though in your state of honour I am perfect. 65

49–50, 58–59. Two lines of verse in Ff. Pope printed as prose.

63. LADY MACDUFF | Wife $F_1 F_3 F_4$ | Son F_2.

64. "This messenger was one of the murderers employed by Macbeth to exterminate Macduff's family; but who, from emotions of pity and remorse, had outstripped his companions, to give timely warning of their approach." — Heath. "This messenger may come from Lady Macbeth." — Libby. "The messenger is a dramatic device to represent Macbeth's murderous net closing around Lady Macduff." — Liddell.

65. Perfectly acquainted with your honourable rank and character.

I doubt some danger does approach you nearly :
If you will take a homely man's advice,
Be not found here ; hence, with your little ones.
To fright you thus, methinks I am too savage ;
To do worse to you were fell cruelty, 70
Which is too nigh your person. Heaven preserve you !
I dare abide no longer. [*Exit*]

LADY MACDUFF. Whither should I fly ?
I have done no harm. But I remember now
I am in this earthly world ; where to do harm
Is often laudable, to do good sometime 75
Accounted dangerous folly : why then, alas,
Do I put up that womanly defence,
To say I have done no harm ? — What are these faces ?

Enter MURDERERS

1 MURDERER. Where is your husband ?

LADY MACDUFF. I hope, in no place so unsanctified 80
Where such as thou mayst find him.

1 MURDERER. He 's a traitor.

SON. Thou liest, thou shag-ear'd villain !

1 MURDERER. [*Stabbing him*] What, you egg !
Young fry of treachery !

SON. He has kill'd me, mother :
Run away, I pray you ! [*Dies*]

[*Exit* LADY MACDUFF, *crying* ' Murder ! '
Exeunt MURDERERS, *following her*]

78. Two lines in Ff.
82. [*Stabbing him*] Rowe | Ff omit.
84. [*Dies*] Capell | Ff omit. — [*Exit* | Exit crying Murther Ff.

82. **shag-ear'd**: with shaggy, hairy ears. For this, the Folio reading, Steevens suggested ' shag-hair'd.' Cf. *2 Henry VI*, III, i, 367.

SCENE III. *England. Before the King's palace*

Enter MALCOLM *and* MACDUFF

MALCOLM. Let us seek out some desolate shade, and there
Weep our sad bosoms empty.

MACDUFF. Let us rather
Hold fast the mortal sword, and, like good men,
Bestride our down-fall'n birthdom. Each new morn
New widows howl, new orphans cry, new sorrows 5
Strike heaven on the face, that it resounds
As if it felt with Scotland, and yell'd out
Like syllable of dolour.

MALCOLM. What I believe, I 'll wail;
What know, believe; and what I can redress,
As I shall find the time to friend, I will. 10
What you have spoke, it may be so perchance.
This tyrant, whose sole name blisters our tongues,
Was once thought honest: you have lov'd him well;
He hath not touch'd you yet. I am young; but something

SCENE III | Scene IV Pope. — *England . . . palace* Dyce | Ff omit.

4. down-fall'n Globe | downfall $F_1F_2F_3$.

4. Bestride: bravely defend. To stand over a fallen comrade and defend him was a special bravery of friendship. Cf. *1 Henry IV*, V, i, 122; *2 Henry IV*, I, i, 207; *Comedy of Errors*, V, i, 192. — **birthdom**: native land. Some take it in the sense of 'birthright.'

8. Like syllable of dolour: a similar cry of pain.

10. to friend: friendly, favourable. Cf. *Julius Cæsar*, III, i, 143.

14–16. You may see what sort of a man Macbeth is from my sad experience, and learn from me the wise policy of offering up, etc. Most modern editors have accepted Theobald's change of the text. But "'deserve' for 'discern' makes nonsense out of the latter part of the passage. 'I am young,' which is in contrast to the thought

You may discern of him through me, and wisdom 15
To offer up a weak, poor, innocent lamb
T' appease an angry god.

MACDUFF. I am not treacherous.

MALCOLM. But Macbeth is.
A good and virtuous nature may recoil
In an imperial charge. But I shall crave your pardon ; 20
That which you are, my thoughts cannot transpose :
Angels are bright still, though the brightest fell :
Though all things foul would wear the brows of grace,
Yet grace must still look so.

MACDUFF. I have lost my hopes.

MALCOLM. Perchance even there where I did find my doubts. 25

15. discern F_3F_4 | discerne F_1F_2 | deserve Theobald Globe Camb. — me, and Ff | me ; and Camb | me ; 't is Hanmer.
25. Two lines in Ff.

which ' but ' introduces, is meaningless with ' But you deserve something through me.' The normal contrast with Malcolm's youth and innocency would be a characteristic of age and experience ; this we have if we take ' discern ' in its Elizabethan sense, ' to learn by discernment ' ; the word in this sense is usually followed by ' of.' " — Liddell. In earlier editions of Hudson's Shakespeare, Theobald's reading was adopted with this interpretation : You may purchase or secure his favour by sacrificing me to his malice ; and to do so would be an act of worldly wisdom on your part, as I have no power to punish you for it.

19–20. May recede or fall away from goodness and virtue under the temptations of a man so powerful to resent or to reward.

21. transpose : transform, change. Cf. *A Midsummer Night's Dream*, I, i, 233.

23–24. Though all bad things should counterfeit the looks of goodness, yet goodness must still wear its own looks.

25. Though Macduff claims to have fled his home to avoid the tyrant's blow, he has left his wife and children in the tyrant's power.

Why in that rawness left you wife and child,
Those precious motives, those strong knots of love,
Without leave-taking ? I pray you,
Let not my jealousies be your dishonours,
But mine own safeties : you may be rightly just, 30
Whatever I shall think.

MACDUFF. Bleed, bleed, poor country !
Great tyranny, lay thou thy basis sure,
For goodness dare not check thee ; wear thou thy wrongs ;
The title is affeer'd ! Fare thee well, lord :
I would not be the villain that thou think'st 35
For the whole space that 's in the tyrant's grasp,
And the rich East to boot.

MALCOLM. Be not offended :
I speak not as in absolute fear of you.
I think our country sinks beneath the yoke ;
It weeps, it bleeds ; and each new day a gash 40
Is added to her wounds : I think withal
There would be hands uplifted in my right ;

33. **dare** F_1F_2 | dares F_3F_4.
34. **The** Ff | His Pope | **Thy** Malone. — **affeer'd** Hanmer | **affear'd** F_1F_2 | afear'd F_3 | afeard F_4.

This makes the prince distrust his purpose and suspect him of being a secret agent of Macbeth. And so, when he says, " I have lost my hopes," the prince replies, Perhaps the cause which has destroyed your hopes is the very same that leads me to distrust you ; that is, perhaps you have hoped to betray me, and this is just what I fear.

26. **rawness** : unprovided condition. Cf. *Henry V*, IV, i, 147.

33. **wear thou thy wrongs.** Does ' thou ' refer to ' country,' to ' tyranny,' or to Malcolm ? ' Tyranny ' is probably the object addressed, and the meaning will be, Enjoy the place and honours gained by your wrong-doing.

34. **The title is affeer'd** : the title you put forward is confirmed.

And here from gracious England have I offer
Of goodly thousands : but, for all this,
When I shall tread upon the tyrant's head, 45
Or wear it on my sword, yet my poor country
Shall have more vices than it had before ;
More suffer, and more sundry ways than ever,
By him that shall succeed.

MACDUFF. What should he be ?

MALCOLM. It is myself I mean ; in whom I know 50
All the particulars of vice so grafted,
That, when they shall be open'd, black Macbeth
Will seem as pure as snow ; and the poor state
Esteem him as a lamb, being compar'd
With my confineless harms.

MACDUFF. Not in the legions 55
Of horrid hell can come a devil more damn'd
In evils to top Macbeth.

MALCOLM. I grant him bloody,
Luxurious, avaricious, false, deceitful,
Sudden, malicious, smacking of every sin
That has a name : but there 's no bottom, none, 60
In my voluptuousness ; your wives, your daughters,
Your matrons, and your maids, could not fill up
The cistern of my lust, and my desire

59. smacking F_1 | smoaking F_2 F_3F_4. 63. cistern F_3F_4 | Cesterne F_1F_2.

43. gracious England : Edward the Confessor, then King of England. Cf. *King John*, III, iv, 8, "bloody England into England."

55. confineless harms : boundless vices. Cf. *Othello*, III, iii, 173, "But riches fineless is as poor as winter."

57. top : surpass. Cf. *King Lear*, I, ii, 21 ; *Coriolanus*, II, i, 23.

All continent impediments would o'erbear,
That did oppose my will. Better Macbeth 65
Than such an one to reign.

MACDUFF. Boundless intemperance
In nature is a tyranny; it hath been
Th' untimely emptying of the happy throne,
And fall of many kings. But fear not yet
To take upon you what is yours: you may 70
Convey your pleasures in a spacious plenty,
And yet seem cold, the time you may so hoodwink.
We have willing dames enough; there cannot be
That vulture in you, to devour so many
As will to greatness dedicate themselves, 75
Finding it so inclin'd.

MALCOLM. With this there grows,
In my most ill-compos'd affection such
A stanchless avarice that, were I king,
I should cut off the nobles for their lands,
Desire his jewels and this other's house: 80
And my more-having would be as a sauce
To make me hunger more, that I should forge
Quarrels unjust against the good and loyal,
Destroying them for wealth.

MACDUFF. This avarice
Sticks deeper, grows with more pernicious root 85
Than summer-seeming lust, and it hath been

86. -seeming Ff | -teeming Theobald | -seeding Steevens.

71. Convey: obtain in secrecy. Cf. *Richard II*, IV, i, 317.

80. his: one man's. Cf. *The Merchant of Venice*, IV, i, 54.

86. summer-seeming: summer-resembling. The passion that burns awhile like summer and like summer passes away is contrasted with

The sword of our slain kings : yet do not fear ;
Scotland hath foisons to fill up your will
Of your mere own : all these are portable,
With other graces weigh'd. 90

MALCOLM. But I have none : the king-becoming graces,
As justice, verity, temperance, stableness,
Bounty, perseverance, mercy, lowliness,
Devotion, patience, courage, fortitude,
I have no relish of them ; but abound 95
In the division of each several crime,
Acting it many ways. Nay, had I power, I should
Pour the sweet milk of concord into hell,
Uproar the universal peace, confound
All unity on earth.

MACDUFF. O Scotland, Scotland ! 100

88. foisons | foysons F_1F_2 | poison F_3F_4.

the other passion, avarice, which grows stronger and stronger to the end of life. Malone calls attention to "winter-seeming summer's night" in Donne's *Love's Alchemy*.

87. Either (1) the sword that has slain our kings, or (2) the evil that has caused our kings to be slain with the sword. "For that crime the most part of our kings have been slaine and brought to their final end." — Holinshed.

88. foisons : plenty, abundance. See Murray. Cf. *Sonnets*, LIII, 9.

89. mere: absolutely. Cf. line 152.— **portable**: endurable. Cf. *King Lear*, III, vi, 115 : "How light and portable my pain seems now."

92. verity : honesty. Cf. *As You Like It*, III, iv, 25.— **temperance** : restraint. Cf. *Hamlet*, III, ii, 8 ; *Measure for Measure*, III, ii, 251.

93. perseverance. Accented on second syllable. The Elizabethan pronunciation. Similarly the verb 'persever' was accented on the penult, rhyming with 'ever' in Spenser's *Amoretti*.

96. division : variation. A musical term. Cf. *Romeo and Juliet*, III, v, 29, and 'ravishing division' in *1 Henry IV*, III, i, 211.

99. Uproar : fill with tumult. — **confound** : destroy. Cf. II, ii, 11.

MALCOLM. If such a one be fit to govern, speak :
I am as I have spoken.

MACDUFF. Fit to govern !
No, not to live. O nation miserable,
With an untitled tyrant bloody-scepter'd,
When shalt thou see thy wholesome days again, 105
Since that the truest issue of thy throne
By his own interdiction stands accurs'd,
And does blaspheme his breed ? Thy royal father
Was a most sainted king : the queen that bore thee,
Oftener upon her knees than on her feet, 110
Died every day she liv'd. Fare thee well !
These evils thou repeat'st upon thyself
Hath banish'd me from Scotland. O my breast,
Thy hope ends here !

MALCOLM. Macduff, this noble passion,
Child of integrity, hath from my soul 115
Wip'd the black scruples, reconcil'd my thoughts
To thy good truth and honour. Devilish Macbeth
By many of these trains hath sought to win me

102–103. One line in Ff.
107. **accurs'd** | accurst $F_2F_3F_4$ | accust F_1.
109. **sainted king** | Sainted-King $F_1F_2F_3$ | Sainted King F_4.
113. **Hath** Ff | Have Rowe.

106. **Since that.** 'That' as a conjunctional affix. Cf. line 185. See Abbott, § 287.

111. Cf. *1 Corinthians*, xv, 31, "I die daily." "Every day of her life was a preparation for death." — Clar.

118. **trains** : lures, devices of circumvention. "A technical term both in hawking and hunting : in hawking, for the lure thrown out to reclaim a falcon given to ramble . . . and in hunting, for the bait trailed along the ground, and left exposed, to tempt the animal from his lair or covert, and bring him fairly within the power of the lurking huntsman." — T. S. Baynes.

Into his power; and modest wisdom plucks me
From over-credulous haste: but God above 120
Deal between thee and me! for even now
I put myself to thy direction, and
Unspeak mine own detraction; here abjure
The taints and blames I laid upon myself,
For strangers to my nature. I am yet 125
Unknown to woman, never was forsworn,
Scarcely have coveted what was mine own,
At no time broke my faith, would not betray
The devil to his fellow, and delight
No less in truth than life: my first false speaking 130
Was this upon myself. What I am truly,
Is thine and my poor country's to command;
Whither, indeed, before thy here-approach,
Old Siward, with ten thousand warlike men,
Already at a point, was setting forth: 135
Now we 'll together; and the chance of goodness
Be like our warranted quarrel! Why are you silent?

126. woman F_1 | women $F_2F_3F_4$.
133. thy $F_2F_3F_4$ | they F_1.
135. Already Ff | All ready Rowe.
— forth : | foorth : F_1 | foorth ? F_2.

128–129. If he would not betray the devil to his friend, much less would he betray him to his enemy.

133. here-approach. Cf. 'here-remain,' line 148. See Abbott, § 429.

134. "In the mean time, Malcolme purchased such fauor at King Edwards hands, that old Siward earle of Northumberland, was appointed with ten thousand men to go with him into Scotland to support him in this enterprise." — Holinshed.

135. at a point: ready, prepared. Cf. *Hamlet*, I, ii, 200, "Armed at point exactly, cap-a-pe"; *King Lear*, I, iv, 347.

136–137. May the chance for virtue to succeed be as good, as well warranted, as our cause is just. For 'quarrel' in the sense of 'cause' cf. *2 Henry IV*, IV, v, 169.

MACDUFF. Such welcome and unwelcome things at once
'T is hard to reconcile.

Enter a DOCTOR

MALCOLM. Well; more anon. — Comes the king forth, I
pray you? 140

DOCTOR. Ay, sir; there are a crew of wretched souls
That stay his cure: their malady convinces
The great assay of art; but at his touch,
Such sanctity hath heaven given his hand,
They presently amend.

MALCOLM. I thank you, doctor. 145
[*Exit* DOCTOR]

MACDUFF. What 's the disease he means?

MALCOLM. 'T is call'd the evil:
A most miraculous work in this good king;
Which often, since my here-remain in England,
I have seen him do. How he solicits heaven,
Himself best knows: but strangely-visited people, 150
All swoln and ulcerous, pitiful to the eye,

140. Scene V Pope.

142. **convinces**: overcomes. Cf. I, vii, 64.

143. **assay**: attempt, effort. See Murray. — **art**: professional skill.

146–159. This episode, really irrelevant to the action of the play, is usually construed as a courtly compliment to James I, who was always pleased to exercise the power of 'touching' for the 'king's evil,' as scrofula was called. The description of Edward the Confessor is from Holinshed: "As hath bin thought he was enspired with the gift of Prophecie, and also to haue hadde the gift of healing infirmities and diseases. Namely he vsed to help those that were vexed with the disease, commonly called the Kyngs euill, and left that vertue as it were a portion of inheritance vnto his successors the Kyngs of this Realme."

The mere despair of surgery, he cures,
Hanging a golden stamp about their necks,
Put on with holy prayers: and 't is spoken,
To the succeeding royalty he leaves 155
The healing benediction. With this strange virtue,
He hath a heavenly gift of prophecy,
And sundry blessings hang about his throne,
That speak him full of grace.

Enter Ross

MACDUFF. See, who comes here?
MALCOLM. My countryman; but yet I know him not. 160
MACDUFF. My ever-gentle cousin, welcome hither.
MALCOLM. I know him now. Good God, betimes remove
The means that makes us strangers!
ROSS. Sir, amen.
MACDUFF. Stands Scotland where it did?
ROSS. Alas, poor country,
Almost afraid to know itself! It cannot 165

159. Scene VI Pope.

153. "Each person touched received a gold coin. Sir Thomas Browne wrote sixty years later, 'The King's Purse knows that the King's Evil grows more common.'" — Herford. In Shakespeare's day the coin given (the 'evil-gold') was an 'angel.' Cf. *The Merchant of Venice*, II, vii, 55–57:

They have in England
A coin that bears the figure of an angel
Stamped in gold.

162–163. Malcolm at first distrusts Ross, just as he had before distrusted Macduff: but he has given his confidence unreservedly to Macduff, and now he has full faith in Ross as soon as he sees how Macduff regards him. The passage is very delightful. — **means**: cause. Either singular or plural in Elizabethan English.

Be call'd our mother, but our grave: where nothing,
But who knows nothing, is once seen to smile;
Where sighs and groans and shrieks that rend the air,
Are made, not mark'd; where violent sorrow seems
A modern ecstasy: the dead man's knell 170
Is there scarce ask'd for who; and good men's lives
Expire before the flowers in their caps,
Dying or ere they sicken.

MACDUFF. O, relation
Too nice, and yet too true!

MALCOLM. What 's the newest grief?

ROSS. That of an hour's age doth hiss the speaker; 175
Each minute teems a new one.

MACDUFF. How does my wife?

ROSS. Why, well.

MACDUFF. And all my children?

ROSS. Well too.

MACDUFF. The tyrant has not batter'd at their peace?

168. **rend** Rowe | rent Ff.
170. **dead man's** Johnson | Dead-mans F_1F_2 | Dead-man's F_3F_4.
173. **ere** Ff | e'er Rowe.
173–174. **O, relation . . . too true** one line in Ff.

170. **modern ecstasy**: ordinary, common, disturbance of mind.

174. **nice**: particular, elaborate. Having too much an air of study and art, and so not like the frank utterance of deep feeling. See Murray.

175. That which is but an hour old seems out of date, and causes the narrator to be denounced as tedious.

177–179. This use of 'well,' not as a mere equivoque, but as a euphemism for 'dead,' is illustrated in *Antony and Cleopatra*, II, v, 31–33:

> MESSENGER. First, madam, he is well.
> CLEOPATRA. Why, there 's more gold.
> But, sirrah, mark, we use
> To say the dead are well.

ROSS. No; they were well at peace when I did leave 'em.
MACDUFF. Be not a niggard of your speech: how goes 't?
ROSS. When I came hither to transport the tidings 181
Which I have heavily borne, there ran a rumour
Of many worthy fellows that were out;
Which was to my belief witness'd the rather,
For that I saw the tyrant's power a-foot: 185
Now is the time of help; your eye in Scotland
Would create soldiers, make our women fight,
To doff their dire distresses.
MALCOLM. Be 't their comfort
We are coming thither: gracious England hath
Lent us good Siward and ten thousand men; 190
An older and a better soldier none
That Christendom gives out.
ROSS. Would I could answer
This comfort with the like! But I have words
That would be howl'd out in the desert air,
Where hearing should not latch them.
MACDUFF. What concern they?

195. they? Theobald | they, Ff.

183. **out**: in arms, in open revolt. "He was out wi' the Hieland-men in Montrose's time." — Sir Walter Scott, 'Wandering Willie's Tale,' *Redgauntlet*. What follows means that the 'rumour' is confirmed by the fact that Macbeth has put his troops in motion.

188. **doff**: put away. 'Doff' is from 'do off' as 'don' from 'do on.' Cf. 'dup' (*Hamlet*, IV, v, 53) from 'do up.'

192. **gives out**: shows. This expression with this meaning occurs often in Shakespeare. Cf. *Twelfth Night*, III, iv, 203; *Othello*, III, iii, 209; *The Winter's Tale*, IV, iv, 149.

195. **latch**: catch. Cf. *Sonnets*, CXIII, 6. But 'latch' in *A Midsummer Night's Dream*, III, ii, 36, is probably a different word, meaning 'moisten.' See Murray under 'latch' and 'leach.'

The general cause? or is it a fee-grief 196
Due to some single breast?
  ROSS. No mind that 's honest
But in it shares some woe; though the main part
Pertains to you alone.
  MACDUFF. If it be mine,
Keep it not from me, quickly let me have it. 200
  ROSS. Let not your ears despise my tongue for ever,
Which shall possess them with the heaviest sound
That ever yet they heard.
  MACDUFF. Hum! I guess at it.
  ROSS. Your castle is surpris'd; your wife and babes
Savagely slaughter'd: to relate the manner, 205
Were, on the quarry of these murder'd deer,
To add the death of you.
  MALCOLM. Merciful heaven!
What, man! ne'er pull your hat upon your brows;
Give sorrow words: the grief that does not speak
Whispers the o'er-fraught heart and bids it break. 210
  MACDUFF. My children too?
  ROSS. Wife, children, servants, all
That could be found.
  MACDUFF. And I must be from thence!
My wife kill'd too?
  ROSS. I have said.
  MALCOLM. Be comforted:

203. **Hum!** Rowe | Humh: Ff Humph! Malone | Ha! Hunter.

211–213. **Wife . . . too?** | two lines in Ff, first ending **found.**

196. **fee-grief**: private, individual sorrow. "A grief held 'in fee' by a single owner."—Herford. Another of the many legal terms in *Macbeth*.

206. **quarry**: heap of slain. See note, I, ii, 14. Cf. *Hamlet*, V, ii, 375.

Let 's make us medicines of our great revenge,
To cure this deadly grief. 215

MACDUFF. He has no children. — All my pretty ones?
Did you say all? O hell-kite! All?
What, all my pretty chickens and their dam
At one fell swoop?

MALCOLM. Dispute it like a man.

MACDUFF. I shall do so; 220
But I must also feel it as a man:
I cannot but remember such things were,
That were most precious to me. Did heaven look on,
And would not take their part? Sinful Macduff,
They were all struck for thee! naught that I am, 225
Not for their own demerits, but for mine,
Fell slaughter on their souls. Heaven rest them now!

MALCOLM. Be this the whetstone of your sword: let grief
Convert to anger; blunt not the heart, enrage it.

MACDUFF. O, I could play the woman with mine eyes, 230
And braggart with my tongue! But, gentle heavens,

225. struck Rowe | strooke F_1F_2.

216. He has no children. This is most likely said of Malcolm, and with reference to what he has just spoken, though it is commonly taken as referring to Macbeth, and in the idea that, as he has no children, there can be no adequate revenge upon him. But the true meaning probably is, that if Malcolm were a father, he would know that such a grief cannot be healed with the medicine of revenge. Cf. *King John*, III, iv, 91. Besides, it would seem that Macbeth has children, else why should he strain so hard to have the regal succession "stand in his posterity"? And Lady Macbeth knows "how tender 't is to love the babe that milks me" (I, vii, 55).

220. **Dispute it**: strive against it, resist it.

225. **naught**: wicked, worthless. Not to be confounded with 'nought.' Cf. 'naughty' in *The Merchant of Venice*, V, i, 91.

Cut short all intermission ; front to front
Bring thou this fiend of Scotland and myself ;
Within my sword's length set him ; if he scape,
Heaven forgive him too !
MALCOLM. This tune goes manly. 235
Come, go we to the king ; our power is ready ;
Our lack is nothing but our leave. Macbeth
Is ripe for shaking, and the powers above
Put on their instruments. Receive what cheer you may :
The night is long that never finds the day. [*Exeunt*]

235. **tune** Rowe | time Ff.

235. The little word ' too ' is so used here as to intensify, in a very remarkable manner, the sense of what precedes. Put him once within the reach of my sword, and if I don't kill him, then I am as bad as he, and may God forgive us both ! — **tune.** Liddell defends the Folio reading here, but as has been often pointed out, ' time ' and ' tune ' would be very easily confused in Elizabethan manuscript. — **manly.** Adjectives ending in -ly are used as adverbs in Elizabethan English without any change of form.

237. Nothing remains to be done but to take our leave.

239. **Put on their instruments** : set their agents to work.

ACT V

Scene I. *Dunsinane. Ante-room in the castle*

Enter a Doctor *of Physic and a* Waiting-Gentlewoman

Doctor. I have two nights watch'd with you, but can perceive no truth in your report. When was it she last walk'd ?

Gentlewoman. Since his majesty went into the field, I have seen her rise from her bed, throw her night-gown upon her, unlock her closet, take forth paper, fold it, write upon 't, read it, afterwards seal it, and again return to bed : yet all this while in a most fast sleep. 7

Doctor. A great perturbation in nature, to receive at once the benefit of sleep, and do the effects of watching ! In this slumbery agitation, besides her walking and other actual performances, what, at any time, have you heard her say ? 12

Dunsinane Capell | Ff omit. — *Ante-room in the castle* Globe | Ff omit.

3. **went into the field.** Steevens calls this one of Shakespeare's oversights. In the preceding scene, Macbeth was said to have his " power a-foot " (line 185) against " many worthy fellows that were out " (line 183). Probably the coming of the English forces induced him to withdraw his troops from the field and put them within the strong fortress of Dunsinane.

4. **night-gown :** dressing-robe. Cf. II, ii, 70.

9. **do the effects of watching :** act as in her waking hours. Shakespeare often uses ' effects ' for ' actions.' Cf. *King Lear*, I, i, 188 ; *Hamlet*, III, iv, 129. See Schmidt.

GENTLEWOMAN. That, sir, which I will not report after her.

DOCTOR. You may to me; and 't is most meet you should.

GENTLEWOMAN. Neither to you nor any one; having no witness to confirm my speech. 16

Enter LADY MACBETH, *with a taper*

Lo you, here she comes! This is her very guise; and, upon my life, fast asleep. Observe her; stand close.

DOCTOR. How came she by that light? 19

GENTLEWOMAN. Why, it stood by her: she has light by her continually; 't is her command.

DOCTOR. You see, her eyes are open.

GENTLEWOMAN. Ay, but their sense are shut.

DOCTOR. What is it she does now? Look, how she rubs her hands. 25

GENTLEWOMAN. It is an accustom'd action with her, to seem thus washing her hands; I have known her continue in this a quarter of an hour.

LADY MACBETH. Yet here 's a spot. 29

17 *Enter* LADY MACBETH . . . Enter Lady . . . Ff.

23. sense are Ff | sense is Rowe.

24–25. Ff print as verse.

14. "The speeches of the Doctor . . . have a certain cadence verging on blank verse, without quite gliding into it." — Delius.

18. **stand close**: keep concealed. Cf. *Julius Cæsar*, I, iii, 131.

20. Contrast this with her invocation, "Come, thick night, And pall thee in the dunnest smoke of hell," I, v, 48–49. So the "washing her hands . . . a quarter of an hour" as compared with "A little water clears us of this deed," II, ii, 67.

23. **sense are.** This, the Folio reading, is usually changed to 'sense is,' the 'are' being regarded as a printer's repetition of 'are' just above. But 'sense' is a plural in *Sonnets*, CXII, 10. Cf. 'balance' as a plural in *The Merchant of Venice*, IV, i, 255. See Abbott, § 471.

DOCTOR. Hark! she speaks: I will set down what comes from her, to satisfy my remembrance the more strongly.

LADY MACBETH. Out, damned spot! out, I say! — One, two; why, then 't is time to do 't. — Hell is murky! — Fie, my lord, fie! a soldier, and afeard? What need we fear who knows it, when none can call our power to account? — Yet who would have thought the old man to have had so much blood in him? 37

DOCTOR. Do you mark that?

LADY MACBETH. The thane of Fife had a wife; where is she now? — What, will these hands ne'er be clean? — No more o' that, my lord, no more o' that: you mar all with this starting. 42

DOCTOR. Go to, go to; you have known what you should not. 44

GENTLEWOMAN. She has spoke what she should not, I am sure of that: heaven knows what she has known.

LADY MACBETH. Here 's the smell of the blood still: all the perfumes of Arabia will not sweeten this little hand. Oh, oh, oh. 49

35. account F_3F_4 | accompt F_1F_2.
43–44. Ff print as two lines of verse.
47. the blood F_1F_2 | blood F_3F_4 Rowe.

33. **Hell is murky!** Some commentators, following Steevens, think that Lady Macbeth imagines her husband to utter these words, and repeats them after him as in ridicule or reproach of his fears.

41–42. She is alluding to the terrors of Macbeth on seeing the Ghost of Banquo in the banquet scene, III, iv, 63.

47–48. Upon this passage, Verplanck, after remarking how fertile the sense of smell is in the gentler charms of poetry, comments:

But the smell has never been successfully used as the means of impressing the imagination with terror, pity, or any of the deeper emotions, except in this dreadful sleep-walking of the guilty Queen, and in one parallel scene of the Greek Drama, as wildly terrible as this. It is that passage of the

DOCTOR. What a sigh is there! The heart is sorely charg'd.

GENTLEWOMAN. I would not have such a heart in my bosom for the dignity of the whole body.

DOCTOR. Well, well, well, —

GENTLEWOMAN. Pray God it be, sir. 55

DOCTOR. This disease is beyond my practice: yet I have known those which have walk'd in their sleep who have died holily in their beds. 58

LADY MACBETH. Wash your hands; put on your nightgown; look not so pale. I tell you yet again, Banquo's buried; he cannot come out on 's grave.

DOCTOR. Even so? 62

LADY MACBETH. To bed, to bed; there 's knocking at the gate: come, come, come, come, give me your hand: what 's done cannot be undone: to bed, to bed, to bed.

[*Exit*]

DOCTOR. Will she go now to bed?

GENTLEWOMAN. Directly. 67

53. the dignity F_1F_2 | dignity F_3F_4.

Agamemnon of Æschylus, where the captive prophetess Cassandra, wrapt in visionary inspiration, scents first the smell of blood, and then the vapours of the tomb breathing from the palace of Atrides, as ominous of his approaching murder. These two stand alone in poetry; and Fuseli, in his Lectures, informs us that when, in the kindred art of painting, it has been attempted to produce tragic effect through the medium of ideas drawn from this 'squeamish sense,' even Raphael and Poussin have failed, and excited disgust instead of terror and compassion. He justly remarks that 'taste and smell,' as sources of tragic emotion, seem scarcely admissible in art or in the theatre.

55. Does the Gentlewoman misunderstand the Doctor's "Well, well, well," or does she mean this as a further hint how dreadful the thing is? At all events, this may be regarded as one of Shakespeare's quiet, unobtrusive master-strokes of delineation.

DOCTOR. Foul whisperings are abroad : unnatural deeds
Do breed unnatural troubles : infected minds
To their deaf pillows will discharge their secrets : 70
More needs she the divine than the physician.
God, God forgive us all ! Look after her ;
Remove from her the means of all annoyance,
And still keep eyes upon her. So, good night :
My mind she has mated, and amaz'd my sight : 75
I think, but dare not speak.

GENTLEWOMAN. Good night, good doctor.

[*Exeunt*]

SCENE II. *The country near Dunsinane*

Drum and colours. Enter MENTEITH, CAITHNESS, ANGUS, LENNOX, *and* Soldiers

MENTEITH. The English power is near, led on by Malcolm,
His uncle Siward, and the good Macduff :
Revenges burn in them ; for their dear causes
Would to the bleeding and the grim alarm
Excite the mortified man.

ANGUS. Near Birnam wood 5
Shall we well meet them ; that way are they coming.

The country near Dunsinane Capell | Ff omit.

73. annoyance : doing violence to herself. Cf. *Richard II*, III, ii, 16 ; *Troilus and Cressida*, I, iii, 48. See Murray. This foreshadows the " taking off " her life " by self and violent hands," V, viii, 70–71.

75. mated : bewildered. Still used in ' check-mated.' See Skeat.

4–5. Would rouse and impel even a hermit to the war, to the signal for carnage and horror. By ' the mortified man ' is meant ' a

CAITHNESS. Who knows if Donalbain be with his brother?
LENNOX. For certain, sir, he is not: I have a file
Of all the gentry: there is Siward's son,
And many unrough youths, that even now 10
Protest their first of manhood.
MENTEITH. What does the tyrant?
CAITHNESS. Great Dunsinane he strongly fortifies:
Some say he 's mad; others, that lesser hate him,
Do call it valiant fury: but, for certain,
He cannot buckle his distemper'd cause 15
Within the belt of rule.
ANGUS. Now does he feel
His secret murders sticking on his hands;
Now minutely revolts upbraid his faith-breach;
Those he commands move only in command,
Nothing in love: now does he feel his title 20
Hang loose about him, like a giant's robe
Upon a dwarfish thief.

10. unrough Theobald | vnrufle F_1F_2 | unruff F_3F_4.

religious man,' one who has mortified his passions, is dead to the world. Cf. *Love's Labour's Lost*, I, i, 28–31.

8. **file**: list, catalogue. Cf. 'the valued file,' III, i, 94, 101.

10. **unrough**: beardless, smooth-faced. Cf. *The Tempest*, II, i, 250.

11. **Protest**. Cf. III, iv, 105. — **first of manhood**. Cf. III, i, 117.

12. "But after that Makbeth perceiued his enimies power to increase, by such aid as came to them foorth of England with his aduersarie Malcolme, he recoiled backe into Fife, there purposing to abide in campe fortified, at the castell of Dunsinane." — Holinshed.

15. He cannot keep his disorganized party within control. For the metaphor, cf. *Troilus and Cressida*, II, ii, 30. In previous editions of Hudson's Shakespeare, Collier's emendation of 'course' (i.e. 'course of action') for 'cause' was adopted.

18. **minutely**: occurring every minute. Accent on first syllable.

MENTEITH. Who then shall blame
His pester'd senses to recoil and start,
When all that is within him does condemn
Itself for being there?
CAITHNESS. Well, march we on, 25
To give obedience where 't is truly ow'd:
Meet we the medicine of the sickly weal;
And with him pour we in our country's purge
Each drop of us.
LENNOX. Or so much as it needs
To dew the sovereign flower and drown the weeds. 30
Make we our march towards Birnam. [*Exeunt, marching*]

SCENE III. *Dunsinane. A room in the castle*

Enter MACBETH, *the* DOCTOR, *and* Attendants

MACBETH. Bring me no more reports; let them fly all:
Till Birnam wood remove to Dunsinane
I cannot taint with fear. What 's the boy Malcolm?

27. medicine | Med'cine Ff | med'cin Hanmer | medecin Steevens.
31. Birnam | Birnan F_1.
Dunsinane. A room in the castle Capell | Ff omit.
2. Birnam F_3F_4 | Byrnane F_1.

23. **pester'd**: troubled. Another word that has degenerated in meaning. — **to recoil and start**. Infinitive used gerundively.

27. **medicine**. This undoubtedly refers to Malcolm, but is the word to be taken as meaning 'physician' (Fr. *médecin*; cf. *All's Well that Ends Well*, II, i, 75), or 'remedy,' as the next line seems to suggest? Probably the word is used in the double sense here; cf. 'sovereign,' in line 30, in the sense of 'royal' and 'powerful remedy.' Malcolm was the lawful prince, and in the olden time the best remedy for the evils of tyranny, or the greater evils of civil war, was thought to be a king with a clear and unquestioned title.

3. **taint**: be infected. A transitive verb used intransitively.

Was he not born of woman? The spirits that know
All mortal consequences have pronounc'd me thus: 5
'Fear not, Macbeth; no man that's born of woman
Shall e'er have power upon thee.' Then fly, false thanes,
And mingle with the English epicures:
The mind I sway by and the heart I bear
Shall never sag with doubt nor shake with fear. 10

Enter a SERVANT

The devil damn thee black, thou cream-fac'd loon!
Where got'st thou that goose look?

SERVANT. There is ten thousand —

MACBETH. Geese, villain?

SERVANT. Soldiers, sir.

MACBETH. Go prick thy face, and over-red thy fear,
Thou lily-liver'd boy. What soldiers, patch? 15
Death of thy soul! those linen cheeks of thine
Are counsellors to fear. What soldiers, whey-face?

11. loon F_3 | Loone F_1F_2 | Lown F_4. 12. goose look | Goose-looke Ff.

5. An Alexandrine verse. — **me.** Probably an ethical dative.

8. Cf. this passage from Holinshed:

For manie of the people abhorring the riotous manners and superfluous gormandizing brought in among them by the Englyshemen were willing inough to receive this Donald for their King . . . bicause he had beene brought up in the Iles, with old customes and maners of their ancient nation without tast of the English likerous delicates.

11. **loon.** This word of uncertain origin is still in common use in Scotland and the north of England in the sense of 'lad' or 'loafer.' In the sixteenth century it often meant 'a man of low birth,' as in the phrase 'lord and loon'; cf. *Pericles*, IV, vi, 19.

17. **lily-liver'd**: cowardly. Falstaff in *2 Henry IV*, IV, iii, 110–114, says: "The second property of your excellent sherris is the

SERVANT. The English force, so please you.
MACBETH. Take thy face hence. [*Exit* SERVANT]
Seyton! — I am sick at heart,
When I behold — Seyton, I say! — This push 20
Will cheer me ever, or disseat me now.
I have liv'd long enough: my way of life
Is fall'n into the sear, the yellow leaf;
And that which should accompany old age,
As honour, love, obedience, troops of friends, 25
I must not look to have; but, in their stead,
Curses, not loud but deep, mouth-honour, breath,
Which the poor heart would fain deny, and dare not.
Seyton!

19. [*Exit* SERVANT] Ff omit.
21. cheer F_3F_4 | cheere F_1F_2 | chair Percy Dyce. — disseat Steevens | dis-eate F_1 | disease $F_2F_3F_4$.

warming of the blood; which, before cold and settled, left the liver white and pale, which is the badge of pusillanimity and cowardice." Cf. *The Merchant of Venice*, III, ii, 86; *King Lear*, II, ii, 17; IV, ii, 50. — **patch**: clown, fool. Cf. *The Tempest*, III, ii, 71.

21. One of the textual *cruces*. But the reading of the text makes satisfactory sense, Will bring comfort to me for the rest of my life, or will dethrone me now, once for all. Furness would hyphenate the 'disease' of the later Folios, and interpret, Will bring at once permanent relief or affliction. In previous editions of Hudson's Shakespeare, Percy's substitution of 'chair' for 'cheer' was adopted, with the interpretation, Will seat me firmly on the throne, or else unseat me utterly.

22. **my way of life**: the course of my life. Johnson suggested 'May' for 'way,' and, as a parallel, Clar quotes *Richard II*, III, iv, 48–49.

23. Cf. *Sonnets*, LXXIII, 1–4:

That time of year thou may'st in me behold
When yellow leaves, or none, or few, do hang
Upon those boughs which shake against the cold,
Bare, ruin'd choirs, where late the sweet birds sang.

Enter SEYTON

SEYTON. What 's your gracious pleasure?
MACBETH. What news more?
SEYTON. All is confirm'd, my lord, which was reported.
MACBETH I 'll fight, till from my bones my flesh be hack'd. 32
Give me my armour.
SEYTON. 'T is not needed yet.
MACBETH. I 'll put it on.
Send out moe horses, skirr the country round; 35
Hang those that talk of fear. Give me mine armour.
How does your patient, doctor?
DOCTOR. Not so sick, my lord,
As she is troubled with thick-coming fancies,
That keep her from her rest.
MACBETH. Cure her of that.
Canst thou not minister to a mind diseas'd, 40
Pluck from the memory a rooted sorrow,
Raze out the written troubles of the brain,
And with some sweet oblivious antidote

32. be F_1 | is $F_2F_3F_4$.
35. moe F_1F_2 | more F_3F_4.
36. talk of F_1 | stand in $F_2F_3F_4$.
39. Cure her $F_2F_3F_4$ | Cure F_1. — of F_1F_2 | from F_3F_4.
42. Raze F_1F_2 | Raise F_3 | Rase F_4.

35. moe : more. Middle and Elizabethan English 'mo' or 'moe' (from Anglo-Saxon *má*) usually indicated number; 'more' (from Anglo-Saxon *mára*) had specific reference to size. — skirr : scour. In *Henry V*, IV, vii, 64, the verb is used intransitively.

42. Delius notes that this figure occurs in *Hamlet*, I, v, 98–103.

43. oblivious : causing forgetfulness. Cf. *Paradise Lost*, I, 266–267:

> The associates and co-partners of our loss,
> Lie thus astonished on the oblivious pool.

Cleanse the stuff'd bosom of that perilous stuff
Which weighs upon the heart ?
DOCTOR. Therein the patient 45
Must minister to himself.
MACBETH. Throw physic to the dogs, I 'll none of it.
Come, put mine armour on ; give me my staff.
Seyton, send out. Doctor, the thanes fly from me.
Come, sir, dispatch. If thou couldst, doctor, cast 50
The water of my land, find her disease,
And purge it to a sound and pristine health,
I would applaud thee to the very echo,
That should applaud again. Pull 't off, I say.
What rhubarb, senna, or what purgative drug, 55
Would scour these English hence ? Hear'st thou of them ?
DOCTOR. Ay, my good lord ; your royal preparation
Makes us hear something.
MACBETH. Bring it after me.
I will not be afraid of death and bane,
Till Birnam forest come to Dunsinane. 60
DOCTOR. [*Aside*] Were I from Dunsinane away and clear,
Profit again should hardly draw me here. [*Exeunt*]

44. stuff'd | stufft F_1 | stuft $F_2F_3F_4$ | full Pope. — stuff F_3F_4 | stuffe F_1F_2 | grief Collier.
46. to F_1 | unto $F_2F_3F_4$.
48. mine $F_1F_2F_3$ | my F_4.
55. senna F_4 | Cyme F_1 | Cæny F_2F_3 | clysme Badham conj. | sene Wellesley conj. | sirrah Bulloch conj.
60. Birnam | Birnane F_1.
61. [*Aside*] Hanmer | Ff. omit.

44. stuff'd . . . stuff. Such a repetition is thoroughly Shakespearian.
48. staff. Either ' general's baton ' (Clar) or ' lance ' (Schmidt).
50. Come, sir, dispatch. Spoken to the armourer.— cast: inspect.
54. Pull 't off. To the armourer. The " Bring it after me " of line 58 has reference to this piece of armour just ordered to be pulled off. These orders, so effective in stage representation, show Macbeth's agitation and impatience.

SCENE IV. *Country near Birnam wood*

Drum and colours. Enter MALCOLM, *old* SIWARD *and his* SON, MACDUFF, MENTEITH, CAITHNESS, ANGUS, LENNOX, ROSS, *and* SOLDIERS, *marching*

MALCOLM. Cousins, I hope the days are near at hand
That chambers will be safe.
MENTEITH. We doubt it nothing.
SIWARD. What wood is this before us ?
MENTEITH. The wood of Birnam.
MALCOLM. Let every soldier hew him down a bough,
And bear 't before him : thereby shall we shadow 5
The numbers of our host, and make discovery
Err in report of us.
SOLDIERS. It shall be done.
SIWARD. We learn no other but the confident tyrant
Keeps still in Dunsinane, and will endure
Our sitting down before 't.
MALCOLM. 'T is his main hope : 10

Country near . . . Globe | Ff omit.

2. chambers will be safe. This refers, probably, to the spies and informers whom Macbeth keeps in the noblemen's houses, prowling about their private chambers, and listening at their key-holes. Or it may have reference simply to Duncan's murder.

4–5. Holinshed thus describes the incident :

Malcome following hastilie after Makbeth, came the night before the battell vnto Birnane wood, and when his armie had rested a while there to refresh them, he commanded every man to get a bough of some tree or other of that wood in his hand, as big as he might beare, and to march foorth therewith in such wise, that on the next morrow they might come closelie and without sight in this manner within viewe of his enimies.

For, where there is advantage to be given,
Both more and less have given him the revolt,
And none serve with him but constrained things,
Whose hearts are absent too.

MACDUFF. Let our just censures
Attend the true event, and put we on 15
Industrious soldiership.

SIWARD. The time approaches
That will with due decision make us know
What we shall say we have and what we owe.
Thoughts speculative their unsure hopes relate,
But certain issue strokes must arbitrate ; 20
Towards which advance the war. [*Exeunt, marching*]

SCENE V. *Dunsinane. The castle*

Enter MACBETH, SEYTON, *and* Soldiers, *with drum and colours*

MACBETH. Hang out our banners on the outward walls ;
The cry is still, 'They come.' Our castle's strength
Will laugh a siege to scorn ; here let them lie

11. **given** Ff | gone Capell | got Steevens conj. | taken Keightley (Chedworth conj.) | ta'en Walker Dyce.
14-15. **just censures Attend** F_1 | best Censures Before $F_2F_3F_4$.

Dunsinane. The castle | Ff omit.
1. **banners on the outward walls ;** | Banners on the outward walls, Ff | banners ! on the outward walls Keightley.

11. Various substitutes for 'given' have been proposed. Probably 'to them' should be supplied after 'given.'

12. more and less : high and low, nobles and commons.

14–15. Let our judgments wait for the actual result, the issue of the contest, in order that they may be just. A proleptical form of speech.

18. What we have as rights and what are our duties.

19–20. There is no use speculating or talking about it ; nothing but fighting will settle the matter.

Till famine and the ague eat them up.
Were they not forc'd with those that should be ours, 5
We might have met them dareful, beard to beard,
And beat them backward home. [*A cry of women within*]
What is that noise?

SEYTON. It is the cry of women, my good lord. [*Exit*]

MACBETH. I have almost forgot the taste of fears:
The time has been, my senses would have cool'd 10
To hear a night-shriek, and my fell of hair
Would at a dismal treatise rouse and stir
As life were in 't: I have supp'd full with horrors;
Direness, familiar to my slaughterous thoughts,
Cannot once start me.

Re-enter SEYTON

Wherefore was that cry? 15

SEYTON. The queen, my lord, is dead.

MACBETH. She should have died hereafter;
There would have been a time for such a word.
To-morrow, and to-morrow, and to-morrow,
Creeps in this petty pace from day to day, 20

8. [*Exit*] Dyce | Ff omit. 10. cool'd Ff | quail'd Collier.

5. **forc'd**: strengthened, reënforced. This sense of 'force' was common in the sixteenth century. Collier suggested 'farced,' i.e. 'stuffed.' Cf. 'forcemeat,' corruption of 'farce-meat.'

11. **To hear**: at hearing. Infinitive used gerundively. — **fell.** The original meaning of 'fell' is 'skin' or 'hide' of an animal, and thus Shakespeare uses the word in *King Lear*, V, iii, 24.

12. **dismal**: tragic. Cf. I, ii, 53. — **treatise**: story. Cf. *Much Ado About Nothing*, I, i, 317; *Venus and Adonis*, 774.

17–19. If she had not died now, she would have died hereafter; the time would have come when such intelligence had to be spoken.

To the last syllable of recorded time ;
And all our yesterdays have lighted fools
The way to dusty death. Out, out, brief candle !
Life 's but a walking shadow ; a poor player
That struts and frets his hour upon the stage 25
And then is heard no more. It is a tale
Told by an idiot, full of sound and fury,
Signifying nothing.

Enter a MESSENGER

Thou com'st to use thy tongue ; thy story quickly.
MESSENGER. Gracious my lord, 30
I should report that which I say I saw,
But know not how to do 't.
MACBETH. Well, say, sir.
MESSENGER. As I did stand my watch upon the hill,
I look'd toward Birnam, and anon, methought,
The wood began to move.
MACBETH. Liar and slave ! 35
MESSENGER. Let me endure your wrath, if 't be not so :
Within this three mile may you see it coming ;
I say, a moving grove.

23. dusty F_1 | study $F_2F_3F_4$ Rowe Pope Capell | dusky Hanmer (Theobald conj.).

30. Gracious my F_1 | **My gracious** $F_2F_3F_4$.

37. may you F_1F_2 | you may F_3F_4.

21. recorded time : the record of time. A proleptical expression.

24–28. To these lines Coleridge prefixes this note :

Now all is inward with him ; he has no more prudential prospective reasonings. His wife, the only being who could have had any seat in his affections, dies : he puts on despondency, the final heart-armour of the wretched, and would fain think every thing shadowy and unsubstantial ; as indeed all things are to those who cannot regard them as symbols of goodness.

MACBETH. If thou speak'st false,
Upon the next tree shall thou hang alive,
Till famine cling thee : if thy speech be sooth, 40
I care not if thou dost for me as much.
I pull in resolution, and begin
To doubt th' equivocation of the fiend
That lies like truth : ' Fear not, till Birnam wood
Do come to Dunsinane ' ; and now a wood 45
Comes toward Dunsinane. Arm, arm, and out !
If this which he avouches does appear,
There is nor flying hence nor tarrying here.
I 'gin to be a-weary of the sun,

42. pull Ff | pall Johnson conj. **48. nor flying F_1F_2 | no flying F_3F_4.**

40. cling: wither, shrivel. See Murray. — **sooth**: truth. See Skeat.

42. In previous editions of Hudson's Shakespeare Johnson's conjecture ' pall in ' was adopted in place of the ' pull in ' of the Folios. ' Pull in ' may be interpreted as either (1) ' check,' ' restrain,' the probable meaning here ; or (2) ' draw back.' Cf. Fletcher's *Sea Voyage*, III, i : " All my spirits, As if they had heard my passing-bell go for me, Pull in their powers and give me up to destiny."

46–52. Dowden thus sums up his character study of Macbeth :

The soul of Macbeth never quite disappears into the blackness of darkness. He is a cloud without water carried about of winds ; a tree whose fruit withers, but not even to the last plucked up by the roots. For the dull ferocity of Macbeth is joyless. All his life has gone irretrievably astray, and he is aware of this. His suspicion becomes uncontrollable ; his reign is a reign of terror ; and, as he drops deeper and deeper into the solitude and the gloom, his sense of error and misfortune, futile and unproductive as that sense is, increases. . . . Finally his sensibility has grown so dull that even the intelligence of his wife's death — the death of her who had been bound to him by such close communion in crime — hardly moves him, and seems little more than one additional incident in the weary, meaningless tale of human life. . . . Macbeth remembers that he once knew there was such a thing as human goodness. He stands a haggard shadow against the hand's-breadth of pale sky which yields us sufficient light to see him.

And wish th' estate o' the world were now undone. 50
Ring the alarum-bell! Blow, wind! come, wrack!
At least we 'll die with harness on our back. [*Exeunt*]

SCENE VI. *Dunsinane. Before the castle*

Drum and colours. Enter MALCOLM, *old* SIWARD, MACDUFF, *and their* Army, *with boughs*

MALCOLM. Now near enough; your leavy screens throw down,
And show like those you are. You, worthy uncle,
Shall, with my cousin, your right noble son,
Lead our first battle: worthy Macduff and we
Shall take upon 's what else remains to do, 5
According to our order.

SIWARD. Fare you well.
Do we but find the tyrant's power to-night,
Let us be beaten, if we cannot fight.

MACDUFF. Make all our trumpets speak; give them all breath, 9
Those clamorous harbingers of blood and death. [*Exeunt*]
[*Alarums continued*]

Dunsinane. Before the castle | Ff omit. 1. Two lines in Ff.

52. **harness**: armour. So 'harness'd' in *Troilus and Cressida*, I, ii, 8. Cf. 'joints of the harness,' *1 Kings*, xxii, 34.

1. 'Leavy' is the earlier and more normal form of 'leafy.' Cf. *Much Ado About Nothing*, II, iii, 75; *Pericles*, V, i, 51. 'Leavy labyrinth' occurs in Milton's *Comus*, line 278, as originally printed.

4. **first battle**: foreguard, vanguard. Cf. *Julius Cæsar*, V, i, 4, 16. Holinshed uses 'battle' in the sense of 'battalions': "When his whole power was come together, he divided the same into three battels."

SCENE VII. *Another part of the field*

Enter MACBETH

MACBETH. They have tied me to a stake ; I cannot fly,
But, bear-like, I must fight the course. What 's he
That was not born of woman ? Such a one
Am I to fear, or none.

Enter young SIWARD

YOUNG SIWARD. What is thy name ?
MACBETH. Thou 'lt be afraid to hear it.
YOUNG SIWARD. No ; though thou call'st thyself a hotter name 6
Than any is in hell.
MACBETH. My name 's Macbeth.
YOUNG SIWARD. The devil himself could not pronounce a title
More hateful to mine ear.
MACBETH. No, nor more fearful.

SCENE VII | Scena Septima Ff | Rowe Pope continue the scene. — *Another part of the field* Globe | Ff omit.

2. **the course**. This was a phrase of bear-baiting, where the bear was tied to a stake, and then the dogs set upon him ; the poor bear could not run, and so had no way but to fight it out. Cf. *King Lear*, III, vii, 54 ; *Julius Cæsar*, IV, i, 48.

The end of Macbeth is savage, and almost brutal, — a death without honour or loveliness. He fights now, not like 'Bellona's bridegroom lapp'd in proof,' but with a wild and animal clinging to life. His followers desert him ; he feels himself taken in a trap. The powers of evil in which he had trusted turn against him and betray him. His courage becomes a desperate rage. We are in pain until the horrible necessity is accomplished. — Dowden.

YOUNG SIWARD. Thou liest, abhorred tyrant; with my sword 10
I 'll prove the lie thou speak'st.

[*They fight, and young* SIWARD *is slain*]

MACBETH. Thou wast born of woman.
But swords I smile at, weapons laugh to scorn,
Brandish'd by man that 's of a woman born. [*Exit*]

Alarums. Enter MACDUFF

MACDUFF. That way the noise is. Tyrant, show thy face!
If thou be'st slain, and with no stroke of mine, 15
My wife and children's ghosts will haunt me still.
I cannot strike at wretched kerns, whose arms
Are hir'd to bear their staves: either thou, Macbeth,
Or else my sword, with an unbatter'd edge,
I sheathe again undeeded. There thou shouldst be; 20
By this great clatter, one of greatest note
Seems bruited. Let me find him, fortune!
And more I beg not. [*Exit. Alarums*]

Enter MALCOLM *and old* SIWARD

SIWARD. This way, my lord. The castle 's gently render'd:
The tyrant's people on both sides do fight; 25
The noble thanes do bravely in the war;
The day almost itself professes yours,
And little is to do.

22. **bruited**: noised abroad. Cf. *Hamlet*, I, ii, 127; *1 Henry VI*, II, iii, 68. See Murray. Wherever Macbeth goes, he has a strong guard or escort attending him; and the clattering of so many feet and swords would indicate his approach.

MALCOLM. We have met with foes
That strike beside us.
SIWARD. Enter, sir, the castle. 29
[*Exeunt. Alarum*]

SCENE VIII. *Another part of the field*

Enter MACBETH

MACBETH. Why should I play the Roman fool, and die
On mine own sword ? whiles I see lives, the gashes
Do better upon them.

Enter MACDUFF

MACDUFF. Turn, hell-hound, turn !
MACBETH. Of all men else I have avoided thee :
But get thee back ; my soul is too much charg'd 5
With blood of thine already.
MACDUFF. I have no words,

SCENE VIII Dyce | Scene VII Pope | Ff continue scene. — *Another part of the field* Globe | Ff omit.
2. whiles Ff | whilst Rowe.

29. **That strike beside us** : who take pains not to hit us, who only sham as they fight against us, for their hearts are on our side. Cf. *3 Henry VI*, II, i, 129–132.

1. Brutus, Cassius, and Antony, in Shakespeare's great Roman plays, commit suicide. Cf. *Julius Cæsar*, V, iii, 89, where Titinius, as he kills himself, says, " This is a Roman's part." In the same play, V, i, 101–103, Brutus, referring to the suicide of Marcus Cato, says :

> Even by the rule of that philosophy
> By which I did blame Cato for the death
> Which he did give himself.

2–3. While I see living foes, it is better to be exercising my sword upon them than upon myself.

My voice is in my sword ; thou bloodier villain
Than terms can give thee out ! [*They fight*]

MACBETH. Thou losest labour :
As easy mayst thou the intrenchant air
With thy keen sword impress as make me bleed : 10
Let fall thy blade on vulnerable crests ;
I bear a charmed life, which must not yield
To one of woman born.

MACDUFF. Despair thy charm ;
And let the angel whom thou still hast serv'd
Tell thee, Macduff was from his mother's womb 15
Untimely ripp'd.

MACBETH. Accursed be that tongue that tells me so,
For it hath cow'd my better part of man !
And be these juggling fiends no more believ'd,
That palter with us in a double sense ; 20
That keep the word of promise to our ear,
And break it to our hope. I 'll not fight with thee.

MACDUFF. Then yield thee, coward,
And live to be the show and gaze o' the time :
We 'll have thee, as our rarer monsters are, 25

8. [*They fight*] Malone | Fight : Alarum Ff.

9. **intrenchant** : indivisible. 'To trench' is 'to cut.' Cf. 'the air invulnerable,' *Hamlet*, I, i, 145. For active participles in a passive sense, see Abbott, § 372.

12. **charmed** : secured against human assault by the might of magic spells. Cf. *Cymbeline*, V, iii, 68–69.

20. **palter** : equivocate. Cf. *Antony and Cleopatra*, III, xi, 62–63.

25–27. An advertising practice of the time. Cf. *Much Ado About Nothing*, I, i, 267 ; *The Tempest*, II, ii, 28–34. "Therewithal he stept unto him and slue him. Then cutting his head from his shoulders he set it upon a pole and brought it unto Malcolm." — Holinshed.

Painted upon a pole, and underwrit,
' Here may you see the tyrant.'
MACBETH. I will not yield,
To kiss the ground before young Malcolm's feet,
And to be baited with the rabble's curse.
Though Birnam wood be come to Dunsinane, 30
And thou oppos'd, being of no woman born,
Yet I will try the last : before my body
I throw my warlike shield : lay on, Macduff ;
And damn'd be him that first cries, ' Hold, enough ! '
[*Exeunt*, *fighting*. *Alarums*]

Retreat. *Flourish*. *Enter with drum and colours*, MALCOLM, *old* SIWARD, ROSS, *the other* Thanes, *and* Soldiers

MALCOLM. I would the friends we miss were safe arriv'd.
SIWARD. Some must go off ; and yet, by these I see, 36
So great a day as this is cheaply bought.
MALCOLM. Macduff is missing, and your noble son.
ROSS. Your son, my lord, has paid a soldier's debt :
He only liv'd but till he was a man ; 40
The which no sooner had his prowess confirm'd
In the unshrinking station where he fought,
But like a man he died.

34. After *Alarums* Ff have *Enter Fighting, and Macbeth slaine.*

35. Scene VIII Pope. — *Retreat.* | Retreat, and Ff.

34. him. " Perhaps ' let,' or some such word, was implied." — Abbott, § 208. — " To cry ' hold ' " was an authoritative way of separating combatants, according to the old military rules and regulations. Cf. I, v, 52.

36. go off. A not unusual Elizabethan euphemism for ' die.'

42. unshrinking station : the place where he unshrinking fought.

SIWARD. Then he is dead?

ROSS. Ay, and brought off the field: your cause of sorrow
Must not be measur'd by his worth, for then 45
It hath no end.

SIWARD. Had he his hurts before?

ROSS. Ay, on the front.

SIWARD. Why then, God's soldier be he!
Had I as many sons as I have hairs,
I would not wish them to a fairer death:
And so his knell is knoll'd.

MALCOLM. He 's worth more sorrow, 50
And that I 'll spend for him.

SIWARD. He 's worth no more:
They say he parted well, and paid his score;
And so God be with him! Here comes newer comfort.

Re-enter MACDUFF, *with* MACBETH'S *head*

MACDUFF. Hail, king! for so thou art: behold, where stands
Th' usurper's cursed head: the time is free. 55

54. Two lines in Ff.

47. This Spartan bearing is thus described by Holinshed:

When his father heard the newes, he demanded whether he receiued the wound whereof he died, in the forepart of the bodie, or in the hinder part: and when it was told him that he receiued it in the forepart: I reioise (saith he) euen with all my heart, for I would not wish either to my sonne nor to myselfe any other kind of death.

52. parted: departed. So "a parted . . . at the turning o' the tide," *Henry V*, II, iii, 12. — score: reckoning. The allusion is to a traveller taking leave of an inn. The old inn accounts were commonly kept either by marking down the items with chalk on a board, or by cutting, 'scoring,' notches on a stick.

I see thee compass'd with thy kingdom's pearl,
That speak my salutation in their minds;
Whose voices I desire aloud with mine:
Hail, King of Scotland!

ALL. Hail, King of Scotland! [*Flourish*]

MALCOLM. We shall not spend a large expense of time
Before we reckon with your several loves, 61
And make us even with you. My thanes and kinsmen,
Henceforth be earls, the first that ever Scotland
In such an honour nam'd. What 's more to do,
Which would be planted newly with the time, 65
As calling home our exil'd friends abroad
That fled the snares of watchful tyranny;
Producing forth the cruel ministers
Of this dead butcher and his fiend-like queen,

56. pearl F_3F_4 | Pearle F_1F_2 | peers Rowe.

56. pearl: choicest ornament. 'Pearl' is here a collective noun and is used as such by Milton. The metaphor describing the worthiest nobles is a string of pearls encircling the neck, or the head, of royalty. The expression seems to have been a not unusual one. In Dunbar's *The Thrissill and the Rose*, 1503, we have:

Welcome to be our princes of honour,
Our perle, our plesans, and our paramour.

62–75. The matter of Malcolm's last speech is in this passage from Holinshed:

Malcolme Cammore thus recouering the relme (as ye haue heard) by support of king Edward, in the 16 yeere of the same Edwards reigne, he was crowned at Scone the 25 day of Aprill, in the yeere of our Lord 1057. Immediatlie after his coronation he called a parlement at Forfair, in the which he rewarded them with lands and liuings that had assisted him against Makbeth, aduancing them to fees and offices as he saw cause, & commanded that speciallie those that bare the surname of anie offices or lands, should haue and inioy the same. He created manie earles, lords, barons, and knights.

Who, as 't is thought, by self and violent hands 70
Took off her life ; this, and what needful else
That calls upon us, by the grace of Grace,
We will perform in measure, time, and place :
So, thanks to all at once and to each one,
Whom we invite to see us crown'd at Scone. 75

[*Flourish*. *Exeunt*]

75. *Exeunt* | Exeunt omnes Ff.

Manie of them that before were thanes, were at this time made earles, as Fife, Menteth, Atholl, Leuenox, Murrey, Cathnes, Rosse, and Angus. These were the first earles that haue beene heard of amongst the Scotishmen, (as their histories doo make mention).

70. self : own. ' Self ' is here used as an adjective. Cf. III, iv, 142.

71. For the ellipsis of ' there be ' after ' else,' see Abbott, § 286.

72. grace of Grace. " This is an expression that Shakespeare is fond of." — Malone. Cf. *Two Gentlemen of Verona*, III, i, 146; *All's Well that Ends Well*, II, i, 163.

74–75. " There can be little doubt that the actor, in speaking these lines, addressed the audience rather than the *dramatis personæ*, and made this utterance of thanks serve as a sort of epilogue." — Manly.

INDEX

I. WORDS AND PHRASES

This Index includes the most important words, phrases, etc., explained in the notes. The figures in heavy-faced type refer to the pages; those in plain type, to the lines containing what is explained.

II. QUOTATIONS FROM HOLINSHED